ADVANCE PR

C000155996

"Erlijn Sie presents insightful learnings from some of the world's most inspiring changemakers dedicated to a more inclusive financial system, and offers compelling and practical ways for all of us – business leaders, social innovators and funders – to join the movement."

Pei Yun Teng, Global Director, Social Impact, Kearney

"*Reimagining Financial Inclusion* provides invaluable insights into how system changes inspired by social entrepreneurs can resolve the longstanding challenge of financial services not serving those who need it most. As the global financial services industry is facing disruptive transformation globally, Erlijn Sie's book proves that all of us can be part of the solution, offering powerful and refreshing perspectives on how we can reimagine ourselves."

Paul de Kroon, Chairman of the Supervisory Board,
Aegon Bank (labels Knab and Aegon Bank), CEO 34 Capital
and former CEO, Royal Bank of Scotland, Turkey and Israel

"How do you get a loan if you have no salary paperwork? The two billion people whose incomes come from the informal sector have none. This is but one part of an invisible finance wall ensuring continued inequality. Erlijn Sie's book is a gift: you will see the wall and how to tear it down as she introduces you to the leading social entrepreneurs everywhere who are building the alternates."

Bill Drayton, Founder and leader of Ashoka, thought leader
in the field of social innovation and entrepreneurship

Published by
LID Publishing
An imprint of LID Business Media Ltd
The Record Hall, Studio 304,
16-16a Baldwins Gardens,
London EC1N 7RJ, UK

info@lidpublishing.com
www.lidpublishing.com

A member of:

BPR ⊛
businesspublishersroundtable.com

© Erlijn Sie, 2021
© LID Publishing, 2021

Printed by Severn, Gloucester
ISBN: 978-1-911671-52-7
ISBN: 978-1-911671-53-4 (ebook)

Cover and page design: Caroline Li

REIMAGINING FINANCIAL INCLUSION

TACKLING THE FLAWS OF OUR FORMAL FINANCIAL SYSTEM

ERLIJN SIE

MADRID | MEXICO CITY | LONDON
NEW YORK | BUENOS AIRES
BOGOTA | SHANGHAI | NEW DELHI

CONTENTS

PREFACE

"A mind that is stretched to a new idea never returns to its original dimensions." The American author and physician Oliver Wendell Holmes said that about a hundred years ago, and it expresses exactly how I felt when I read *Reimagining Financial Inclusion* and thought about the impact the book will have in the financial community.

Reimagining Financial Inclusion inspires. It's about breakthrough innovations, courageous entrepreneurs on a mission, about immaculate execution and success at scale. But most importantly, the book is a recipe for change with massive impact, changing the lives of billions of low-income people.

The financial system is often presented as the utility system of the economy. Obviously, this does not reflect the sector's importance. Beyond any doubt, money is the lifeblood of the economy and society. Consequently, the financial system is the cardiovascular system.

The financial sector plays a key part in the social and economic development of every community, country or continent, and in personal development as well. Although most people may not realize it, financial services are at the heart of the daily lives of individuals and businesses. An ever-growing part of medical costs is covered by insurance. A vast number of businesses is financed by banks. The use of money is an essential part of daily life; it is a key to protection and to a better future.

Now, unfortunately, most people do not have access to these kinds of financial services. They are completely absent in the rural villages, in the slums or on the streets where low-income people live. The consequences are immense. If you don't have access to, for instance, health insurance, it is more difficult to stay healthy. And when one of your family members gets seriously ill, there is a fair chance to be thrown back into poverty. It is these kinds of vicious circles that keep billions of families around the globe from building a better life. Yes, billions.

The issue is the financial system: the laws and regulations, the written and unwritten rules, the assumptions and industry conventions. Most probably all developed with good intentions, aimed to provide protection. But at the end of the day, the resulting procedures are not geared to the daily lives of low-income people. Consequently, they are working against inclusion, in fact even excluding the majority of the people on our planet.

In *Reimagining Financial Inclusion*, author Erlijn Sie is not just pointing at the flaws in the system: "Because that won't fix it," she argues. Instead, she handpicked 13 social enterprises from across the globe, each giving access to financial services to sometimes millions of customers already – customers that were previously considered unbankable and uninsurable.

Unconventional enterprises by nature venture to question the industry conventions. Each of the great entrepreneurial minds behind these 13 success stories did not take the formal system for granted. They realize that if you want to play the game, you need to change the rules. They uncovered underlying assumptions and proved them to be false or obsolete. Each of the game changers thought outside the current system to solve or bypass the flaws, creating an alternative and effective pathway to financial inclusion.

A key issue of the formal financial system, for instance, is that many rules are products of mistrust. Mistrust distracts from the main purpose. It is therefore preferable to take the principles as the single most important point of departure, rather than the rules. It is inspiring to see how this thinking results in different solutions with almost immediate impact without compromising the core principles.

Rather than describing each of the 13 best practices according to the obvious business model canvas, *Reimagining Financial Inclusion* decodes what makes all of them so successful. The author did a great job revealing the essential keys to success they all have in common. On the one hand, the framework she presents refers to Simon Sinek's well-known and much used *why-what-how*, which makes it easy to understand. On the other hand, the framework precisely and comprehensively captures what makes all 13 successful in creating financial inclusion at scale, making it also very actionable.

Reimagining Financial Inclusion reads as a recipe book of famous chefs. While reading you start imagining the taste, and you feel like you can't wait to make it yourself. The framework elements not only make it easy to understand the magic and the new paradigms the social enterprises work with. They also introduce a new and inspiring vocabulary. They serve as design principles that can be used by other social entrepreneurs as well as by established incumbents – which in turn accelerates to grow to a world in which all of us are financially included.

In general discussions about innovation in financial services, industry executives seem to always look at 'the usual suspects,' like Ping An and Lemonade in insurance, and DBS and N26 in banking. The companies featured in *Reimagining Financial Inclusion* definitely make a fine addition to the list of examples everyone should learn from. The 13 who made it into *Reimagining Financial Inclusion* are of a totally different category. They offer a new perspective on successful business models, with truly being part of everyday life, customer empowerment, ecosystem thinking, open innovation and continuous loops of learnings in their veins. Moreover, they are missioned to have massive impact.

More and more established financial institutions are looking for ways to increase their social and economic impact. Some by planting trees to reduce the carbon footprint, others by already leveraging the sometimes hundreds of billions of euros of assets they have under management. Virtually all incumbents realize that all great challenges we are faced with in the coming decades – from climate change, water and energy to providing healthcare for ageing populations – require solutions in which financial institutions play a key role; and that their customers are longing more than ever for institutions that care.

Having said that, it is remarkable that financial inclusion is not top of the agenda at most financial institutions. Which is a shame in view of so many people who could benefit. The 13 innovators in *Reimagining Financial Inclusion* show that it is possible to reach the base of the pyramid at scale and create a sustainable business in the process. Unlocking the potential of billions of people also unlocks massive new markets for financial institutions – which should be an attractive strategic incentive to give financial inclusion much more emphasis. Just imagine using a small part of all the creativity, intelligence, manpower and financial means that incumbents have on board to work together with these social entrepreneurs and create an impact for the billions that are part of the base of the pyramid worldwide. The world would be a better place.

Reimagining Financial Inclusion tells exactly how to seize the opportunity.

Roger Peverelli
Author on the future of financial services and
co-founder, Digital Insurance Agenda

INTRODUCTION

We live in a strange world in which you cannot live your life without money, but the majority of the people in the world do not have access to it. They make a modest living, the way they save is by putting their money under the mattress, the way they invest is by buying golden bangles or a cow, the way they get extra money is through money lenders, and the way they spread risk is across a support network of family and friends. People with low or no income do not use formal financial services like a bank account for savings and payments, loans or credit cards, let alone have access to insurances for health or business-related risks, or a pension or mortgage. Financial inclusion in the broadest sense is that everybody in the world has access to those financial services to develop to their full potential. Our current formal financial system is intrinsically excluding low-income people, who actually make up the majority of the world.[1] Many of us believe in democracy; however, in financial services it's not the majority ruling – the majority is excluded. This is fundamentally wrong.

But it can change. Professor Muhammad Yunus, acknowledged as the Banker of the Poor and awarded the Nobel Peace Prize for Peace for founding the Grameen Bank, has pioneered microcredits and shown that the poor can work to bring about their own development with access to small loans. Likewise, Jeroo Billimoria, founder of Aflatoun and Child &Youth Financial Inclusion, has pioneered financial education for children and has shown that this financially empowers the next generation. Matt Flannery and Jessica Jackley, founders of Kiva, a peer-to-peer platform, have pioneered a new model of lending to low-income families, and have triggered a revolution in peer-to-peer lending around the globe.

These people are game changers, and their respective organizations are system-changing social enterprises. Grameen and Kiva actually changed the formal financial system. Microcredits and giving a loan to a poor person was previously thought of as impossible. By thinking out of the box, as game changers, they came up with a new inclusive solution. By showing it could work with their social enterprises and inspiring others to tag along to start doing the same, they made a lasting change.

We take the formal financial system for granted, but we'll need to think outside of the current system to solve the flaws of it, to reach financial inclusion. The examples in this book are game changers like Grameen, Aflatoun and Kiva. They do just this: they are rethinking the current financial system and tackling some of the roots of its flaws. They are acting on behalf of current and future generations that are excluded and unable to live their lives to the fullest. Aflatoun and Child & Youth Financial Inclusion both brought financial education to our children and youth, a prerequisite for financial inclusion. They, too, like Grameen and Kiva, have trigged a transition to a new inclusive way of offering financial services to previously excluded low-income people. What these examples have in common is that they tackle some of the systemic barriers. And the good news is there are many more of them out there! This book is about game changers like Professor Yunus and Jerroo Billimoria. It studies what flaws they identified and how their financial solutions are flipping the system, in what way they created an alternative pathway to financial inclusion, how they triggered or are triggering transition to a new normal, and how their innovative solutions work and include those who previously have been excluded. It describes what their inclusive solutions look like, how exactly their social enterprises tackle existing flaws of the formal system, how they organize their social enterprises, and how they aim to reach a point of no return from the old and excluding ways.

Photo by Ymke Sie

This book aims to inspire you to contribute to transition to a world in which we all have access to the money we need to live a fruitful and meaningful life. If you are a social entrepreneur or innovator, starting and growing, feel free to digest these new ways of organizing and take forward what suits the growth of your mission best. Banks, insurers, financial service providers, please be appetized to explore and support new models for financial services in collaboration with partners 'out there.' Big businesses in energy, water and food, fashion, electronics – and not to forget fintech and insurtech – I hope you see you're needed, and it is possible for you to make a difference and become partners in financial inclusion. Please be invited to take a leading role, get inspired to explore, and support new and inclusive financial models. Don't try to do it all yourself; tag along with these game changers. Last but not least, for funders and impact investors, and the corporate venture arms, CSR and foundations, grow your impact to a system-changing level by collaborating with social entrepreneurs such as these; invest, fund, and share resources with pioneers and those social innovators who are scaling; and take the long-term view, since changing the system takes time.

7

This book will showcase carefully selected game changers and their social enterprises. What they do, why they do it and how they are doing so. These game changers come from all corners of the world; each one of them has an impressive track record of success (i.e. profoundly impacting the lives of so many), many of them with startling scale. Unique to their selection is their approach to changing the system. They present a diverse mix of uniquely and intrinsically inclusive solutions. Each chapter consists of several game changers, tackling at least one, but regularly a few flaws of our system. For those who also want to understand the magic of a system change and how this comes about, I've provided a framework that evolves around five levers. It captures why and how a system change comes into being, and therefore, too, answers the question why these game changers have been selected. After these five levers are presented to you, each lever will be illustrated by a number of cases of the game changers and their social enterprises. Each one of the game changers checks the boxes of this framework. The framework is actually based upon their work, and therefore gives a snapshot of how they are jointly reimagining financial inclusion.

This book is the result of an exciting and educational journey I've experienced. In the past 15 years, I've started two social ventures. The first one, Micro Credit for Mothers, provides small loans to enterprising women to invest in income-generating activities, operating in 10 countries in South and Southeast Asia, reaching thousands of the excluded families every year. In doing so, I've gained some understanding in the meaning of 'remote' and how that translates to being financially excluded. 'Remote' meaning way more than with a large physical distance from a bank, meaning also not being able to read or compute, meaning no internet, or roads being flooded or inaccessible due to monsoon rains during four months of the year. More recently, I've founded Credits for Communities, aiming to innovate financial services for groups of enterprising low-income people who not just generate (more) income for themselves, but also increase the wellbeing of their own village. This adventure is deepening my insight and gives me hands-on experience of how to pilot an inclusive financial solution and then further develop and scale it through collaboration with partners in the formal financial system.

My time with the Banking with the Poor Network (BWTP) – a network of Asian microfinance institutions – and more recently with Ashoka, the world's largest international network of system-changing social entrepreneurs, has given me the opportunity to learn from and collaborate with so many amazing social entrepreneurs and innovators. Some of them are featured in this book. I was privileged to witness the way they think and work. I'm grateful they gave me an insider view. Both networks, Ashoka and BWTP, provided fertile soil for speaking to some of the most provocative thought leaders on different matters related to financial inclusion. These years with Ashoka and BWTP were super-fruitful in attesting and validating new social business models and hybrid value chains to reach and serve the poor.

Before I became a social entrepreneur or worked for Ashoka, I worked for over a decade with big businesses, including Philips, KLM, IBM and ABN-AMRO. Being educated with a Master of the Science of Industrial Engineering and Business Management empowered me to analyse and distil the learnings and approaches of these game changers. The concepts in this book are imagined and implemented by the social innovators featured – all credit goes to them. My humble contribution is the distilling of lessons learned and levers, serving the purpose of growing to a world in which all of us are financially included. The beauty is that this collection of game changers jointly paints a clear picture with similar colours, shading and contours. They present to us a promising picture of our future. If we could only collectively commit to contributing to inclusive solutions like these ... the world would be a better place.

CHAPTER 1

FIVE LEVERS IN A FRAMEWORK TO FLIP THE FORMAL FINANCIAL SYSTEM

The world is changing at an increasing speed, with COVID, Black Lives Matter and Greta's "our house is on fire" spearheading these developments and showing the growing urgency. We've witnessed the damage of 'them-against-us,' the destruction of not being inclusive. But how do we progress? What's next? Studying game changers in the space of financial inclusion at large offers a window of opportunity to picture ourselves how the world would look when you offer financial services fully adapted to the needs of the low-income people. It offers a view of the potential financial system that could work for all of us, flipped inside out and upside down. By distilling what issues these social entrepreneurs are solving, by capturing what their inclusive solutions look like, and by abstracting the key features of how they do it, this framework was developed. The five levers are essentially the five key flaws of the current formal financial system; each game changer aims to overcome at least one of them. The first clog wheel in this framework is therefore about these systemic issues. However, by just pointing to the cracks in the system that need to be glued, we don't fix the system. It's in the how to do this, where the magic is. That's where the other two radars of the framework come in. Since this framework, including the five levers, is based upon the work of these game changers, let me start by introducing them to you, short and sweet. I will categorize them using the five levers.

THE FIVE LEVERS

Some rules in our system make it very hard for the low-income people to progress out of poverty. Hence, 'Changing the rules' of the game is the first lever. These three game changers are inspiring examples of how this can be done. Shivani Siroya, the founder of Tala, is on a mission to expand access to financial products to the emerging middle class globally. She is rewriting creditworthiness through radical trust by using the mobile phone. Willy Foote is founder of Root Capital, which has revolutionized access to finance for the small-scale farmers of our food by using potential earning as collateral. Hamse Warfa is co-founder of BanQu, a supply chain solution for multinationals and an economic identity platform for refugees and people in extreme poverty. BanQu has invented a so-called economic passport to vouch for hard-work, as a solution to inclusion.

Inclusion, by nature, means *everybody*. I will highlight two elements of this second lever. Firstly, all of us – men and women – need to be included. For this to happen, secondly, we need more partners, not just banks and insurers, to join the game of financial inclusion. The following three innovators demonstrate how we can make sure that *'Everybody plays.'* Katherine Lucey, founder of Solar Sisters, offers an innovative last-mile distribution solution for clean energy technologies. She is beating the gender balance by tapping into the power of female entrepreneurs in the villages in rural Africa. Brett Matthews, the founder of My Oral Village, is on a mission to increase numeracy. As reading is for education, numeracy is a prerequisite for financial inclusion. Rebecca van Bergen is the founder of Nest; she is committed to the social and economic advancement of the informal workforce of fashion and home decoration and accessories industries. Nest is financially including home-based artisans and their workers, mostly women, in close collaboration with big brands.

The use of money is rooted in daily life; however, our formal financial services are absent in the slums, the rural villages and on the streets where low-income people live. The third lever is, therefore, *'Daily life as the playground.'* It starts with income, and thus it's all about jobs, jobs, jobs. Gojek, co-founded by Nadiem Makarim, and at the heart of this solution Mapan, founded by Aldi Haryopratomo, are on a mission to empower the huge informal sector, creating more income and, while doing so, formally financially including them, in South and Southeast Asia, at the moment people need it, at the place they need it. Joost van Engen, founder of Healthy Entrepreneurs, is building rural health markets, selling healthcare products and services from mobile mini-pharmacies in remote villages in Uganda, Ghana, Kenya and Tanzania. He brings income-generating activities with the adjoining financial services, while simultaneously accelerating access to health products and services.

Our formal system offers financial services; however, it's not integrated with the fulfilment of daily needs of low-income people, during the harvest, at the market or when one falls ill and needs insurance, or needs to replenish stock for a petty shop. For this to happen, we need to *'Link all players,'* so we can offer integrated financial services. This fourth lever is demonstrated by Gustaf Agartson, founder of BIMA, a leading mobile-delivered health and insurance player in emerging markets, offering protection through the phone, in close collaboration with mobile network providers and insurers. Tienda Pago, founded by Dan Cohen, offers inventory loans for petty shop owners in Mexico and Peru. He is doing so in close collaboration with fast-moving consumer goods companies that get access to mobile cashless payments. George Kuria, CEO of ACRE Africa, offers farmers a solution to manage agricultural risks, at the place and the moment they need it in their farming business, with micro-agricultural insurances.

Another crack in the system is that it is fully geared to support individuals, or an organization acting as 'one.' Social interaction and groups are not taken into account in our formal financial system, whereas groups, villages and social capital are uniquely well positioned as a lever to ignite inclusion. This fifth lever, *'Play as a group,'* is illustrated beautifully by Sebastian Groh, founder of SOLshare, who's growing a network of village solar power grids, empowering solar power prosumers – a household that produces and consumes – rural village by rural village in Bangladesh. Kumar Shailabh, founder of Uplift Mutuals, has developed a community model for healthy living and health micro-insurances in India.

THE FRAMEWORK

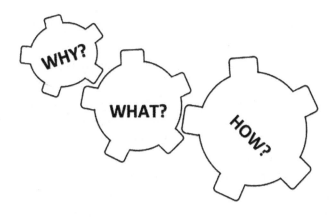

Like Simon Sinek[2] says, it starts with why. So, first, what flaws are they tackling? The *why*. As you've read, these game changers leverage five key principles, solving five cracks of the current formal financial system. The approach these game changers apply is unique; they take a system change approach. To help us understand what makes them unique and how they do this, I will distinguish between the innovative solutions they have developed, the *what* and the way they organizing to deliver their innovative solution – the *how*. These are intertwined with each other; one does not happen without the other. They both intertwist with the *why* too, like cog wheels. So, the first and foremost cog wheel is the *why*, with the five levers as its teeth. The second cog describes the *what*, the five features characterizing their inclusive innovation. This provides insights into what makes the inclusive solution different in itself. Distilling these features helps for the financial innovation to be scaled through adoption, replication and joining forces with partners. Many game changers put in considerable effort to encourage others to adopt and replicate their inclusive solution and invite partners to join in using 'their' inclusive solution. The future forwardness of the game changers anticipates accelerating inclusion through sharing and adoption of the inclusive solution itself and of the features these inclusive solutions share.

This attitude in inviting others to join using their inclusive solution is so different from 'business as usual.' It's based upon collaboration, the opposite of competition. This is a great example of the fact that the *what* and the *why* are so intertwined with the *how*: a whole new way of thinking and doing is put into practice by these game changers. So, third is the *how*. Each and every innovator gets their inclusive solution in place by applying new ways of organizing. The social innovation is created, produced, distributed and delivered by organizing their enterprise in an alternative way. It is never just the inclusive financial innovation in itself, but always in combination with other ways of developing, producing and delivering, that makes inclusion possible. The operation of their social enterprise, *how* they organize and manage, is fundamentally different. The second cog, the inclusive innovation, cannot take place without the third wheel, another way of organizing. I have found five distinct characteristics of these new ways of organizing, the five teeth of this third cog wheel.

It is exactly this magic mix of an inclusive innovation – the *what* – with an alternative way of producing it and bringing it to the low-income families – the *how* – that provides them with the power to change the game. It makes it possible for them to put their mission to be inclusive – their *why* – into practice. These three cog wheels, operating together, make up the framework.

WHY?

Let's start with the five key principles these game changers leverage to tackle the main flaws of the current formal financial system that keep so many excluded. Before doing so, I like to point out that all of the game changers are putting more than just one of these five principles into practice; they are all tackling several fundamental issues at the same time. They are by no means applied one by one nor exclusively.

CHANGING THE RULES OF THE GAME

If we take a closer look at the rules of the game, we can see two different sets. On the one hand, we see values and norms, let's say the unwritten rules. Most of them are implicit, some based upon biases. Obviously, all being local, culture and often country specific. We can call these unwritten rules together a mindset; they are baked in everywhere. In some countries, women are not allowed to inherit or own land and have to stay at home and take care of the children. Or, on the other side of the same coin, men have to provide an income and are not considered to be true men if they care for their kids. Another example of unwritten rules, less gender stereotyping, is that low-income people cannot afford insurance. Mindsets are based upon implicit assumptions. In most countries, there's a strong bias that you can only trust a person (with a loan or bank account) when she has an identity card or a written proof of income. These are examples of covered assumptions that have crept into the finance sector. More often than not, we only take written proof of income as evidence for the ability to pay. Mind you, it's not just with banks and insurers;

it is in many other institutions too. In many, perhaps even most jurisdictions, one needs to work in a factory or in an office to be protected against malpractice, such as non-payment or an unhealthy workspace, and to assure you earn a decent salary and get a form of work guarantee. These unwritten rules are based upon underlying assumptions, which are most of the time incorrect. Each one of the game changers in this book uncovers an underlying assumption and proves it to be false. What we call 'the system' is actually this set of rules. That's what makes our current formal financial system so exclusive.

On the other hand, another set of rules are written down in laws and regulations. Many, perhaps even most, are aimed to provide protection. This is, of course, in essence a good intention. However, decades of application of these laws and regulations have resulted in procedures that turn out to be also working against inclusion. Some elements of the procedures resulted in hurdles that hinder low-income people to grow out of poverty. Decades of application made them rigid. Because they are infused in the whole system, and not owned by anyone anymore, they are an integral part of the system. The rules apparently work better for those who already have built up capital and a formal job in an office with a tangible salary slip to show, while, although unintended, they do not work for low-income people to prosper and thrive. Not being able to get a loan, because you do not have a formal job or an identity card, prevents you from growing your income from your own enterprise, a vicious circle keeping a person from progressing. Not being able to get health products, services and insurance keeps a family from staying healthy, which propels millions of families back into poverty when a family member gets seriously ill. This is another vicious cycle keeping families from building a better life. In this way, low-income people are excluded just because they do not have written

proof that they exist, such as an identity card or a birth certificate. UNICEF estimates that a quarter of the children
under five worldwide are unregistered.[3] According to the
UN, two billion people earn their livelihood in the informal sector,[4] not having a formal job. Which means that
they do not have the salary slip to apply for a loan in our
formal financial system. This is not a minor issue. These
written rules work better for those who have built up capital, work in offices with permanent contracts, can identify
with an id card and – not unimportant –can read. You can
do the math: it's only the happy few who have all of these.
Many mechanics of the operating of our formal financial
system are based upon a combination of these written and
unwritten rules. And while originally meant to protect, we
witness that they've resulted in excluding the majority of
the people on our planet. Which is what nobody wants.

Each of these game changers prove one or more of these
underlying assumptions behind these rules to be wrong. You
do not necessarily need a salary slip to trust someone with a
loan; you can use behavioural data, too. Identification usually goes with a fixed home address, identity card and signature, while you can identify differently with an economic
passport or by other people vouching for you. All of the
social entrepreneurs show that the die-hard assumption
that poor people cannot afford financial services is false.
Farmers can afford replanting guarantees, communities
of low-income people can afford health micro-insurances.
A sneaky assumption that you cannot be protected against
non-payment or earn a proper income while working from
home, that you do not have to be in an office or factory
for that, has slowly proven to be incorrect. These social
innovators provide evidence that remote villages can be
developed to be markets for food, transportation, solar,
housing and health-related products, too. And another
covered-up assumption, that only banks and insurers can

deliver financial services, is steadily losing ground. Unusual suspects turn out to be excellent partners to bring those markets into being, to financially serve those market players, and ultimately be strong players and contributors for financial inclusion.

Now is the time to rethink those rules, because we have new insights and new technologies. It has become possible to rewrite the rules without adding too much risk, due to new technological developments. Let's avoid these excluding rules in the application of new technologies. And what is more, it is possible to rewrite these rules, benefitting low-income people. Several examples have shown us that technology-powered developments can bump up financial inclusion. Take, for example, aadhaar in India – the world's largest biometric ID system – a brand-new system for identification built in the past decade. Or, for example, Mpesa – a leading mobile-phone-based money transfer service – has reached and improved inclusion for millions in less than two decades through the rise of (smart) phones. Mind you, of the unbanked adults in the world, about two-thirds have a mobile phone.[5] Changing the rules can only be done while empowering other partners to join too. Just think of the microcredits. Triggered by Professor Yunus' Grameen bank, it has spread globally mainly due to the fact that it was taken forward and replicated by so many others, in just a few decades. What is key to these examples that have changed the rules is that they have taken a system-change approach, for which partnerships and work in ecosystems is key.

These examples also demonstrate that the transition from coins, bills and wallets to digital money and online transaction processing can be turned into a massive force for good for inclusion. Which in itself offers a huge potential to serve all of us. Especially when we empower other partners to join in financial service provisions. Shifting the rules so that these three extremely powerful mechanisms – new insights, new technologies and new partners – can ignite financial inclusion. Big businesses are more and more committing to the United Nations Sustainable Development Goals (SDGs). However, *"while 84% of companies participating in the UN Global Compact are taking action on SDGs, only 46% are embedding them into their core business."*[6] It's time to focus on the actual behavioural changes required to support each person in the world to transact and store value, to make a living and live a productive life.

EVERYBODY PLAYS

Most money mechanisms in most society are male dominated: ownership of land, inheritance, use of mobile money, making money. While money is required to care for kids, buy groceries, marriage and building a safe home, this is, in many regions and cultures, the domain of women. A widely acknowledged root cause of our failing system is this gender disbalance. World banks' Global Findex numbers are telling: women in developing economies remain 9% less likely than men to have a bank account; 56% of all unbanked adults are women; and among the unbanked, women are more likely than men to be out of the labour force.[7]

At the same time, there's another element of this lever too. It is a different side, but from the same coin, no pun intended. Tradition has it that our current formal financial system is made by giant banks, global leaders in insurance, and world trade institutions. Those giants are in faraway places from where the majority of the people live, work, eat, pray and play. Those who actually transact with low-income people on a day-to-day basis are around the corner: at the market, where they buy their food or fertilizer, in school teaching their children, receiving the produce of their hard-working hands, providing phone credits. They are the ones who know and transact with low-income people daily. So, they are the ones that can financially include them, too. The time and technology has come to think – and act – outside the giant financial institutions. We need to link in low-income people at the market around the corner to hook them up through their phones. This requires that we capacitate many more players, those who are already knocking on their doors, to also deliver financial services.

The lever *Everybody plays* has therefore two elements: we knock on all the doors and everybody who knocks is capacitated to deliver financial services.

DAILY LIFE AS THE PLAYGROUND

Money is meant as a medium of exchange, to facilitate transaction and to store value in case you need it at a later moment in life. Basic needs are the first and foremost reason to transact, exchange and store value. Money should have strings attached: strings to daily life. Nowadays, formal financial services are disconnected from the basic needs of the poor. The majority of the world, those living with little income, need money to get their basic needs fulfilled on a daily basis. Delivery of financial services is needed at the place where and at the moment when basic needs arise and are supplied. A mother needs cash when and where she buys food. Where a farmer sells produce, that is the place to save money. When an entrepreneur wants to start a business, or take a large order, that is the moment to provide a loan. When seeds are bought for a new season of planting is the moment risk needs to be covered for bad weather with insurance. When a child has a cough is the moment a family should be able to buy health insurance and get access to medicines and a family doctor to avoid the high cost of a hospital visit. The playground for financial inclusion is at the doorsteps. It arises in the daily lives, not at a separate place, not at a separate moment. Then and there is where the financial service should be delivered, attached to daily life.

The way to offer financial services – at the doorsteps or around the corner – is by integrating it with the fulfilment of basic needs. We need to grasp the helping hand of peers and partners who are currently already delivering essential resources to excluded families. It's time to take to the villages, the slums and the streets.

LINKING ALL PLAYERS IN EQUALITY

Most of our food, fashion and flights are made in global and complex supply chains, the same as with many other services and products. We've gained many benefits from this so-called globalization. However, also some flaws crept in that make finance for all, hard to establish. Consumption at large scale is incentivized, which makes sustainable production at small scale close to impossible. A perception of people as consumers has rooted deeply, and our trust in people as producers is becoming weaker with the day. The link between 'our' soil, sun and natural resources at a certain place, and the fulfilling of needs in another place, is weak or broken. All of these factors contribute to making it hard to keep a global balance in our complex set of global supply chains. The question is not how to stop globalization, but how do we reestablish those linkages to find a better balance that benefits all of us? A rebalancing act after which each partner in global chains gets its fair share.

The game changers studied in this book suggest three clear directions to solving this. One is being fully transparent in the global chains, closing the loop with the mining, producing, generating people of our population, usually the families with low income in far-away places. This allows for making the mechanisms in the diffuse global chains more visible and taking corrective actions, paving the way for more sustainable mining, sourcing and production practices, while simultaneously financially including low-income families too. Secondly, the direction in which the financially included – the beneficiaries so to say – are treated as equals, and do not necessarily fully pay for the inclusive services, others contribute too. We need revised cost recovery mechanisms or, in old-school terminology, new business models for inclusive solutions. Many of the game changers have developed a so-called blended business model to deliver financial services integrated with the fulfilment of the daily needs of the hard-working people at the start of our global supply chains. Lastly, there's the direction of closing the loop between consumption and production locally, at least partially. Which, in business terms, means we allow for and stimulate more local value creation. And, of course, an application of any of the three in combination. Some innovators apply new cost-recovery structures in their social enterprises, while radically transforming global chains with transparency. Other game changers are linking consumption and production locally, for and by low-income families, while delivering financial services on the go.

The three directions these game changers have taken have one matter in common: they join forces with partners to create transparency, to apply a blended business model, to link consumption and production locally. Only by joining forces can we integrate financial service delivery to excluded people. New grounds – or in old-school terminology, markets – can be discovered with joint effort, integrating the players in the chain. Each game changer has shaped a last-mile infrastructure by differently trying together existing players.

PLAY AS A GROUP

There is a unique power of a group: it stems from its cohesion, it contains a unique knowledge and understanding of the context, it is based on solidarity and it's facilitated with social capital. Our current system is not fully geared to 'use' this innate group nature; it's barely incorporating our social context: the family, the village, the farmers or miners connected through their fields or mine, neighbours, the people in one address book, the shopkeepers or home-based artisans, as a group. Recognizing the strengths of a group, using it as new pathways to inclusion, is an opportunity not to miss. *Play as a group* is huge for financial inclusion. Look at what happened with microcredit, acknowledging and incorporating solidarity in a new lending practice, which proved to be a great way to give a loan to a poor person. This was a unique feature of a group that Professor Yunus' approach was based upon, and now millions across the globe are reached, financially included, by others who started to replicate the same solidarity lending practice. Similarly with self-help-groups, groups that are empowered to take savings of their members and distribute loans from their collective savings. In India, a programme of the National Bank for Agricultural and Rural Development (NARBARD's) is linking these self-help-groups to banks, and has financially included over 2 million groups, with an estimated 40 million people reached. Massive inclusion happened just by allowing to *play as a group*. How can we incorporate these strengths of a group even more to allow all of us to be included? There is still a lot to discover here. Not surprisingly, many of the game changers developed their inclusive solutions by taking the group as a premise.

They have built their inclusive solution based upon the strengths of the group, of the communities they serve. They have done parts of the development of the solution with the communities. What's more, the communities they financially include are often part of their social enterprises; they take on parts of the delivery and distribution. Many game changers have incorporated this sense of community, the relationships of low-income people in their financial solution. These game changers have engaged group members to identify others, to capture needs, to determine rules that aligned with their social context, to raise awareness, to educate other group members, to sell, to evaluate services and to monitor progress. By integrating one, some or all of these functions performed by members of the groups and communities, you can see communities taking and getting ownership, which results in protection by the same people. Protection by peers and taking some functions over through self-organizing are powerful mechanisms that ignite inclusion. And by doing so, their solution becomes intrinsically inclusive. This is what makes empowerment to *play as a group* so strong, and one of the ways to go for financial inclusion.

These five principles provide an outline of the picture of how the world would look like if we adapt the financial services fully to the needs of low-income people and fix some cracks in the system. But, of course, we also want to know how they did it. It's always a combination of a unique financial innovation – the *what* – on the one hand, and the way of producing and delivering it, on the other hand – the *how*.

WHAT?

The five features that characterize each and every financial innovation of these game changers are easy to grasp but not as easy to implement, because they intertwine with the why and the how. These game changers dedicate considerable amounts of their time and effort to assure easy access for others to join, replicate or adopt their inclusive solution. The uniqueness lies in the fact that the financial innovation is framed in such a way that it appetizes others to follow suit, to collaborate in several ways, to join and adopt it for another country or community. The financial solution is not meant to be kept in isolation; the game changers actively seek to spread it, aiming to realize an irreversible change. Unlike 'business-as-usual,' the approach to change the system is based upon spreading the social innovation in itself. And that is partly why these financial innovations are considered to be the game changers. Studying them provided insight in the key features of their innovations. The following five Ps are the features that can be recognized in all financial innovations of these game changers.

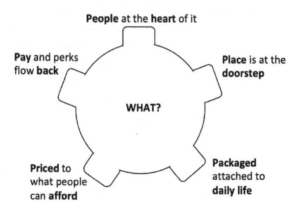

PEOPLE AT THE HEART OF IT

In each of the game-changing solutions, it's low-income people who are at the heart of the solution. Sometimes they are targeted as farmers, in other cases as the villagers or the artisans working from home, but the solution is made to serve a (previously) excluded part of the population, a community of low-income people. The inclusive solutions are built to empower the families they target; they serve no other purpose! The innovation is always empowering them, by education and through connections. The innovations come with education. The people served are taught how to apply governance, how to take ownership. To do so, all solutions are based on trust, trust in the people. Trust is reciprocal by nature, so they trust the people they serve, and therefore the people who bring the solution to them are trusted partners. The people are often part of the solution, part of how the solution is delivered.

PLACE IS AT THE DOORSTEP

Delivery of the solution is at home or around the corner, where the need for money, saving, taking a loan or manage risk arises. The people they serve are not asked to travel to a far-away place. The game changers offer the solution at their doorstep: in the village, the refugee camp, at the farmers' produce drop-off point. Each part of the process of a financial service is brought close to the low-income people. Through their phones they can get a loan. Through their neighbours or friends, they can be identified. Their closest peers are included in the solution: their village head or a member of the saving group they join weekly vouches for a short-term loan. From the distributor who delivers their inventory, they can get pre-finance and pay cash-less. Where and when they take a gig, they get a work guarantee. At the farmer's shop they weekly visit, they can get insurance.

The innovation of the financial service is actually most of the time due to the fact that it is delivered at nearby places in their daily lives.

PACKAGED ATTACHED TO DAILY LIFE

What's even more, it is delivered and accessible for exactly what the people need it for. It is adapted exactly to and integrated with the fulfilment of the daily needs of that moment. When they earn some income with producing and selling solar power, the financial inclusion comes from allowing them to save that money, for a later moment in time the family needs it. The solution is adapted to their local reality. The family is enabled to keep the money at their home and use it at another moment when they need it, for example, when they saved enough to invest in a solar power panel. Health insurance is adapted to this local reality, it solves the issues for the family, providing access to doctors and affordable medicines for each family member. The micro-health insurance is packaged in such a way that it includes access to a doctor, affordable medicines and includes the whole family. Similarly, when taxi drivers take a gig, they need immediate assurance they will get paid, offering protection at the moment when and at the place where the gig happens. The innovation in financial services is due to the fact that it is integrated in the products and services they need the money or financial service for.

PRICED TO WHAT PEOPLE CAN AFFORD

It's surprising to witness that most of the financial innovations are priced based upon what a low-income family, farmer or refugee worker can afford. Old-school cost-based pricing mechanisms don't work when you aim for financial inclusion. By no means does this imply that those social enterprises are not financially sustainable. Here's where the new ways of organizing come into the picture – see the *how* in the next paragraph – due to which this affordable pricing becomes possible. The unique feature here is the fact that the price is set based upon what the family can afford. How the inclusive offering is produced and distributed is reversely engineered back to this price. This is often done with the help of technology, but mind you, this is just a part of the solution. Most of the time, costs related to the product development, or the delivery, are carried by others or shared with others. Very often, the end consumer does not carry all the costs alone. That is the unique feature these game changers bring: blended business models to ensure affordable prices. Many of the game changers demonstrate that the 'old-school' precept of the-user-pays-all won't do. The key takeaway here is: offering the service for a price a low-income family can afford is a prerequisite.

PAY AND PERKS FLOW BACK TO THE FAMILY OR COMMUNITY

Many of the solutions to inclusion of these system-changing social innovators close the loop locally between income generation and/or cost savings for the end-consumer. The income generation, the benefits of an investment made, or the cost savings as a result of using the financial service are channelled back into the local context: within the family or the family business, within the village, or the farmers' or insurance group. Every financially inclusive innovation of the game changers has pay or other perks – financially related – flowing back to the family or community, directly or indirectly. For example, a petty shop owner can take a loan for inventory, based upon the increased earnings as a result of it. A community receives access to health advice and affordable medicines by joining a health insurance scheme or by getting health-entrepreneurs in the village.

What's even more, the mechanisms, the rules, how it flows back and how much flows back locally are sometimes jointly decided by the community members themselves and realized in close collaboration with them.

HOW?

Many of the above features of the inclusive financial solution are no-brainers. Still, it holds true that most of today's financial services fail to be inclusive because they don't check the boxes for these five P-elements. Apparently, it's quite a challenge to make financial services inclusive, so let's have a look at how these game changers manage to realize it. There are no fixed recipes (yet) to do so. The secret is actually in the kitchen. The magic mix is in the making of the inclusive solutions. It lies in the processes of development, production and delivery of these inclusive solutions. All the system-changing social entrepreneurs apply unique ways of organizing; they organize differently to reach their beneficiaries and serve these low-income people. Rooted in their commitment to an inclusive mission, they manage, operate and innovate differently than business as usual. It's in how they redistribute work in the supply chain – in order to attach financial services to the fulfilment of daily needs – where you can see the difference. It's their entrepreneurial attitude to collaboration that distinguishes their way of organizing. You can see this back in the joint delivery or networked way of distribution, in close collaboration with partners and with the beneficiaries. You can find it in their approach to innovation, most of them reverse engineer their solution to meet low-income families' needs. You can witness it in how they recover costs for their full operation with blended business models and in hybrid value chains. It's in production and delivery through partnerships that you can see that their social enterprises barely acknowledge boundaries and can be better viewed as networks. I've coined the following five characteristics, the five Cs, to capture their alternative ways of organizing to serve the hard-to-reach and previously excluded groups of people.

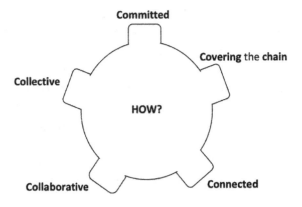

COMMITTED

Above all, the leaders and the teams use motivation as the main driver to organise. A motivation derived from the commitment to their mission. It's the commitment to their inclusive mission that keeps them on their toes to continuously innovate to overcome whatever challenge they come across. It's commitment to the low-income families they aim to include that make them reengineer reversely, adapting products and services to their needs. The founder's commitment is often so contagious that team members can get partners on board. The leaders know and act upon the fact that the system does not change if the organization does not change, and that their organization does not change if the people don't change. So, they put human resources practices in place to select committed people and to stimulate through motivation and instil trust, both equally important to bring change about.

How do they do this? At many of their social ventures, they have put a practice in place of bringing your whole self to the workplace. They cherish their talent as whole human beings, not just as professionals. Those organizations don't manage or control, they lead with trust, following their belief that when you are committed, you can be trusted to take the right actions, to make the right decisions. In case it turns out to be the wrong decision, you learn a lot. To grow commitment, as well as trust, empathy is needed, so regularly empathy is considered as a core competence in these organizations. Through empathy, the hearts of team members and clients are connected, through which the commitment becomes unbreakable. A whole lot of encouragement of entrepreneurial behaviour takes place at their social enterprises, with the commitment to an inclusive mission as the northern star. Enterprising attitudes are required to overcome whatever challenge you run in to. And by the nature of the job, which is ultimately changing the game, only one thing is certain: that is the fact that you need to overcome many challenges. All team members are required to solve challenges they will run into, without knowing beforehand what it will be. This means that the team needs to be empowered to go out, explore, try and adapt. And if it does not work, the team learns to fail fast. Failing is learning. For all of this experimenting, testing and failing, you need a safe space. A place where you feel safe and trusted to fail and learn. For a big chunk, this safe space is shaped by sharing one mission. Sharing one mission is not to be mistaken for like-minded team members; it's the opposite, actually. It's often through diverse teams, linked by their commitment to the same mission. Learning and innovation happen when you are challenged by a diverse group of team members. This is what you will see back at most of those game-changing organizations. You can only challenge the status quo and come up with new ideas and test new ways if you dare to disagree and try differently, while trusting you're all committed to reach the same outcome: inclusion.

COVERING THE CHAIN

Because the game changers aim to make a difference in the lives of the low-income families they serve, they usually have to change the next player upstream or downstream in the chain too. Business as usual did not work out well, so won't work now. Therefore, the suppliers, and the suppliers of the suppliers, have to change too. Most of the innovators tweak, reform or disrupt parts of the value chain they are part of, from raw materials to finished goods. They either shift power, restructure incentives, or make parts more efficient or fair. They do so while often adding a step or two: building an effective channel to reach the last mile, allowing smallholder farmers, low-income families or day laborers to be reached by insurers, for example. Or, making the producer at home, migrant miner or front shop store visible for big brands, by tracing produce or products when it goes from their hands to distributors, middlemen and transportation partners in the chain. Other game changers show how they can bring affordable, good quality medicines, health screenings or solar power to remote and rural villages, by adding some elements to the supply chain, the so-called 'last mile,' for which they restructure some other parts to make sure that the whole chain continues to operate. The point being that this reach-out to the people who live in remote areas cannot be done without integrating, influencing and feeling accountability for what happens in other parts of the full chain. These game changers demonstrate a deep insight and drive to deliver the required change into the whole chain, for which they will connect, collaborate and create collective actions – see last of the five Cs, below. This is what they see as part of their 'job.' They acknowledge that their work doesn't stop where their enterprise stops; they know that this is actually where it all starts. Most of the game changers act as supply-chain integrators and coordinators;

they orchestrate the players in the chain for the benefit of the hard-working hands at the base of the production chain. They accept that they have to impact the full chain for the change required to include the low-income families to take root.

CONNECTED

Most of the organizations of the game changers aiming for financial inclusion have a sort of blurred boundaries. Their organization, the service they offer or channel they've built is usually heavily wired with other partners, and therefore operates more like a network. Sometimes they reach the last mile through a network of local micro-entrepreneurs selling medicines or solar solutions while creating awareness and educate about healthy living or clean energy. Other cases show an inclusive service offering, in combination with the service(s) of their partner(s). For example, health screenings and consultations in combination with health insurances through mobile phones, offered in partnership with mobile network operators, doctors and insurers. Other game changers offer investments to grow small-scale farmers' businesses through farmers' cooperatives on the one side, impact and grant funding partners on another side, and large food companies contracting the farmers on yet another side, in a triangle-shaped network. Or, for instance, a network of mom-and-pop shops on the one side of the social venture offering inventory pre-finance in close collaboration with fast-moving consumer good companies and their distributors on the other side. The new ways of organizing demonstrated by many of those social innovators have integrated their business to such an extent with multiple strategic partners that it makes them act as a network. The social venture acts as supply chain coordinator and connector.

It is the networked nature of their approach and organizations that makes their financial solution innovative, inclusive as well as financially sustainable. Through this connectedness, they manage to finance and fund their full operation, allowing them to offer the inclusive services priced affordably to the low-income family, farmer or refugee. It's the connected nature of their business that allows them to be sustainable, through a so-called blended business model. A business model that is far away from traditional cost-based pricing and the user-pays-it-all-model. This blended model is a new business model that often applies cross-subsidization schemes internally to keep the prices to the base-of-the-pyramid family affordable. The blended model mixes different types of income, philanthropic and impact funds, sales revenue and fee for services, with different types of cost compensation such as joint development, volunteering and pro-bono services. The connectedness offers the basis for the new business model, a blended model.

It's also through this connectedness that the game changers shift the power balance in their supply chain, realizing transparency, adapting incentives, redistributing income streams and reforming attitude and mindset in the chain – ultimately, including and empowering the low-income people they serve. The game changers see it as their role to assure that every party gets a fair share, including low-income people. They take these coordinator and connector roles seriously and build the required trust to act on behalf of low-income people and create understanding between all other partners engaged. They use the connectedness to develop affordable products, to distribute to low-income people, to offer the service at the moment the rural family needs it and attached to 'primary' products they need. It's through a bundled offering with primary products fulfilling daily needs that they make financial services tangible. It is through the connectedness with low-income families that the members of the community are incorporated in the production and distribution of the solution, which results in being intrinsically inclusive. It is only through this connected way of operating that they can serve the poor.

COLLABORATIVE

This connectedness is an organizational characteristic that comes into being through collaboration. It's not that you have a few account managers in your organization that deal with some partners, it is in the DNA of the organizations of these game changers. Their whole social enterprise is geared toward collaboration. A strong ability to collaborate sits with each and every team member working in the organization and beyond. What makes those game changers unique is that they hardly act upon competition; it's all about collaboration. Everything is done in collaboration. It is actually the system-changing approach underpinning the financial innovation they are developing: to facilitate others to join and step in the same game with them. It's not about keeping it to themselves so they can benefit from a competitive advantage. It's the opposite – it's all about how to collaborate in such a way that more partners can contribute. Their work in the chain is open to adapt to what their partner needs, what their partner's strength is. It's a continuous search to find the sweet spot in their collaboration, acknowledging they both come with their own core business and strengths, seeking where the synergies are. When they have separate units or legal entities within their organization, it is to assure focus, either on a specific expertise, functionality or geographic area. However, this focus of each separate unit is meant to optimize trade-offs in dialogue, ultimately beneficial to the target group: the low-income family.

Several features return frequently in their social enterprises that contribute to them being strong and entrepreneurial collaborators: they are transparent and ask this of their partners. They are strong communicators and practice deep listening. Their commitment – to their inclusive mission – works contagiously, which is why partners want to collaborate with them. They know how to think big, but start and act small. And this applies to everybody in their organization: leadership is distributed, everybody is asked to be transparent, strong in communication and able to translate big visions into actionable steps. An organizational capacity to collaborate, whether it is inside or outside your own organization, as long as it is serving the inclusive mission, functions as the oil in the larger operating of the machine.

COLLECTIVE

Closely related, but definitely different to the connectedness and collaboration, is the strong urge to take it forward collectively. These game changers have built their organizations on a collective learning journey. Because they don't know how the financial inclusive future looks like, they share the learnings while exploring and discovering what works and what does not. Their teams are encouraged to continuously learn, always in collaboration with the low-income customer, as well as with their strategic partners. Talent is explicitly selected for their growth mindset. Teams are dynamic – they change over time – and are assembled to facilitate learning. Most of their organizational processes include regular feedback loops with both customers and partners. The solutions and tools they develop, test and use are often openly shared and not kept for themselves. Platforms are built to welcome other partners to join. These social innovators know that this is the way to collectively include more low-income people. These game changers acknowledge that the gain – for financial inclusion – is in the collective learning. That is: learning that goes way beyond the boundaries of their own organization. That is why the learnings during the development and pilots of their inclusive solutions are explicitly shared with others, not just with their strategic partners and/or funders, but with others who could be inspired and benefit from it too.

It's not 'just' collective learning; they often go far beyond that and walk the extra mile to facilitate others to also take action. These game changers often assemble councils and establish associations to grow momentum to not only collectively learn, but also get into action to 'use' the inclusive solutions, the new lending practice, the alternative way of identifying, the building of formal transaction history, the protection to work from home and so on. They invite others to join and follow suit: use the same solution, replicate it and adapt it to the needs in another geographical region, or at least take the learnings forward. They invite others to join in the platform, collaborate to use the same tools, learn from the same pilot, adopt the features of their product and take it to another community, to another area. All just for the sake of growing financial inclusion. That's what I will call collective action, often orchestrated by these system-changing social entrepreneurs.

They apply a strategy of building evidence, developing collective actions and co-creating joined advocacy and awareness raising, as to scale inclusiveness to a point of no return. All of these strategic steps go beyond benefits for their organization only. Don't be mistaken: this is not done out of pure altruism; it's rooted in a deep understanding of the nature of inclusiveness that it accelerates with each partner that joins the network. Or in business terminology: *the network effect*. Most of these system-changing social innovators show a unique sense of collective responsibility, which often translates into a power to push for collective actions. These game changers act as pace makers of the network effect to accelerate inclusion.

WHO?

Last, but not least, all these social enterprises have coura-geous leaders, often the founders, with an open mind and on an inclusive mission. They have an idea, an innovation, and apply their entrepreneurship to get it into practice. None of them is guided by being solely profitable; all of them are driven by the impact: the growth to an inclu-sive society. They don't necessarily seek to grow their own organization; instead, they aim to grow the change they see required to grow toward full financial inclusion. They will never stop reinventing, adding and adapting inclusive solutions, and inviting others to join, just because there is so much left to do to make the transition to a truly inclu-sive financial system. Hopefully this clarifies, too, why I call these game changers social entrepreneurs. They blend the good of doing business with the development spirit on their mission to financial inclusion. Doing business is what makes it sustainable; the development spirit is what makes it inclusive. Combining the two is what's required to reim-agine a world in which nobody is left out. Until then, for them the game isn't over.

Although it goes without saying, those leaders apply the above-described new ways of organizing with their teams as second nature. For the purpose to learn from them, how they organize, I've also looked at how they instil their values, their ways of dealing with the system's flaws, in their teams. We could call this a new style of leadership that they have developed. One that is focused to instil openness, trust and empathy in their teams. One that encourages innovation, to think out of the box, to take risks and to be entrepreneurial.

It's interesting to see that most of the social innovators are nurturing and developing similar kinds of organizing principles in their social ventures. A practice full of learning and listening, with little management and control, valuing the whole human being at work. The teams in their social enterprises are diverse and dynamic, the members have fluid roles. In different ways, most game changers have built a strong user base in their organizations. And, also remarkable, they treat those who generate revenue – partners and funders – equally with those who receive the benefits – customers and beneficiaries – demonstrating high standards when it comes to equality.

Frederic Laloux coined this type Teal organizations in his book *Reinventing Organizations*. This Teal organization reveals three breakthroughs, according to Laloux. Firstly, *"Teal organizations have found the key to operate effectively with a system based upon peer relationships, without the need for either hierarchy or consensus."* Secondly, *"Teal organizations have developed a consistent set of practices that invite and bring all of who we are to work."* Thirdly, *"Teal organizations are seen as having a life and a sense of direction of their own."*[8] Many of the commonly shared cultural elements encountered by Laloux in the pioneering Teal organizations I found back with these game changers too: trust, open information sharing and decision-making, all are equal, a safe and caring workplace, recognition that we are all deeply interconnected (empathy), every problem is an invite to learn, every failure is an opportunity to learn, collective purpose, in the long-run there are no trade-offs between purpose and profit, if you focus on purpose, profit will follow.[9] Like Laloux's Teal organization, these game changers too illustrate that they break with doing business as usual and invent a new set of management principles and practices, a new style of leadership that better fits their purpose, their inclusive mission.

Let's just have a closer look. The following chapters will describe the game changers leveraging the five key principles, each tackling one or more of the cracks in the system. You will recognize the five P features of their innovative solutions, and many of the five C features in the way they organize. None of them show none of these features, none of them show all. All of them could have been described in one of the other chapters, since they usually leverage multiple of these principles simultaneously. They are tackling each and every of the systemic barriers in their own way, not one by one but holistically.

CHAPTER 2

CHANGING THE RULES OF THE GAME

One of the major challenges in our current formal financial system is that there is a huge gap between those who own most of the capital and have access to information, and those who are desperately in need of money and financial services. Those with the capital and the information – usually the big banks, global insurers, governmental bodies and big brands with global supply chains – play a big role in determining the rules. The rest is left with marginal roles of following rules and order. This is not done by anyone with bad intentions, this is due to global presence of these big players, and therefore long chains and rigid procedures. On top of this, it is reinforced by a lack of transparency and traceability. This is the system we're caught in, all of us.

People who are excluded by the system make out the majority. If we take a closer look, such a person would generate an income of a few dollars a day, either as a day labourer or selling products or produce. Such a person would need money to transact at the market and would have built up some savings in a sealed clay pot. Such a person would open this clay pot to pay with the savings for the education of their children or to invest in a home-based business, like weaving baskets. Such a person would take a loan from a family member or money lender, when granny falls ill and needs medicines or has to go to a health centre in the closest town. Such a person, a mom of five, would love to insure her crop, when it is time to buy seeds at the start the planting season. All we know for sure is that such a person is very unlikely to be supported with all these financial dealings by our formal financial system. This system is not built for her. The system does not know who she is, let alone supports her with any of her financial needs. The rules intrinsically exclude her.

Each game changer in this book is battling a different devil in disguise. All of them are changing the rules, whether they are implicit, baked in our mindset or explicitly written down in policies and regulations. Each one shows that one or more underlying assumptions are false. Do we really need collateral or formal (i.e. written) proof of income to trust someone with a loan? Tala and Root Capital – and Tienda Pago described in a later chapter –are redefining how credits can be provided to people without monetary collateral or permanent job contracts. Tala is building a new model to lend to low-income people, based upon radical trust, just by sharing data on their mobile phones. Without requiring a fixed home address, identity card and signature to verify their identify. Rewriting the rules and algorithms make them equal for everybody who applies. Making parts of the formal procedures obsolete, which are often invasive and unnecessary when you apply new technologies. Tala's model demonstrates positive outcomes for the poor, providing the evidence that enterprising low-income people are trustworthy clients for credit. Infusing the system with a revolutionary equal way of credit assessment, based upon behavior instead of static data only.

Root Capital identified an unexpected ally in the provision of an alternative to collateral for our small-scale food farmers with an appetite to grow their farmer's business. Fixed-priced forward contracts with large consumer brands prove to be a good alternative to collateral, enable loan provision and financial and business education. Root Capital has provided the evidence that their potential earnings work as well as a pathway to sustainable business growth. Root Capital has revolutionized the chain of finance for our food farmers by showcasing how those new rules work. Their new lending method, based upon this alternative for collateral, has positive results. Not just for Root Capital, although it is a sustainable social enterprise; it's benefitting low-income farmers and their communities. Without too much risk for the financing party. And on top of that, it improved the environmental impact.

BanQu, the third game changer described in this chapter, is putting the power of information in the hands of the migrant factory worker, the refugee miner, the family farmer. Replacing the formal salary slips as the only means to vouch for hard work. Finding an ally in the big business, offering transparency in their global value chain. An unprecedented transparency that works both ways. For the big business it creates insights all the way through the global chain to the hard-working hands of the producers at the base, on the one hand. But also – the other way around – empowering low-income people with their own information, providing them with an alternative means of identification and proof of their hard work. In this way, BanQu is tackling information biases too, solving lack of information, while empowering the small-scale producer by owning their own identity, by building a transaction history in a so-called economic passport. Tackling implicit assumptions about who owns your data, and what can prove your hard-work, and therefore your trustworthiness.

The new practices from these innovators bring a new game board into existence. With their inclusive solutions – a new way of identification, a new way of credit assessment, a new lending method – an enormous number of people can be financially included. BanQu and Root Capital demonstrate that other partners can step into the game of financial inclusion. Big businesses can become trustworthy partners in financial inclusion, big banks turn out to be able to change their procedures to include low-income people. What is key is that financial inclusion is for all of us to do. Every one of us is in the business of changing mindset – implicit values and norms – written and unwritten rules and therefore financial inclusive behaviour. The sooner we realize this, the faster we can shift to full financial inclusion.

Let's have a look.

2.1 TALA – REWRITING CREDITWORTHINESS THROUGH RADICAL TRUST

A phone as a credit card for lower-income families and radical trust as credit score. What if you trust to give your phone identity in return for credit? Entrepreneurial lower-income people who cannot enter banks for their cash flow issues are willing to do so to pre-finance small inventory loans or educational loans for their children. Radical trust goes both ways and can work as an alternative to formal credit scores. This proves to be a promising way to link in, hook-up and bridge the gap with millions of previously unbanked or only partially banked people.

Tala[10] is on a mission to prove the potential of poor people through providing credit based upon past behaviour, which is demonstrated by their smartphone records. Tala takes the risks in order to put more power in the hands of lower-income families. Disbursing loans from US$20 to US$500 to people without formal credit history, based upon the trust people give to share their past behaviour stored on their smartphone. A person with a modest income applies for a loan and gets a decision after several minutes, at the doorstep on their phone. The loan has a one-time fee and a term between 20–90 days. Tala disrupts, in essence, *"the perception of risk that society has – not just banks – that these customers are not creditworthy, that they don't have the capacity, that they don't have the potential,"* according to Shivani Siroya, the founder and CEO of Tala.[11] She defines her own objective as *"to develop financial identity through the data on their smartphones... proving a person's financial potential"*[12] for an emerging middle class so far underserved by our formal financial system.

Photo by game changer

Reaching over 4 million people (2020) with credit and personalized financial education in Kenya, Philippines, India and Mexico, six years since they started shows the power of Tala's new approach. Although roughly over half of their clients are formally employed, the other half is in the informal sector, earning between US$2 to US$19 a day.[13] Providing 9 million loans of US$100 each, with a repayment rate of 92%, repaid roughly in a month, it is becoming the 'credit card' of the unbanked.[14] The majority of Tala's clients start with a one-off fee of 15% per loan, a fee that will decrease to a minimal 5% when they build their credit history with Tala. Apart from an 8% fee for an extension of the loan term, there are no hidden costs for the customers. Tala looks for patterns that shows consistent behaviour, in the 'collateral,' i.e. the data the client chooses to share with Tala on their smartphone. Once a customer takes and gets a loan, repayment history is built up, which will become the most important factor for future lending.

PRICED TO WHAT THE PEOPLE CAN AFFORD

Data that Tala uses are phone usage, communication patterns and habits. Tala's approach is enabled by information technology to keep the prices affordable. It uses scrupulous data-mining techniques to answer basically three questions that can be deduced from the data on a smartphone. Firstly, are you who you say you are? This is the alternative identity check, ruling out you are not a fraud. Secondly, what can you afford? In most of those emerging countries, the way your utility providers, employers or others like suppliers interact with you goes via text messages. So, most receipts of transactions can be found on the phone, and based upon this data, consistency of your transaction related behaviour is used to estimate how much you can afford. Thirdly, what is the likelihood of repayment and what is the long-term nature of the relationship? This will be answered based upon behavioural data on the smartphone. For example, if Tala gives you the opportunity to review your application data, do you actually use the opportunity to review it? If you review it, do you quickly flip through it, or do you actually read the answers you've typed in, and even add or adjust it? The time when you call or apply, all this information provides good indicators to answer this third question. Tala made the need for human evaluation obsolete, through technology, and keeps in this way the prices affordable for the enterprising family.

EVERYBODY PLAYS

Fully automated processes for identification and credit assessment do not only allow for affordability, they also assure equality. Everybody can apply for credit and is judged in the same way. It allows everybody to play. Each person is evaluated against the same criteria in a fully automated process using tested algorithms. There are two big plusses of this way of assessing. Firstly, no persons are involved to judge, which makes the process less prone to implicit and personal biases, and therefore more equal. And, since Tala has built the credit scoring mechanism from scratch, gender, race and other discriminating factors such as religion or mere location are explicitly kept out of the algorithms. As a result, also built-in biases of the past are bygones. Admittedly, there's currently still a gender and age bias baked into the actual ownership of a smartphone, and the usage of mobile payment solutions.[15] The numbers of people Tala reaches show this too, mostly male and young people (under 35). However, at the core of this solution, gender, age, race, ethnicity, religion, sexual orientation, medical (handicap) and political bias are non-existent.

Obviously, customer data protection is of the utmost importance in this behavioural data-driven solution. Tala asks permission upfront, and has an ethical data policy in place assuring they do not share any personalized data with others outside of their company, except for complying with local law and reporting to national credit bureaus. Even before the potential client is downloading the app, Tala informs them what exactly they take as information and what they do and don't do with it.

PACKAGED ATTACHED TO DAILY LIFE

In addition to the loan, the clients get access to a personalized financial education app and to the Tala Community, through which they can access multiple financial education courses for free, and learn from each other. In this community of peers, there are regularly pilots for free financial coaching and favourable health insurances. A survey[16] from Tala shows that the app is well received and valued. According to this survey, the mobile learning platform is the top choice for receiving financial advice – beating even family and friends. Peers become advisors in financial decisions to be made. And 78% of respondents say they plan to change their financial habits, very promising information demonstrating Tala's success in becoming a trusted partner in daily life. Tala is expanding financial access, bringing choice and control into the daily lives through the phone. With an uptake of their financial service by millions of low-income people, it shows the value add to their daily lives.

COLLECTIVE

Next to the added value in the daily lives of so many, Tala facilitates collective action to take ethical lending forward. It shows how Tala sees finance as a tool for empowerment. When in Kenya, in 2019 indebtedness was on the rise, Tala launched a campaign not to take another loan. The message was to use budgeting instead as a tool to manage Christmas holiday spending. Acknowledging that large scale behavioural change is required, Tala has spearheaded the foundation of the Digital Lenders Association of Kenya (DLAK), launched in June 2019 with 11 other digital lenders. Members of DLAK are committing to a code of conduct, self-regulating the larger industry they are part of. By early 2020, this association has put its weight behind regulation for the digital lending industry, regarding consumer privacy protection, advocating for an institutionalizing of a formal credit reference channel applicable for the whole industry.[17]

Being part of a larger ecosystem, and act on behalf of it, is important when you are on a mission to expand financial access to the underserved people globally. *"What we're doing is not focused just on the product, but we're actually focused on changing systems,"*[18] according to Shivani Siroya. *"We are not building a company, we are solving a problem."*[19] And the DLAK shows their conviction that they cannot do that alone. For Tala it is not about scaling the organization per sé, it's about scaling the required change.

COMMITMENT IS CONTAGIOUS

At Tala, trust is key. When you trust people, people trust you. Tala's free marketing, the way their financial service spreads, is through their clients. Take Edwin, one of their clients from Kenya: *"Tala is transforming lives. I've shared Tala with everybody in my phone book. Each week I get a message that someone I have referred has repaid their loan and I get a bonus. It's not about the money, it's the fact that I helped someone somewhere. I feel it and I know it. That's the beauty about it."*[20] Over 60% of Tala's customers come in through referrals.[21] What's impressive is that this trust-based approach delivers positive financial results too. Tala's completely 'unsecured' individual loans have similar repayment rates as in the microfinance sector, where the loans are mainly secured by social capital by ways of lending to members of a group. Tala is providing the evidence that there is an alternative way of lending to lower-income people. This alternative way to individual lending is based upon trust. Both the sharing of data, and the social context and referrals, are key to Tala's success. Tala's commitment is contagious; it is what makes Tala grow the communities it serves. This results in a sense of shared ownership by their clients, and other clients of the mobile learning platform become their peers in the Tala community. Ultimately, this is resulting in protection (of Tala's capital) by peers. The financial positive outcome is 'only' a consequence of this commitment; it's not an aim in itself.

IT TOOK YEARS ... TO REVERSE ENGINEER IT TO MEET THE NEEDS

Let me take you back a few years, before Tala came into being. With the pre-runner of Tala, called InSight, many of the elements and underlying assumptions of Tala's current market and service proposition were tested and experimented with.

In these preceding years, an incredible experience was built up in the field: in the streets, the villages, among low-income people in India, in close collaboration with microfinance institutions (like Vistaas Finance and Muthoot) and Self-Help Groups (SHGs).[22] Insights were gained, assumptions were tested, similar services were piloted in interaction with the people and with partners. An invaluable amount of feed-back was collected, directly coming from the community members. These years of experience, and piles of feedback, helped to reengineer the financial service offering of Tala back to fulfil the needs that arise in the daily lives of low-income people.

DAILY LIFE AS THE PLAYGROUND

Pilots helped to figure out how to build cash flow records for micro-entrepreneurs, and how to assess creditwor-thiness with existing track records people have already (on their phones). A reservoir of insight was built up how – to practice and instil financial literacy in daily routines. Basically, the three components of the model Tala has today – the mobile app, the database of algorithms, the web portal with dashboards – have absorbed all lessons learned from those years of piloting, testing and going to the streets. Also, Tala's recruitment model can be viewed as an offspring of the 'Maitris' model (meaning trusted friend in Hindi) that InSight (the pre-runner of Tala in India) tested. In this Maitris model, local female entrepreneurs on the ground supported the users to keep accurate track of their micro-business records. These local entrepreneurs also recruited new users for which they would receive five rupees per new user.[23] Due to all those years of piloting, Tala's current product/market combination is spot on to the daily needs and integrated in their daily lives.

A BLENDED MODEL IS AN ENABLING FACTOR ...

In the early days in Kenya, Tala performed 'blind lending' to around 10,000 customers to find algorithms and general rules applicable in this market.[24] They intentionally went out and took on both good and bad customers during this 'blind lending' period, because if you cannot figure out the behaviour of bad customers, you will not develop the right model.[25] This is quite an upfront investment, willingness and trust before being able to launch Tala. It's important to recognize that these initial investments were made to understanding the market, the people, their needs, their daily life, their routines, their literacy levels, their lending and repayment behaviour, the trust-building mechanisms, before Tala came into being. Bear in mind that none of those costs for exploring, developing and building the right proposition will ever be repaid by Tala's current customers, nor the shareholders in the largest sense of the word. In this way, over time, Tala has a **blended model**, in which a lot of assumptions are tested and parts of the solution are developed and piloted with granted money, before the commercially viable social enterprise Tala is nowadays, can come into being for a new market segment at the base of the pyramid.

PEOPLE AT THE HEART OF IT

To demonstrate the reciprocal nature of the trust at Tala's, as well as the deep connection made with the daily needs of the people they serve, it's worth sharing what happened during the COVID-19 crisis in 2020. Within no time, Tala offered health information with their community – how to check if you are infected, how to protect yourself and your community members, all kinds of prevention measures in local languages, etc. Tala established a COVID-19 Rebuild fund, offering 0% interest loans for small businesses that provided essential support, such as healthcare products and services, clean water, food or education to their communities. For their clients, Tala offered flexible repayment plans. Interestingly enough, the economic downturn due to COVID-19 did not result in Tala's bankruptcy, what one could have expected, with rising defaults and late repayments. However, after an initial tough period, things stabilized, according to Shivani: *"We think that in some ways the customer base that we serve, because they are the underserved and they are already facing very volatile lives, know how to get through these circumstances."*[26] Another factor might very well be that Tala's services are invaluable in the daily lives of their clients. It comes as no surprise that this crisis led Tala to look into developing saving and insurance products for their clients, too, to empower them even more to cope with risks, keeping the people truly at the heart of it.

COMMITTED

How does Tala, as an organization, assure all work is toward this inclusive mission? What organizational features are contributing to its success? What sticks out is a strong focus on innovation to reach their objectives. An organizational **culture of innovation**, through hackathons, is part of **continuous learning** instilled in the company. Most important for this culture of innovation is the belief that the products and services need to be designed from the customer's needs up. The innovation is just a mean to reach the full potential of the underserved people. *"We're unlocking trust,"*[27] according to Shivani, which is what drives the product development. For which you need to go out and connect with your customers' needs to really understand it, to grasp the social context in which the need arises.

How do you unlock trust to create an attitude to challenge the status quo, to dive deeper, to go further and beyond?

Trusting your 'own' people is where it starts. Believing in people starts with **listening** to them. Listen to their ideas in haccathons, for example, but also have them go regularly into the (client) communities and listen to clients and their needs. A prerequisite for trust is the acceptance of the full human being, not just the part that shows up at work. Embrace the **full human being** at work. Another organizational feature found at Tala: a strong focus on celebrating life outside of work. This is what creates a supporting workplace to grow trust. At Tala, you can see an exceptional lot of attention celebrating family, family time and holidays. From this business culture based upon trust, you can start to challenge your (own) limits. You cannot solve the problem without going out there and **making mistakes**. A big **risk appetite** is part of the business. It's not about making money; it's about solving the problem together, according to Shivani: *"It's like being a fearless romantic – you have to be willing to put yourself out there and know that you will get your heart broken ... but the more open and willing you are with sharing your ideas ... people are just willing to come with you on that journey."*[28]

Another huge contributor to their success is baked into the role they envision for themselves; Tala aims for a system change that goes beyond their organization as such. *"At the end of the day we are not a financial service provider,"* Shivani says. *"What we are is a customer-focused technology and data science company that is ultimately focused on changing financial systems as a whole."*[29]

2.2 ROOT CAPITAL – A NEW LENDING METHOD TO INCLUDE THE MISSING MIDDLE

In the past 50 years, we have seen a steady increase of financial inclusion through microfinance, basically offering financial services – savings and loans – to poor people and families for their personal and micro-business needs. But with farmer businesses in particular, what happens is that they often join in agricultural enterprises, like cooperatives, since the soil, water and other inputs for farming are shared with the larger community and are therefore better managed by community as a whole. These farmer communities, as agricultural enterprises, are no longer micro-enterprises. What if you wish to grow the agricultural enterprise? You need investment in in order to grow your business. You're too big for microfinance, but too small or too risky for formal banks, since those banks in general only provide loans to those who already have built up capital, i.e. collateral in their business. In the past few decades we have also seen an upsurge of ethical and environmentally conscious consumers and related fair-trade brands, such as the Bodyshop, Lush, Ben & Jerry's, Fairtrade coffee and bananas. Those brands usually use so called fixed-price forward contracts to buy from ethical and environmental conscious producers. What if you could get a loan to grow the agricultural business in a sustainable manner, by using those fixed-price forward contracts as a collateral?

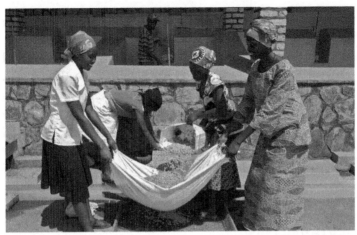

Photo by game changer

COVERING THE CHAIN

Root Capital[30] is an organization that started doing exactly that, using forward contracts as an assessment of earning potential and creditworthiness of small and growing agricultural enterprises, to provide them with credit and financial education they need to grow their business. In this way, Root Capital links in rural enterprises previously considered unbankable. These enterprises are the so-called missing middle of our food chain. Next to providing loans to this missing middle, Root Capital also offers a range of advisory services to agricultural enterprises, including specialized financial management training to better equip cooperatives and their farmer-members to realize their full potential. The third part of Root Capital's approach is influencing and engaging other capital providers through sharing this new lending methodology with them. This approach demonstrates their role, and capacity to 'tweak' the full chain, from small scale family farmer, to cooperatives, to big brands and to big banks, with the ultimate goal of transforming rural communities and the agricultural value chains that sustain them.

Root Capital offers agricultural enterprises a growth path into the formal financial system. After Root Capital demonstrated the viability of lending to agricultural enterprises in Rwanda, for example, a local bank in Kigali extended financing to some of these same clients.[31] *"By helping these businesses grow, a significant percentage have graduated from our direct lending and accessed additional capital from other sources. More than 40% of our clients graduate to commercial financing after three years of working with us,"*[32] according to Willy Foote, founder of Root Capital.

COLLABORATIVE

Root Capital does all of this by actively seeking for collaboration with partners in the agricultural chain. Nowadays, two decades into their journey, Root Capital continues to form new partnerships and establish joint ventures to share and replicate this new lending methodology. Root Capital was the founding partner of the Finance Alliance for Sustainable Trade (FAST, founded in 2007), established to develop a long-term vision for small and growing business financing. FAST was preceding the establishment of the Council of Smallholder Agricultural Finance (CSAF, founded in 2012), an alliance of social lending institutions focused on agricultural businesses that lack sufficient access to capital in developing countries. Well-known financial institutions like Oikocredit, Rabobank and Triodos Bank are members of this council today.

It all started two decades ago with a loan to a coffee cooperative in Guatamala. Fast-forward, by 2020 Root Capital is supplying agricultural small and growing businesses in Latin-America, sub-Saharan Africa and Southeast Asia with capital and financial training. Root Capital reached a cumulative 2.3 million farmers (which impacted the lives of 10 million family members) in the world's most vulnerable communities. Of the farmer households reached, 69% are living on less than US$5.50 a day. The agricultural businesses they support are supported for years, and show on average an annual growth of 20–25%. This growth allows the farmers to invest in more sustainable production methods and improve livelihoods for other farmers and related small agricultural businesses in their community. Mind you, in 2020, 95% of their clients operate in environmental vulnerable hotspots – in terms of biodiversity, water, soil or climate change. And 99% of their clients invest intensively in social or environmental services for the small-scale farmers in their community, impacting 2.7 million hectares with sustainable cultivation. All of this with a 99% repayment rate! While Root Capital is applying this new lending model, they allow cooperatives and agricultural businesses to build formal track records of their loans and repayments. These track records provide an in-route for them to become borrowers of (formal) local banks after several years. In this highly collaborative spirit, with partners in the food supply chain, Root Capital has built an alternative pathway to financially including smallholder farmers.

EVERYBODY PLAYS

The above describes from a bird's eye view Root Capital's journey to financially including small-scale food farmers organized in agricultural enterprises. However, it took years to **reengineer it back to meet the needs** of the farmer communities, to assure everybody is included. One important factor in succeeding was to keep going to the farmers' fields, listen to their needs and to do whatever is required to adapt the financial service to what the farmers, their families and their communities need. Let's illustrate this with an example. Root Capital noticed, during many of their field visits, that women were often not seen as main contributors and influencers in the agricultural enterprise. When this surfaced, they acknowledged that this needed to change, so they started to focus on gender-inclusiveness. They developed, adapted and established a gender-inclusive lending practice, integrating it in their lending model. This resulted after several years in the fact that by 2020, 46% of Root Capital's clients were gender-inclusive businesses, and 48% have specific programmes in place to support female farmers and employees, from child care facilities to credit offerings. It's an inspiring illustration of assuring that everybody plays, as well as an example of how Root Capital continuously reengineers their lending practice to the needs of the farmers.

COLLECTIVE

Key to Root Capital's approach, on top of this so-called direct services to the missing middle, is their leading role in mobilizing the industry as a whole, showing a deep sense of collective responsibility. Root Capital is by now acknowledged as a leader building a global movement, partly because they were a shaping force behind CSAF (Council of Smallholder Agricultural Finance). This alliance of social lending institutions provided US$669 million in loans to 655 small- and medium-sized businesses across 61 countries in 2019,[33] collectively reaching millions of farmers and their families in deprived communities. The council members drafted a set of responsible lending principles for other impact-first agricultural lenders, influencing the larger finance sector. It's estimated that Root Capital, other social lenders and local banks meet 40% of the demand from smallholder farmers in export-oriented value chains.[34] Root Capital invested heavily in building this collective action, mobilizing and facilitating others to join, because they had a system change approach from the start. The alliance and council are aiming for collective learning; both have built a movement that openly and jointly drives the change with financial industry players to become more inclusive.

CHANGING THE RULES OF THE GAME

Root Capital took a couple of hard-core no-gos in the industry and started to do things differently, aiming to include those who were excluded. Creditworthiness has always been assessed based upon risk; the formal system manages risk mainly through built-up capital, i.e. collateral. These rigid rules of the formal financial system (only managing risks with built-up capital) meant that millions of small-scale famers organized in agricultural enterprises with an ambition to grow were facing a gap between microfinance and meso-finance from formal banks. Just because they were not able to build up collateral in the traditional way. Root Capital came up with collateral in another shape – namely, potential earning. Root Capital started doing it differently and generated the evidence that those cooperatives of farmers are worth investing in, using a different kind of collateral, one that takes potential earnings into account. As an idea, this was perhaps not entirely new, but it was definitely new for this segment of the market. Walking the extra mile, backed with a strong belief in positive outcome on the longer term, Root Capital figured out a way to make this new lending practice successfully benefit low-income farmers. Root Capital proved those agricultural enterprises are worth investing in.

They first and foremost did so on behalf of the local producer communities and set out on this inclusive mission. Their mission never was to serve them all directly by themselves; their approach was to change the system, and therefore they invited others to tag along, to see and learn from what happens. Twenty years down the road, the change in the communities they worked with is all round: they've reduced poverty, empowered women, employed youth, peace is cultivated and sustainable practices are piloted and built to fight climate change. Those who joined to see what happened got convinced by the early evidence during the learning journey of Root Capital. As a result, more and more actors started to join, committing to financial inclusion too. This is how Root Capital ended up changing the rules of the game.

Root Capital was never in this game to earn a lot of profit. Being a social enterprise, all the **financial returns flow back in the farmer communities**. The fact that income and many other benefits flow back into the communities infused trust in the communities and in their relationship with Root Capital. This was key for Root Capital's success. The evidence Root Capital created supported to convince 'the industry' that it can be done differently, building up for a change to become irreversible.

Root Capital has demonstrated how we can grow to a 'new normal,' in this case showing how integrating the supply chain could pay off in terms of financial inclusion. How earning potential works as collateral too. Challenging another implicit assumption in the current system simultaneously: why should the farmer carry all the burden for sustainable farming and being inclusive? If big brands shoulder related risks, it's a win-win-win. The agricultural business can grow – income and produce – and practice more sustainable farming. The big brand wins because it can deliver on a consumer promise: ethical and sustainable production of ingredients, and guarantees production of the ingredients they need on the long term. The consumers, and all of us – society – win due to less destructive and depleting farming practices, and in the longer run even positively change to contribute to water management, biodiversity and our environment.

DAILY LIFE AS THE PLAYGROUND

But keep in mind, it all started and is strongly rooted in the daily life of the farmers. In fields where the farmers work and live, all the issues of low income, no loans, irregular repayment, and low yield, bad water management and bad quality of their soil are not single issues but integrated. All those issues together keep them in a place where they are left behind. Linking the financial support, the new lending practice, to this daily reality is key. Understanding this local complexity and being there, while also being able to lift it back and link it to an ecosystemic level, is a unique skill of Root Capital. And this starts with acknowledging, accepting and respecting the local reality on the ground. According to the founder of Root Capital, Willy Roote: *"Local communities are forced into short-term survival tactics, like illegal logging and slash-and-burn agriculture."*[35] Unsustainable practices continue not because the local farmer communities want to, but, even if those family farmers team up in cooperatives, they do not have the capital to invest in better equipment, allowing for more income and more sustainable farming practices. Root Capital took this reality of the farmers very seriously and provided the credit to invest in equipment to the farmers' communities.

Photo by game changer

But Root Capital also facilitated with the buying contracts from large fair trade brands, like Starbucks, acting on behalf of the farmers' communities, empowering the whole community to invest, grow income, become more sustainable, employ more youth and so on. Of course, Root Capital also provides training, an integrated education attached to the credit, as well as training in climate-smart agricultural practices. The point being, Root Capital took it from the ground up, taking the daily life as a premise and adapting the financial service exactly to the fulfilment of the farmers' needs, and that of the agricultural enterprise.

LINKING ALL PLAYERS IN EQUALITY

For this to happen, Root Capital needed to 'tweak' the chain. Another key to their success: integration. Horizontal integration of the local issues at hand in the daily realities of the farmers; joining local communities for the longer term, solving them holistically with the capital provided in collaboration with the famers communities. Vertical integration of the agricultural value chain, connecting the contracts from big brands directly (as collateral) of the local farmer communities in their lending practice. And funding-wise – internally at Root Capital – integrating philanthropic funds with impact investments and the like to allow for the risk capital needed to support these farmers. Their approach shows a deep local involvement, based upon trust and long-term vision, in combination with a highly collaborative approach to linking all players in these complex food and finance chains.

COMMITTED

"*Seeing the power of agricultural businesses as a sustainable 'impact engine' to uplift communities*" is what has kept Willy on the path and sticking to Root Capital's mission, *"Collateralizing trade finance against forward contracts was the first of many levers we've pulled on the road to unlocking the full potential of small and growing agricultural businesses."*[36] Today, indeed, Root Capital's approach is increasingly multifaceted – focused on not just credit, but also capacity building, and building the *resilience* capacity of farmers and their agricultural enterprises through innovative service provision around climate action, gender inclusion, and opportunities for the next generation. But apart from a visionary leadership committed to this inclusive mission, how does commitment take root in the whole organization of Root Capital?

Distributed leadership is one part of the answer. According to Willy, *"We realized early on that our relevance to local farmers, agri-businesses, and markets, not to mention our ability to drive impact and manage risk, has everything to do with being proximate to the communities and clients we serve."*[37] Today the vast majority of the team of Root Capital (which includes local consultants) is located in their six regional offices. Let's have a look at another example of distributed leadership, when they aimed to cultivate a culture of inclusiveness. Some time ago, three leading ladies at Root Capital started to notice that women leaders out there in the fields were often hidden influencers, that they played a critical role but were not recognized for their roles in the success of the rural business. These female leaders at Root Capital took charge to celebrate stories of these unrecognized female farmers. Celebrating their stories further developed into the development of the gender lens in the lending practice of Root Capital and the launch of the Women in Agriculture Initiative, doubling the number of women farmers reached by their programmes.[38] This gender lens also took Root Capital to improve their own **gender balance** in their own leadership team. A nice illustration of how an inclusive practice externally mirrors one internally, and vice versa, as connecting valves.

Secondly, creating a workplace that is conducive for **intrapreneurship** is key to invite staff to **think differently**, to come up with ideas and bring them to fruition. Back in the day, a senior impact director came up with the idea to measure an impact score, next to financial scores for their loan portfolio, and suggested publishing them with their financial scores. According to Willy Foote, founder of Root Capital: "*I was hesitant. Lending in agriculture is always challenging – even more so in the world's most vulnerable places – and some of our past loans had neither made a return nor maximized their impact. That wasn't exactly the type of result I wanted publicized! .... While I was apprehensive about admitting that we had made mistakes in our lending, I recognized that sharing our lending data could help other social lenders achieve impact at scale.*"[39] Root Capital decided to do it anyway, and years of presenting in MBA programmes, a few articles published about their lending practice, and continuous **transparency** of their lending practice, this openness paid off. Leading impact investors have adapted their investment strategies and are balancing social, environmental and financial return accordingly. Willy said: "*I nearly said no. Instead, I swallowed my pride, and gave him the space he needed to develop a stellar idea.*"[40]

Which brings us to the third success factor for growth of the impact of the new lending method – as well as organizational growth – and that is to know when to let go. At a certain moment in time a Chief Innovation Officer (CIO) at Root Capital got the mandate to spend time, expertise and effort to launch, build and grow the CSAF (Council of Smallholder Agricultural Finance). After a few years in this job, building the field, thinking bigger and bolder about the systems change it required, building and nurturing the ecosystem, this role could not be done part time anymore. So, Root Capital's CIO and the members of CSAF decided it was time to take the next step to become independent.

Willy Foote said: "*I initially struggled with this transition, as it implied 'losing' one of our most valuable colleagues to the industry alliance.*"[41] Root Capital accepted the step while losing a valued member of the executive team, knowing the sector became a few steps closer to improving livelihoods for millions of farming families. Letting go is tough and embracing **entrepreneurship** often feels counterintuitive, but when **trusting** the team: everybody wins. "*My colleagues are happier, our organization performs better, and my own vision becomes one step closer to reality,*"[42] according to the founding father of Root Capital, Willy Foote.

A BLENDED MODEL IS AN ENABLING FACTOR ...

A key asset for Root Capital that enables them to take the risks related to lending to this missing middle is working with a blended finance model. Root Capital receives investment support from institutions like the US International Development Finance Corporation and philanthropic support from funders like Mastercard Foundation. Philanthropic funds function as a cushion to mitigate the risks for Root Capital's lenders. For each dollar, Root Capital can borrow US$5 to lend to its clients.[43] Root Capital is not a bank, it's a social enterprise, but legally registered as a non-profit.

At a certain moment in time a crisis happened – due to several situations happening at the same time – Root Capital accidently violated a debt-to-equity ratio for a period of several days, in agreement with some of their investors. They chose to be **transparent** and shared this information with all their lenders. All of them appreciated it and gave them a waiver, apart for one. This one made them slow down in order to improve their financial management and governance. Root Capital could have opted to repay and continue without them, but they did not. They stepped into this conversation, which was not an easy one, but a lot of good came from it.

In the process they agreed on practical and tactical steps, a plan that Root Capital was invited to come up with themselves. *"Finding the right blend of toughness and love in its relationship ..."*[44] was the challenge. Having Root Capital themselves drive the change, playing a catalytic role as a lender not overstepping their role nor being too directive, was a balancing act for both. When you play at the edge of non-profit and function as a bank, and you identify as both, you don't wish to be one or the other – that's what it truly means having a 'blended model.' Stepping into this critical conversation helped Root Capital in figuring out the DNA of their organization, getting to the core again of their being, staying true to being both an impact-oriented non-profit and a bank. Finally Root Capital chose to adapt to a moderate growth, allowing them to stay a leader in the field, staying true to their inclusive mission and being financially responsible, which is required for all of the above.[45] Using the tools and mechanisms of two types of organizations (non-profits and banks), is what it means when you apply blended funding; that's one of the key enabling factors for them to change the system.

COLLECTIVE LEARNING

For a bold change to happen, everybody involved should be empowered to learn, every step down the road. So, **continuous** evaluation and **learning loops** are required. Core to Root Capital's vision is demonstrating the impact investing in small and growing agricultural businesses can have; hence, Root Capital focusses on impact even before they make a loan. To qualify for a loan, enterprises are screened for potential negative social or environmental impact *and* rated on expected positive impact. Their impact assessment does not just look at prices and incomes for farmers, but also at whether enterprises provide community services, environmental certification or benefits to employees, among other things. All of these are meant to allow for learning and growth toward sustainable businesses. It fuels learning for the small agricultural businesses, but also learning for the fair-trade big businesses and the financing partners.

What helps other players in the industry to learn from this too, which turned out to be very convincing, is that Root Capital invites third parties to build the evidence of their impact. Take, for example, the study by Yale's Innovation for Poverty Action, and other external researchers. It provides a credible feedback loop, with independent eyes looking at Root Capitals' work. This research, performed by external researchers, was published in a peer-reviewed economics journal,[46] which supported convincing other financial institutions. A repeating loop of credit education and evaluation fuels collective learning. Feeding the results back to the larger ecosystem to change, too, is how Root Capital drives the change.

SPREADING THROUGH REPLICATION, **TRIGGERING IRREVERSIBLE CHANGE**

Early in 2019, Root Capital steps in a partnership to launch and pilot a new funding mechanism, 'pay-for-impact,' focused on early-stage agricultural enterprises. The innovative funding instrument is co-created with Roots of Impact and SDC (the Swiss Agency of Development and Cooperation) and rewards organizations when they have achieved verified social impact. The partnership allows Root Capital to provide loans to high-risk, high-cost, but high-impact early stage agricultural businesses in Latin America. It's showcasing their continued **commitment** to lend to those businesses that need it most, that nobody would consider lending to, that have a substantial promise for growth and impact. Furthering their track record reaching last-mile farmer enterprises. *"We believe that the only way to unlock* *a sustainable future for all of us is to include those traditionally left behind,*[47] according to Willy. Always done in partnership with others. The more that join the game, the higher the acceleration of change in the financial system.

In early 2020 another initiative was launched, following similar forward-thinking as demonstrated by Root Capital: IDH Farmfit, a fund for smallholder farmer finance aiming to leverage big companies' purchasing power to reduce credit risks to farmers. The initiative is in partnership with several multinationals such as Unilever, Rabobank and Mondelez – better known for its Oreo brand – and funded by the Dutch Ministry of Foreign Affairs, backed by a guarantee of the US government and complimented with a farmer's business support services funded by the UK Department of International Development. And it promises to grow to a billion, meant for funds for farmers.[48] IDH, the Sustainable Trade Initiative, has worked many years with companies sourcing from small farmers. According to Joost Oorthuizen, the CEO, *"We don't believe the farmer is the problem – we believe the private sector environment around it is the problem. The 'last mile' is not happening."* That's why the focus of this smallholder farmers finance initiative is from a value chain perspective.[49] Examples like these show that other players have followed suit.

According to Willy: *"The IDH Farmfit example is core to our 'end game' as Root Capital – namely, replication and adaptation by other institutions, hopefully legions of them, both from private sector and impact-first lenders/investors and trainers. We'd like to think they 'crowd in' thanks to our demonstration effect over the years via blueprinting our practices, policies, products and services, impact measurement, lessons learned (including failures!), etc. – sharing all this through radical transparency spurs replication and adaptation."*[50] This illustrates the leading role Root Capital has in the field and how to nurture the inclusion to becoming irreversible.

2.3 BANQU – ECONOMIC PASSPORTS TO VOUCH FOR HARD WORK

Small-scale producers are everywhere, and you will be surprised how many of the products you use, wear or eat originate from their hard-working hands. Boat families are small-scale fisheries. Gold artisans are small-scale migrant miners. Family farmers of cassava are small-scale food producers. A refugee family with chickens or ducks are small-scale producers of eggs. Fair-trade banana producers, weavers working from home, both small-scale producers, and garbage pickers are small-scale plastic recyclers. Many of them own a small home, boat or a plot of land with a few coffee trees or just some ducks or goats roaming around. Many of them are displaced and have no permanent address or identity card, like the shepherds herding sheep or horses, immigrants digging for cobalt, day labourers picking cotton, nomads producing meat and dairy with goats, slum dwellers recycling big oil drums, migrants rebuilding their lives in factories, youngsters and drop-outs jumping from one job to the other. All of them working hard year after year, usually in unsafe, unhealthy circumstances, with irregular payments, no labour contracts, regularly insecure about getting paid. Very often they move from one place to another, due to monsoons, police riots in slums, and politics or corruption, that being the sole reason why they have nothing to show for their hard work. They are at the base of most of our big brands' global supply chains. Big brands – and indirectly so do you – are all buying raw materials or semi-finished goods from billions of people who live in extreme poverty.

It's time to formally link them in and hook them up, too, and one good option is through these big brands with two-way transparency as a tool for transformation.

Photo by game changer

What if you could give all these hard-working, small-scale producers an identity? What if you could give them the credentials of their hard work, even without having an identity card, labour contract or salary slip? The minimum we could do is making their hard work visible, and to not look away, give them their dignity and credit them for their hard work. Then we could review their credentials and provide them access to financial services. That would allow them to start building something out of their years of hard work, wherever they are. We should treat them as equals, with labour and wage protection, payment directly after sales, upfront guarantee of sales, and we should provide them with proper input and tools. Only then we can start growing toward an inclusive and sustainable global economy. Financial inclusion should not be limited to those who have a fixed address, a passport or birth certificate, or a formal job that comes with a labour contract and salary slip.

COVERING THE CHAIN

And this is exactly what BanQu[51] is doing: shining a light on big brands' entire supply chains all the way to the base, where the hard-working hands deliver their produce. How? By providing the small-scale producers an identity. Each producer gets an identity and starts building a track record of their hard work. Family farmers sell their crops, migrant miners hand in their cobalt and receive an immediate digital proof of sale. In this way, they build a digital trail of orders, sales, payment and income on their mobile phones, even if it is not a smartphone. Suppliers, distributors, recyclers, processors – those who act in between the big brands and small-scale producer – confirm quantities, packaging, assembly and shipping. Built-in timestamps and geo-location tags allow for transparent record management, controlling batch quantities, reconciling inventories, reviewing payments and truck information. BanQu's system provides clarity on where a batch of raw material is, how much it is, and for what price it is bought and sold throughout the whole supply chain, including this so-called last mile. It protects the small-scale producers in this last mile from non-payment and keeps track of actual delivery and payment. Simultaneously, it keeps track of losses due to theft, spoilage or damage, wherever it happens in the whole chain. This is protecting the small-scale producers from false claims.

What's different from other Enterprise Resource Planning (ERP) and supply chain software? At BanQu, the small-scale producer owns their own data, they determine when to access and monetize it, and they themselves set permissions for the use of their own data. No centralized systems pushed down in supply chain of formal player, including the informal workers too. BanQu is setting a new norm of cooperation instead of competition between the brands, suppliers, middlemen and small-scale producers, based upon equality. BanQu's system is using block chain technology, and works as a consensus mechanism for the whole supply chain.

BanQu's services were launched in over 20 countries, among others Brazil, Costa Rica, India, Indonesia, Jordan, Malawi, Somalia, South Africa, Syria, Uganda, the United States and Zambia. Five years after its establishment, BanQu has reached hundreds of thousands of the hard-to-reach producers, within multiple global supply chains of big brands, like food manufacturer Mars, Nestlé and beer maker Anheuser-Busch InBev. Even though BanQu is mainly focused on fashion and food, there's an estimated billion people supplying those chains.

IT TOOK YEARS ... TO **REVERSE ENGINEER IT TO MEET THE NEEDS**

Let's start at the beginning: BanQu's mission is to solve extreme poverty. BanQu does not present itself as a technology provider or a platform; they just use block chain for the good of the vulnerable. It started with an app as a way to connect with the most disadvantaged and disconnected people in the often-developing world. The BanQu app was developed in close collaboration with governments and development agencies. The first step was an app that could connect with a mobile phone, enabling a person to register with BanQu like registering for LinkedIn or Facebook. The second step was to build a mini financial network with banked (often overseas) family members and other parties like microfinance institutions, development agencies and community organizations that connected with the migrant worker, refugee gold miner or female coffee farmer. The third step was to start registering economic transactions from all walks of life, like remote purchases, funded wallets, remittances, credit histories, microfinance loans and cash disbursements. But health records, too, such as immunization records and birth registrations. In this way, BanQu started building the so-called economic passport for the refugee, a person on the move, a goat rearer. A few years down the road, BanQu had developed an inclusive solution supporting Anti-Money Laundry (AML), Know Your Customer (KYC) and suspicious activity monitoring, while keeping the needs of the small-scale producers at the heart. They used the power of block chain to redesign payment and transaction processes, aiming for inclusion.

PEOPLE AT THE HEART OF IT

From that moment on, the farmer selling her crop at the cooperative gets a text message on her phone, including data like weight, quantity, price, etc. She can buy input from the big brand like seeds or fertilizer to ensure continued orders. She is building her own economic history in the supply chain, on her phone, in her daily life. That's where it starts. Tackling one of the fundamental flaws in the whole system: information transparency. Her so-called economic passport demonstrating her hard work is with her, including the four loans she had successfully repaid from different microfinance institutions, the sales at different cooperatives over the years, the remittances received from overseas family members. And this is exactly the power of BanQu: it adds value to the lives of people on the move, for the family fisheries and fruit farmers. It allows them to *"own, access, monetize and give permission for the use of their data,"*[52] a human right challenging even the Facebooks of today, according to Ashish Gadnis, BanQu's co-founder and CEO. This is a very empowering force, which keeps the people at the heart of their service. *"We want the farmer to be empowered with his or her data,"*[53] according to Ashish.

BanQu's solution is rooted in trust. The identity is human-centric based upon trusted community and family networks. The small-scale producer controls her own network and decides who she interacts with and what the level of interaction is, and what data she wants to share. Wherever she goes, she can add new institutions and transactions made, as you would do with Facebook. *"BanQu helps you move materially and psychologically from dependency to independence, freedom, and control,"*[54] according to Hamse Warfa, co-founder of BanQu and a former refugee himself. This is invaluable in the lives of so many people on the move.

LINKING ALL PLAYERS IN EQUALITY

Only then came the closing the loop in the global supply chains, resulting in the current proposition of Banqu: offering a software-as-a-service for a fee to the big brands, subscribing to BanQu's platform to get transparency in their supply chain. The brands also pay for each connection point in their entire chain, such as suppliers, transportation partners and distributors. As of last year, BanQu operates on a model in which the big brands get supply chain transparency, traceability and efficiency, while BanQu grows its customer base of producing family farmers and people on the move. Bringing equality in the chain, by ways of two-way transparency between big brands, distributor, transporter, middlemen and small-scale producers to satisfaction of both sides.

COLLABORATIVE

BanQu works in close collaboration with the big brands. Let's take, for instance, the partnership with AB-InBev, the world's largest brewer. It started with a pilot to support the group of farmers that produce casava in Zambia, aiming to grow from subsistence farming into commercial farming. It is in the interest of AB-InBev to bring other partners in as customers for this group of 2,000 casava farmers, so that they can grow their income and wellbeing. In partnership with BanQu, all casava farmers got an economic passport that became bankable, through which they could get loans to grow and improve their casava farming business. The casava farmers started selling to other parties, showing their good work, and to invest in growing or diversifying their crops. Or they invested in related businesses of a husband or wife, growing family income. In close collaboration with AB-InBev, BanQu and other partners worked together with the farmers to build a path out of poverty. All of this was kick-started by this economic passport, keeping records of their economic activity over years. Similar rollouts followed in partnership with AB-InBev and BanQu in India, Uganda and Brazil, creating economic passports for small-scale farmers allowing for access to financial services.[55]

BanQu is doing the same with RSM Spain, bringing efficiency and traceability to their European clients' supply chains. In partnership with Japan Tobacco International (JTI), BanQu supported to track the eradication of child labour in its supply chain. In a joint programme with BanQu and others, JTI has removed about 51,000 children from child labour.[56] Apart from this unique two-way transparency in their supply chains, BanQu's solution also offers a great opportunity for big brands to report on their achievements related to the UN Sustainability Development Goals, like the JTI example. Just recently Banqu started to collaborate with Coca-Cola, to include thousands of plastic waste-pickers inSouth Africa, jointly optimizing the recyclables value chain.

It has not always been easy to collaborate with big businesses. Big brands can be quite sceptical at the start, but that is normal with new things. According to Hamse: "*Seeing the impact and power of transformative change, after a first pilot, is usually what is shifting the mindset of the top leaders.*"[57] The beauty is that BanQu's solution fits seamlessly into the core business of big brands with global supply chains, while it is highly inclusive. This entrepreneurial approach to collaboration is key to the take-off of BanQu.

DAILY LIFE AS THE PLAYGROUND

Mind you, there's a lot of work to be done out there in the refugee camps, in the rural villages and the slums. BanQu does the outreach, does the train-the-trainer, gets the cooperative or buying station to host camps. At the place where the refugee drops off the product or produce, where the migrant worker comes to work, or where family farmers come to sell their crop, is where they are informed about BanQu. If needed, they get support to register, which can be done online by themselves too. The education is not about block chain, it's about understanding the opportunity that from now on the cassava farmer, migrant jeans seamstress or refugee recycler can get a guaranteed price, quality and quantity, and guaranteed pay-out, with simple text message exchange. With a text message the small-scale producer will receive a code after delivery of the produce. With this code the producer can collect the money at the cash-out station. Nobody can steal money anymore, or claim the producer sold less. And when the producers are forced (again) to migrate back or move to another country, this track record, this economic passport, stays with them. The value for the small-scale producers at the last mile is baked in the BanQu solution, making it intrinsically inclusive. It takes the reality of daily life of the small producer as a premise, and the financial service is fully adapted to the daily needs of the producing migrant homeworker, refugee factory worker or coffee farmer.

Photo by game changer

PAY AND PERKS FLOW BACK TO THE FAMILY

And the beauty of it is that BanQu does not charge the migrant factory worker or the female fruit picker. Putting them at the heart of their service, it's free. And in addition to that, the small-scale producer is no longer dependent on a fragmented set of data that sits with different institutions they transact with. These are the **perks** that **flow back** to the hard-working people.

CONNECTED

BanQu can be best viewed as a network, with on the one side the growing group of beneficiaries, the recipients of the economic passport. On the other hand, the big brands and their supply chains partners. A third side of this network can easily be envisioned with all financial services delivered by partners who are willing to consider the economic passport. With the network of beneficiaries growing, more partners are likely to join too. A crop insurer can come in and look at a farmer's data, same for microfinance institution or local bank. They could all 'consume' the data provided and deliver financial services. And why stop there, why not consider other services too, from a water or utility company? Through the connectedness of all these partners the network effect of BanQu's platform comes to light. With each big brand joining, another group of subsistence farmers or day-job laborers gets identified and empowered, while for BanQu – and therefore the brands – economies of scale kick in. And, for each small-scale producer, and brand, more value is added just by growing as a network. The value of the network grows with each person or partner added.

A **BLENDED MODEL** IS AN ENABLING FACTOR ...

BanQu challenges an implicit assumption in the current system: why should the small-scale producer carry all the burden and costs of being included? At the start of the social venture, costs to develop the inclusive solution, the app and the technology were carried and covered by the financial contribution of corporate foundations. Currently, BanQu has developed a new business model in which the costs of the organization are covered by the multiple collaborations with big brands, while their service to the hard-working low-income people is offered for free. Seen over time, BanQu has a blended model with cross-subsidizing as an element of it, which enables them to be inclusive. The small producers get identified and economic passports, through which they can grow production and income, and potentially practice more sustainable production. The big brands get supply-chain transparency and efficiency, while also delivering on a consumer promise: ethical sourcing of ingredients, fabric and/or recycled materials. This can be done without cutting out the middleman, who delivers value too. Brands can also track their progress on the Sustainable Development Goals (SDGs), for their contribution to eradicate poverty, or like JTI did contributing to fight against human trafficking and fighting child labour. Big brands turn out to be capable partners to progress financial inclusion.

EVERYBODY PLAYS

BanQu's new pathway to poverty alleviation makes it possible for everybody to play. On the one hand there is the empowerment of the producers. Mind you, they might be small in terms of what they produce, but they are huge in terms of numbers: it's millions of them. With BanQu's inclusive innovation, either refugee miner or female farmer can take the phone and go to a financial institution to show the economic track record of produce, income and dealings with big brands. But it works the other way around too. A bank, micro-insurer or microfinance institution that has a relationship with the big brand and can review the financial economic trail of transactions of a farmer and provide financial services. So, BanQu is empowering partners to deliver financial services too. BanQu is building the foundation of a connected ecosystem, connecting diverse partners that together shape the enabling environment for small-scale producers to be financially included.

This is the opposite of the current dominant situation in which all of the humanitarian partners with good intentions – United Nations High Commissioner for Refugees (UNHCR), health development agency, middleman, transporter and employer or big brand – are all in control of different sets of the small-scale producers' data. BanQu has built a system that facilitates other partners to join, resulting in benefits for all of them.

COMMITTED

How does BanQu organize to stay focused on their mission, while maintaining financial sustainability? Fighting extreme poverty, with a focus on both migrant, family farmers and refugee communities, on the one hand, and supply chain transparency and traceability for big brands on the other hand, is quite a stretch. One of the tools to spread the commitment of the founders and to stay mission driven, is to keep track of two key performance indicators: annual recurring revenue and the number of small-scale producers in the last mile connected with. Avoiding mission drift is assured, while reporting on both KPIs, because *"profitability is secondary to our social impact,"*[58] according to Hamse, co-founder. *"Our primary partners are the refugees that are the heart of it all."*[59] By prioritizing one above the other, BanQu stays committed to redistribute the power of information in the global supply chains, ultimately including the small-scale producers in our formal financial system.

CHANGING THE RULES OF THE GAME

Bear with me, to take you back to the hard reality of the lives of the migrants and refugees, unfortunately a growing number of people, who go from one place to another. Each time they move to another place, they have to rebuild their lives from scratch, while they are actually the same people, with the same skills, attitude, expertise and hard-working hands as before. But only because they cannot prove who they are, due to haste of flight and host country's regulation, they lose their identity card, home address and job, due to which they have to start over and over again, after the next move to a new camp, repatriate back home or resettle in another country. According to UNHCR, an estimated 70 million people are forced to flee from their homes. More than half being younger than 18 years old, having their whole lives still before them.[60] A refugee or migrant has years of selling produce, taking multiple loans from microfinance institutions, carrying around one or more identity cards from UNHCR and international development organizations, perhaps even one from the government she's residing in. To put it a bit bluntly, this is often to the advantage of the rest of society; we press their reset button each time they have to make a move, keeping them from accumulating wealth and wellbeing. To the advantage of, let's say 'us,' providing cheap labour, no need to pay for the cost of labour protection, proper work conditions, no need to provide proper contracting, guaranteeing next orders nor payments. Breaking with this practice is very hard, because there is little evidence, little insights. While we all know it's out there and none of us wants this. No one person is accountable. BanQu is disrupting exactly this, taking ownership, feeling accountability, changing the rules of the game.

COLLECTIVE

At the end of the day, BanQu considers it to be a collective journey they are leading: *"When we become collectively committed to a better outcome to all of our citizens, global citizens, there is no limit to what we can accomplish,"*[61] according to Hamse.

CHAPTER 3

EVERYBODY PLAYS

Money is a means of exchange. Centuries ago this was coins and bills and nowadays it is also available as plastic, as a mobile phone, in a bank account, as an insurance, mortgage or pension. Money is a way to store value too. Banks, insurers, pension funds and large finance institutions are here to produce and distribute money and financial services, as well as for determining, adjusting and assuring its value. But they are far away from where the majority of the world, low-income families, are. Obviously, low-income people need money to transact too, to exchange goods and to store value for future use. They usually transact with someone they know: with the tea stall across the street, at the drop-off point for their produce, or with the delivery man of the inventory for their street stall. They transact in places around the corner, at the market, where they get their day job, where they buy phone credits. We should provide money and financial services to everybody, in the place where low-income families go, and through those who already transact with them.

Each game changer in this chapter has an innovation that includes a previously excluded group. Their solutions make sure that women are included, that we don't exclude those who are less numerate, or forget about those who work from home. Each social innovator does so by building the capacity of global partners that join them, integrating the financial service offered to these low-income people. Each one is building a so-called 'last-mile infrastructure,' that on the one hand is empowering big – previously excluded – parts of our population. And on the other hand, is capacitating their partners to join them in financial inclusion. You will see that their cases show both elements this lever consists of: we knock on all doors, and we empower many more partners to knock.

Solar Sister is beating the gender balance by bringing the benefits of solar power into the homes of the families living in remote areas. Not just as 'consumers' of the solar power devices, but also by building capacity and leadership of female entrepreneurs in the same villages. Provision of income and loans, entrepreneurship and business management training grows the decision power of rural female entrepreneurs, and works as an empowering force.

My Oral Village is fully focused on capacitating other players to join in educating everybody to become sufficiently numerate to deal with digital money. New rules of digital money resulted in new behaviour on a whole new playground – with mobile transactions, online loans, mobile wallets, saving apps and insurances one click away. This holds a huge risk to lose a lot when it comes to gender equality; women might be excluded even more. However, it also holds an opportunity to have all players join in making everybody sufficiently numerate to use digital financial services. My Oral Village envisions a radical shift toward a new Know Your Customer: Your Customer Knows How.

Some say "handicrafts" can be seen as the largest employer of the millions of home-based artisans, mainly women. Nest is building a global movement of artisans, with a Guild, a Standard and a Seal. On the one hand, finding an ally in big brands in the fashion, textile and furniture industry, Nest is financially including the artisans working from home. On the other hand, it is igniting gender equality by growing visibility and giving a voice and decision power to the home-based artisans. Nest is redefining how home-based work is playing out, moving it away from exploiting practices, simply because we assume work is supposed to be done in an office or factory.

Let's have a look.

3.1 SOLAR SISTER – BEATING THE GENDER BALANCE

A quarter of our world's population does not have access to energy, and you need energy to lift yourself out of poverty. Solar solutions like a solar lamp, cell phone charger or cook stove show obvious benefits: you save money on costs for diesel or on your electricity bill or you save the time to collect wood before you make breakfast. At the same time, there is no pollution, no smoke in your hut, your children can study and you can work even when it's getting dark. On top of that, you can generate an income with it. You wonder why not every poor person in the developing world already has solar devices.

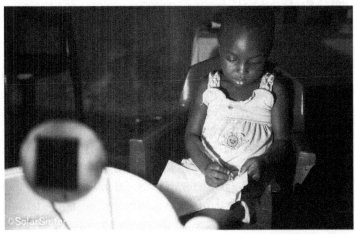

Photo by game changer

According to the World Bank and World Health Organization (WHO), an estimated 650 million people would still be without electricity in 10 years' time with the current rate of progress, with 90% of them in sub-Saharan Africa.[62] Why? Well, because most solar solution providers are just technological solutions and not distributing to low-income people. Most solar solution providers are moving upmarket, away from serving low-income families. Many people live in remote and rural areas, and therefore, reaching them is labour intense and thus costly. A study among 35,000 users of off-grid renewable energy solutions, in 17 countries over three years reports several reasons why it's hard to serve low-income people. Firstly, 34% of these families report challenges with the use of solar solutions. So, after-sales support is very important. Another critique reported in the study is that the price is too high. Mind you, those families live on only a few dollars a day. And even if you deliver the solution with a microcredit, over-indebtedness is a significant issue. All in all, low-income families are not an easy segment to serve. The study highlights too that the off-the grid sector should do more to serve the women; 68% of the users surveyed were men.[63]

EVERYBODY PLAYS

Solar Sister[64] recruits, trains and supports women from energy-poor areas in Tanzania, Nigeria and beyond in Africa. Solar Sister deliberately grows a woman-centred direct sales and after-sales network, supporting the clean energy transition. Solar Sister has over 5,000 micro-entrepreneurs distributing and selling solar devices, of which 86% are female. These so called Solar Sisters reach 1,8 million people, of which 75% live in rural, off-grid communities. These female micro-entrepreneurs increase their weekly income on average 57%, and report a boost in decision-making power and respect in the household. The women entrepreneurs are given a 'business model from a bag,' are taught how to save and run a business, and how to build trust. Some 90% report that someone close to them views them as a role model. A clear sign of a very empowering business! An MIT evaluation shows evidence that Solar Sister's women entrepreneurs are penetrating the last-mile villages that have few alternatives for affordable clean lighting products.[65] Moreover, 14,000 of families started a micro-business thanks to the solar products. Mind you, the village-based, solar micro-entrepreneurs have full autonomy, they decide if they want to participate, how much they want to participate, and what they sell and what not. Some of them are full-scale businesses and some have more occasional sales, a few hours a week or just in the low-season.

Photo by game changer

PAY AND PERKS FLOW BACK IN THE FAMILY
OR COMMUNITY

Bringing solar lamps, cell phone chargers and solar cooking to hard-to-reach families, through women entrepreneurs, is a powerful force. The communities they serve report significant amounts saved (US$200) on kerosine per lamp and 90% reports feeling more safe with solar. An independent study[66] assessing Solar Sister's impact showed that the main reason customers buy from Solar Sister is **trust** (51%), while warranty is another main reason. Putting women at the centre is key for their success; they close the loop of income-generation and cost savings of the families in rural off-grid communities, while reducing pollution. It's not just empowering for the Solar Sisters. The income, cost savings and other perks like less pollution flow back into the families and their communities.

DAILY LIFE AS THE PLAYGROUND

From the perspective of the customer, the Solar Sisters are one of them, not mere salespeople that leave after they made a sale. They talk the same language, and 60% of them also live in a no-grid community themselves, which makes it easy to relate to. Rural villagers place great importance on local, in-person after-sales assistance and close familiarity with the salesperson, much more so than the flexibility of being able to pay in instalments over time, according to the MIT study.[67] Apart from that, the Solar Sisters are trained as entrepreneurs, so they are well placed to inspire other women from off-grid communities to start an income-generating activity with the solar solution too. After the first solar lamp, most demand is for the solar cell phone charger, which could be used to make a small income.

Next to leading by example by the Solar Sisters, you can imagine they also think twice before bringing poor quality or high maintenance solar solutions to the remote villages. They are the ones that will be called when the lamp or stove does not work, so they are basically an additional guarantee for good stuff. In other words, another layer of consumer protection. The network of the Solar Sisters is deeply rooted in the daily life of the communities, and **trust** is the binding factor.

What drives the Solar Sisters is to make a difference in their own communities – next to income generation of course. Woman-to-woman promotion and sales turns out to be very effective at the last mile.

IT TOOK YEARS ... TO **REVERSE ENGINEER IT TO MEET THE NEEDS**

Each Solar Sister is recruited, provided with a branded 'business in a bag' and a year participatory training to kick-start and grow her clean energy business. After this first year, ongoing mentoring is offered. Each one of them will join a peer network, which is hosted and facilitated by Solar Sister as an organization. Mind you, it's quite a heavy up-front investment for Solar Sister as an organization. It took years to build the network of female solar micro-entrepreneurs, while reverse engineering the offering – of the business in a bag and training –to meet the needs of the rural families and the needs of the rural-based solar micro-entrepreneurs. Many solar products were tried, tested and piloted by the rural communities. No solar product that did not meet the needs of the families made it into the 'business bag' of the female micro-entrepreneurs. For those that matched the needs, and allowed for a small margin for the Solar Sisters, warranty, after-sale services and contracts with the solar solution providers were negotiated.

An anecdote Katherine Lucey, founder and CEO of Solar Sister, shared: *"We tested a great solar product once, of good quality, it checked all the boxes, at least, that was what we thought ... but when we asked our Solar Sisters who piloted the sales, they gave it back to us, with the suggestion to change the text on the box that said 'reading lamp' into 'task lamp,' because most women cannot read, and therefore don't want to buy it, while they showed interest when they learned it would help them to perform tasks when dark."*[68]

Solar Sister has built continuous **loops of learning**, providing input for constant improvement of the offering and the network's operation. Two thirds of the Solar Sister micro-enterprises stay in business, but one third quits being a micro-clean energy business. Interviews with those that stopped their micro-business as a Solar Sister show that the three biggest barriers for them were: capital, bad health and moving away. Raising the capital for a next investment, when you started your business with a loan, seems to be a big hurdle. Evidence shows that those who started the business with some personal capital turn out to be more successful as entrepreneur. Loans at the start are not the silver bullet, striking the right balance between investing your own capital and a loan seems to be key. The network of Solar Sisters became sustainable only after a few years of adapting the micro-business model of the Solar Sisters. The feedback of their solar micro-entrepreneurs, from those continuous learning loops, has nowadays become one of Solar Sister's unique strengths.

PRICED TO WHAT THE PEOPLE CAN AFFORD

The solar technology is nowadays getting to the point of affordable prices; however, distribution, especially in the last mile, is still relatively costly. In all those years Solar Sister has figured out a way to make a sustainable business model for their female clean energy entrepreneurs. It's not just a profitable micro-enterprise model; it comes with investing in the women too. Putting both income generation as well as decision power (back) in the hands of the women is the magic trick for Solar Sister. Only then the win-win-win comes into being – Solar Sister building a last-mile network reaching remote villages, affordably priced solar products and a profitable and rewarding income-generation for the businesswomen.

And still, the organizational costs for all of this cannot fully be recovered from the sales and services to low-income families. If Solar Sister would have applied an 'old school' business model of the user pays it all, the solar solutions would have been way too costly to benefit both female solar micro-entrepreneurs, as well as for low-income families. And keeping the prices affordable, for both the rural family as well as for the village-based micro-entrepreneur, allows for some income generation.

A **BLENDED MODEL** IS AN ENABLING FACTOR ...

So, parts of the organizational costs are cross-subsidized by other streams of revenue. Solar Sister is bridging the last mile by cross-subsidizing their marketing, sales and after-sales network, as to assure it's not the low-income people carrying those costs (for reaching them). And to assure that the female clean energy micro-entrepreneurs generate a decent income. Affordability makes Solar Sister to apply a blended business model. Roughly 30% of the revenue from Solar Sister is coming from the margin on top of the sales of the female solar micro-entrepreneur. The other 70% come in through four different types of partnerships: funders, advocacy partners, implementers and collaborators. Some revenue is generated as a fee for development service, some revenue stems from joint campaigning or advocacy, and other income is pure philanthropic.

This blended business model to reach the last mile disrupts doing business-as-usual: Solar Sister does not operate as a for-profit business, nor do they operate as a 'traditional' not-for-profit. Neither pure donation-driven models have helped the poor communities in a sustainable manner to transition to solar, nor did pure for-profit models. Solar Sister's shows that with such a blended model they can grow inclusion. It's a model based upon collaboration, in which you share costs jointly.

CONNECTED

Let's have a look at this collaborative way of operating. Solar Sister as an organization can be best viewed as a network. Each partnership adds value to the clean energy proposition of the Solar Sisters out there in the rural communities. The organization has a network spreading into the rural villages where their Solar Sisters live and work. And the organization has a network on the other side with many partners. Solar Sister has blurred boundaries and is basically a dynamic network of constantly evolving partners on both sides of the organization. It has a highly **agile, flexible and opportunity-based** operation, with the partnerships as the pumping heart and the Solar Sisters as the network of veins. One could not work without the other.

COLLABORATIVE

Let's look at a few examples how partnerships have had ongoing value add to the Solar Sister's proposition. In Tanzania, it's mainly men riding a bike, let alone you come across a female bike mechanic. In partnership with Global Bike – a foundation that uses the power of bicycles to connect women and resources – Solar Sister trained 23 women to ride their (new) bikes and how to carry out repairs and maintenance. And 80 Tanzanian Solar Sisters received branded bikes – with the support of two other partners – expanding their market for their clean energy business. The bikes allowed the entrepreneurs to save on costs for bus rides, supporting them to bring the solar solutions to new places, empowering them to grow their business.

Nigeria is the most populous country in Africa, with half of the population lacking access to energy. In close collaboration with Women to Women International – a foundation envisioning a world in which all women determine the course of their lives and reach their full potential – Solar Sister recruited entrepreneurs among their women-led Village Saving and Loans Groups in Nigeria, offering a viable business opportunity. Of the 496 women receiving the clean energy business training, 82% earned less than US$2 a day. One hundred and five Solar Sister entrepreneurs signed up. This partnership clearly shows the merging of both of their networks' strengths.

Solar Sister also partners with the private sector, for example with Palmetto, a rapidly growing US-based clean technology enterprise targeting the American solar energy market. Palmetto matches the purchases of their customers with a donation to those in need in Africa, through Solar Sister. A charming example of how two companies with the same purpose, operating in different markets, can create a shared value, adding value to both their businesses and clients.

COVERING THE CHAIN

Solar Sister is addressing some serious systemic barriers to the current prevailing system. Unfortunately, most money in the clean energy space still goes to investment in the solar technology – mainly based in non-developing countries – and not in creating the access to clean energy at the base of the pyramid.[69] Whereas the biggest hurdle to tackle the last mile is how to link in and hook up the low-income families often remotely based. Solar Sister is doing exactly this, while simultaneously closing the gender gap. A women-led organization, building a movement of female clean energy entrepreneurs, in a male-dominated system. In that way, they are building an essential – so far missing – link in the chain.

COLLECTIVE

Some partnerships are focused more to drive collective actions. For instance, together with BRAC Microfinance and Signify – former Philips Lighting, a world leader in lighting – Solar Sister launched WE SOLVE 'Women Entrepreneurship through the Solar Value chain for Economic development' in Tanzania. Signify is a global company offering high-quality, reliable and safe lighting products. BRAC Microfinance is providing microloans to purchase solar energy products such as lights and phone chargers. Together they aim in this multipartnership approach to reach 260,000 households, providing over 1 million Tanzanians with clean, renewable energy. WE SOLVE is funded by the Ministry of Foreign Affairs of Denmark. This is a joint approach between a diverse combination of partners from both public and private sector.

Last, but not least, advocacy is an important component to transition to a different inclusive mindset in society. With advocacy partners, Solar Sister grows the impetus to change. For example, Women + Energy, WE Shine, a nationwide storytelling campaign in Tanzania. This campaign was put together in a consortium with Solar Sister, Show the Good, Ripple Effect Images and Energia, an international network on gender and sustainable energy.

COMMITTED

Solar Sister's commitment to their inclusive mission stems from the Solar Sisters themselves. Each one is a social entrepreneur doing business motivated by bringing the benefits of clean energy to her community. *"Knowing her neighbour is never again going to lose her entire thatched roof because they were burning kerosine lamps … or that children in their community won't have burns, having studied too close to the lamp."* That's what drives the Solar Sisters, according to Katherine.[70]

Being a Solar Sister is empowering them; it's highly motivating to be the force of change in your own community. The Solar Sisters together make a highly motivated network, all bringing their drive and their own networks of friends and family. The peer support Solar Sisters offer to each other gives them courage through tougher times. That's what brings resilience and is the strength of the Solar Sister network.

Then there is the organization of Solar Sister, with **local offices staffing local people**, Tanzanians and Nigerian only, showing a relentless drive to seek solutions for and support the network of Solar Sister's village-based micro-entrepreneurs. All partnerships they build are required to help solve their Solar Sisters' daily challenges of difficult roads to travel and selling to customers with little to no cash. It's a balancing act between managing often large international partners, and the needs of the rural family and solar micro-entrepreneur, without putting the one above the other. **Equality** and trust are key in this. The best partners align with Solar Sister's mission, provide new markets or products, and alleviate logistical challenges.[71] However, finding, building and nurturing these partnerships demands a certain talent, attitude and skill set. This is one of the biggest challenges to continue doing what they do, and what is, according to Katherine, their limiting factor to growth: developing the human capacity of their own local staff and team. "*Survival*" is their biggest success so far is what Katherine often says jokingly but seriously, "*continuing to grow*" requires organizational resilience and a constant adapting to the needs of the Solar Sisters and their clients. "*It's a lot harder and it takes a lot longer to get to the last mile than I had ever thought.*"[72]

Bringing in equality and trust in each partnership is hard. Micro-entrepreneur recruitment is time and resource intense. So, how then do they manage to stay motivated?

It's because they see the bigger picture, the longer term. For Solar Sisters it's actually all about – and only about – **investing in female leadership.** This is the deep cultural shift our world requires to become inclusive. We need to understand: *"Where does the answer come from? What are the actions of the Solar Sisters telling us? All of us constantly need to remind ourselves that it is them, the Solar Sisters, they have the answers, and it is just our humble role to get the answer there,"*[73] according to Katherine. To ignite lights in the lives of the poor, it's crucial to invest in female leadership to serve the women entrepreneurs who do the last-mile distribution and delivery. For this to happen you need to shift your own culture internally first, *"of listening, not knowing the answers ... to counter the external culture, which is so different. It's our job to listen, to uncover ... not to force, not to dictate."*[74] All of it while keeping the last-mile customer at the heart of the service delivery. *"Women are more than just the beneficiaries of energy ... they are the key to unlock energy access for all."*[75] Keeping them at the forefront of all that we do is essential, according to Katherine. That's what will ultimately result in **changing the rules** of the solar supply.

3.2 MY ORAL VILLAGE – NUMERACY: A PREREQUISITE

What if you cannot multiply the price of a pair of products? What if it's hard to compute a 10% discount? What if you cannot correctly check what the money lender presents to you is indeed what you have borrowed, minus what you have repaid? It's hard to live in a society based on money, let alone work or run a business. Numbers are as important as letters to live and make a living. Numeracy is a prerequisite, like reading is. However, despite rising literacy rates in the world over the past decades, still an estimated 750 million people are illiterate[76] and most likely innumerate, according to the United Nations Educational, Scientific and Cultural Organization (UNESCO). And most of them are women. Regular financial services are of little support to those who cannot read, write or compute. Even more worrying is the fact that this grows by the day with the shift to mobile financial services. Cash was designed in such a way you could recognize different denominations through colours, pictures, relief and size, but mobile money is not. Moving more and more into a digital economy, with mobile wallets, micro-business bookkeeping apps and online insurances, it becomes harder and harder for the innumerate among us. Let's not refer to them as illiterate or innumerate, characterizing them by what they cannot (yet) do; let's call them as oral people. Acknowledge that there is a whole oral world where history, culture and daily life lead people to trust direct relationships, speech and actions more than writing.

In many countries with low levels of literacy, mobile phone penetration is actually quite high. This resulted in a widespread inability to navigate mobile money interfaces, leading to a rapidly emerging 'over-the-counter' market where the oral people with a mobile phone give their phone and PIN to an agent and pay them to enter the mobile transaction for them. In Pakistan, an estimated 70% to 90% of mobile money transactions happen over-the-counter. We don't know exactly, but the financial inclusion industry is coming more and more to the insight that financial numeracy might be much lower than we've expected so far, hindering acceleration of financial inclusion through mobile technology. This is adding an extra issue to financial inclusion. Research shows that *"Financially numerate adults had nearly 2.5 times greater odds of having a registered mobile money account than the average adult."*[77] As the digital solutions are deepening their imprint in our daily lives, it becomes more and more difficult for oral people to make formal financial transactions. Two large, national randomized control trials in Côte d'Ivoire and Myanmar, testing financial numeracy with over 3,000 people, demonstrated that there are serious numeracy issues. Up to 36% cannot read a number the equivalent of US$50 in their own currency in Myanmar, while UNESCO reports a literacy rate of 90%. A clear indicator that innumeracy is very likely much higher compared with illiteracy rates. When it comes down to innumeracy, we have a huge discrepancy to overcome, especially in those countries where many low-income people live. Women are also less likely to own mobile phones than their husbands. It's very common for low-income rural households to have only one phone, usually in the hands of the man, either due to patriarchal norms, or the fact that the man is more likely to be literate, and hence able to use it more effectively. We risk a widening of the divide due to the mobile tech solutions nowadays.

So, what needs to be done to revolutionize digital finance to include low-income oral people? Adapting the interfaces of digital finance solutions to be safe and easy to use for all oral adults. For exactly this, Orali Mobile will be launched in Pakistan in 2021, providing oral interfacing prototypes and numeracy educational services for mobile money solutions providers. *"The ability to read a long number proved to be a very effective predictor of engagement with mobile money,"*[78] which is a very simple test, according to Brett Matthews, founder of Orali Mobile. With Orali Mobile, Brett will offer a solution for the digital finance providers to increase numeracy skills of oral people, and with that growing the access to financial services. He is on a mission to transition to a new normal in which we collectively achieve universal usability of financial services. His focus is not just universal access – it's usability. Brett aims to transition from Know Your Customer (KYC) to Your Customer Knows How, as to advance financial inclusion.

Photo by game changer

IT TOOK YEARS … TO **REVERSE ENGINEER IT TO MEET THE NEEDS**

The interfacing tools and numeracy educational services Orali Mobile will offer in Pakistan are rooted in the Oral Information Management (OIM) tools for the unbanked that were developed, tested and researched in the past decade by My Oral Village,[79] founded by Brett Matthews too. Oral Information Management (OIM) is the practice of managing information without relying on text. The OIM tools from My Oral Village are based upon images of cash, oral iconography and metaphors for time and space, and work as user interfaces to oral people. Like the finger math counting example as depicted, cash depicting scroll bars for mobile wallets or ATMs, and 'oral' icons that are intuitive, easy to learn and can be adapted to local context.

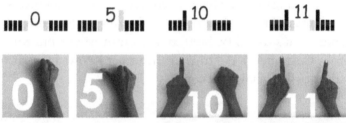

Fingermath counting 0–99.[80]
Photo by game changer

Those oral information tools and services are meant to be integrated in digital financial solutions such as mobile payment platforms, saving account passes, micro-enterprise business apps and the likes. With these tools, oral communities can practice skills to understand numbers, to become numerate. This is empowering the oral people to make mobile transactions, keep loan balances and saving group records on mobile phones. My Oral Village has developed, built and tested those OIM tools for over a decade in oral communities in India, Bangladesh, Cambodia, Tanzania, Timor Leste, Myanmar, Pakistan, Cote D'Ivoire and the Solomon Islands. They've become a centre of expertise regarding what's required to serve and include oral people.

COLLABORATIVE

My Oral Village supplies the expertise and prototypes interfacing with mobile money solutions. They provide access to tools and services such as cash calculators, cash planners, financial numeracy games and mobile wallet games to build the capability of their partners, the providers of mobile financial solutions and services. Their partners support and serve saving groups, self-help groups, enterprising families and micro-entrepreneurs all around the world, growing their financial numeracy.

In collaboration with MicroSave, for example, My Oral Village interactively developed and piloted a Mobile Wallet for Oral (MoWO), and researched the adoption. In India alone, the oral segment includes about 264 million people, including 23 million youth aged 15–24.[81] The MoWO offers a sandbox where oral users can learn numeracy without risking financial loss. The sandbox offers functionalities to send money, request money, add money and pay bills as well, and it has an image-based phonebook.[82] The MoWO was developed based upon the findings of My Oral Village that most oral adults cannot decode multidigit numeral strings, especially four or more digits. One of the key findings of the pilot with MicroSave was that *literate* people are unable to decode place value either. Meaning that even literate people had challenges to put the decimal point correctly. And another key finding indicated that it is actually not getting much better with the younger generation.[83] The clickable prototype for the Mobile Wallet (MoWo) *"now informs the design of applications for several digital finance providers and fintechs in India."*[84]

The OIM proto-tools have been extensively tested, always in collaboration with local partners, for example with UNCDF in the Solomon Islands. Several projects piloted the OIM tools in the Solomon Islands, with its many languages, in collaboration with the Ministry of Women and with the

REIMAGINING FINANCIAL INCLUSION

Anglican church in Melanesia. The "Savings Groups Practice Guide," based upon the pilots applying OIM tools in the saving groups, was adopted by the Ministry of Women and the Mothers Union of the Anglican Church for their savings groups programme.

In partnership with The BOMA project – an NGO that runs a programme in northern Kenya – the OIM proto-tools are being adapted to local context and the many local languages to reach the Kenyan oral people. My Oral Village supported oralizing the business records of enterprising women in Kenya. Pastoralist women micro-entrepreneurs tested the record-keeping system on their phones with a cash calculator, a new ledger book composed of icons representing cash amounts and an 'account box' with colour segmentation – to facilitate cash management. The results of this proof of concept with BOMA in Kenya are looking promising, meaning a high level of usability for oral people.

Photo by game changer

To further facilitate the collaborative approach to fight innumeracy, My Oral Villages is building an open-source repository of OIM proto-tools. Brett envisions that this ignites a growing movement of partners that jointly contribute to this 'new normal' where all institutions providing digital financial services include the oral poor too. Collectively shoulder the transformation to make sure 'Your Customer Knows How To' use your digital financial service. The open-source repository of OIM proto-tools is a means to facilitate financial inclusion of oral people, through partners.

A **BLENDED MODEL** IS AN ENABLING FACTOR …

This repository of OIM tools provides the fertile soil for a network of non-profit and governmental financial education institutions all over the world to grow their contribution and support to bump up numeracy. Next to this, Orali Mobile will target the for-profit digital financial services providers to support them to grow their client base including oral people. Any partner can grow their contribution to Global Sustainable Development Goals by joining either My Oral Village or Orali Mobile. Commercial partners that offer mobile payments, wallets, and other financial payment or savings services, such as telecoms companies, microfinance institutions, banks and remittance firms, can use the oral interface services at the Orali Mobile platform. Orali Mobile will offer a way to include oral people, in a profitable way, with limited risk, using the interfacing through the platform.

Financial inclusion of oral people will be realized in this blended model, through this connecting of partners of My Oral Village on the one hand, and the platform and its partners of Orali Mobile, on the other hand. Through such a network operation all partners jointly shoulder the investment required to ignite numeracy, as a prerequisite to financial inclusion.

The potential is huge, and with the growth of smartphone ownership, the time is now. "*In India, if just 10% of overall monthly expenditures by oral people were transacted* *digitally, it would add up to US$1.6 billion overall for the digital payments industry.*"[85] Through the set-up of these two legs of the network, one partnering with the non-profit and governmental financial (education) institutions, and the other leg to service the commercial partners, a blended model is in place to support the scaling of numeracy.

COLLECTIVE

According to Brett: *"Today, with mixed image, icon and number solutions that do more to help people not only feel safe but learn the financial numeracy skills, it should be considered as a basic human right."*[86] Next to furthering the wiki-like open-source library of those OIM tools, My Oral Village facilitates a collective action to drive numeracy up. It is done by measuring numeracy. The sheer lack of information about numeracy shows how little we know. *" ... absence leads (financial inclusion) practitioners toward the unfortunate working assumption that everyone on earth can read a financial transaction slip or bank statement,"*[87] according to Brett. If we don't know numeracy skills and levels, how on earth do we know if we are progressing? Are we solving the issue at the core: innumeracy? For exactly this objective, My Oral Village is driving a global effort to start measuring financial numeracy. Key to this is a global metric. The Financial Numeracy Indicator (FNI) is in development and piloted by My Oral Village for exactly this purpose. The FNI has been successfully tested in large, nationally randomized surveys in Côte d'Ivoire and Myanmar. Not surprisingly it shows *"In Cote d'Ivoire, where 94% of financially included adults have mobile money accounts, being financially numerate increased the odds of financial inclusion by over 500%."*[88] For this to become a global standard, supporting the acceleration of financial inclusion, My Oral Village is in conversation with the World Bank's Global Findex. The FNI will help to generate more evidence and ultimately drive up the adoption rate of oral information tools. Which is in its turn required to influence public policy regarding consumer protection, as to assure financial institutions present information to oral adults in a way they can understand and use autonomously.

CHANGING THE RULES OF THE GAME

Even if we will never reach inclusion through compliance with formal regulation, which is likely, the OIM tools in combination with a FNI is a huge step toward risk-based supervision. CGAP, Consultative Group to Assist the Poor, acknowledged as independent experts on financial inclusion, suggests to supervise the financial industry based upon the application of instruments that reduce risks for their clients.[89] If we acknowledge the risk of oral people using mobile phones or digital platforms for financial transactions, then each and every institution offering those financial services should be empowered to take action and reduce the risk by application and integration of OIM tools. That's where the pearl in the oyster can be found. These OIM proto-tools are enablers for such a mindset shift: each of us should at least be able to understand the financial transactions we're making. If not through regulatory reforms, there is a moral obligation to incorporate those OIM proto-tools for each and every Financial Service Provider (FSP). The FNI is an additional measure to check how we are progressing on our collective action and moral obligation to grow numeracy. Numeracy as a prerequisite for financial inclusion.

EVERYBODY PLAYS

Obviously, OIM tools and numeracy educational services will counter gender biases, since the majority of the illiterate and innumerate are women. It is a positive trend that the gap of penetration rates of mobile devices is closing in the past decade among women versus men; however, women are still 20% less likely to own a smart mobile phone compared to men in low-and middle income countries.[90] Illiteracy in general, and digital literacy in particular, is still one of the root causes for women why they do not use the mobile phone. Mind you, even if 80% of women globally currently owns a mobile phone in low- and middle-income countries, the true barrier is in the use of it for financial transactions.[91] Not knowing how to use it is the key barrier here. And let's not forget, although millions of households own a mobile phone, you guess who's using it most.

Oral education to ignite numeracy is a must-have, for which My Oral Village and Orali Mobile offer the whole suit of expertise, tools and services to tackle. Firstly, they allow everybody access to digital financial services, creating the universal usability. Secondly, they empower partners to offer it to their (potential) client base. The tools, platform and services are designed to support the giants in the financial inclusion and the mobile finance industry, to join the game – an empowering force to deliver this basic human right to all of us.

COMMITTED

To invite more partners to contribute to making the mobile money, payment and saving, insurance and credit services available for the oral people, Brett Matthews, founder of My Oral Villages and Orali Mobile, constantly seeks to find the right balance between openly sharing and creating the business case to apply OIM tools by the financial service providers, all the while keeping the interests of the oral people as a first priority. Key to solving this delicate balancing act is the team. It's the team members that continuously need to marry a financially sustainable strategy with the growth of the number of oral people truly impacted. For both My Oral Village as well as for Orali Mobile the OIM tools and oral educational numeracy services are meant to serve all oral people; however, to appetize the for-profit financial service providers to join, you need a business case to commercialize it as a service. One way to assure both organizations continue to act on behalf of the oral people is by recruiting people with oral backgrounds in their families. Basically, build a user base in both organizations, My Oral Village and Orali Mobile. At My Oral Village, all their fieldwork requires oral people to be on the team. They never invite urban artists to join; they always rely on village artists, for example. Brett has frequently witnessed a well-intended, but implicit bias toward text with urban artists. *"The process of tools design and adaptation must be client guided,"*[92] according to Brett, the clients being the oral people. Design for the target group is an alternative way to assure commitment to the inclusive mission.

PEOPLE AT THE HEART OF IT

The next step is to assure that the data about daily usage will also contribute to better services for oral people. Orali Mobile's platform approach is designed to leverage the body of data generated through it. Data about the usage of oral numeracy educational services and the numeracy information will in this platform approach keep the information accessible and not just sitting fragmented with each financial service provider. This assures that the further development and application of the OIM tools and services follow the needs of the oral people, and how they prefer to use it **on a daily basis**. It will allow financial service providers to use the service while the usage data will flow back to generate the evidence. The data from the platform will be used and feed back into the designs and adaptation of the next gen open-source OIM solutions for mobile money and digital financial service delivery. The platform is applied with the purpose of keeping **continuous loops of learning**, and to offer a base for oral usability diagnostics.

CONNECTED

Here is where the network effect kicks in and starts to work for the oral people, while as more mobile money service providers are joining the cost per user will decrease, which in its turn will drive usage and reach of number of oral people up. Through this connectedness, numeracy is bound to accelerate. The design of this inclusive innovation geared to systemically changing the financial system.

3.3 NEST – INCLUSION OF HOME-BASED ARTISANS BY BIG BRANDS

Handicrafts can be seen as one of the largest employers of women in emerging countries in the world. These women work from home or in small-scale ateliers and make crafts and textiles. Unfortunately, they are by the nature of where they do this – at home – invisible, most likely not protected, not fairly paid, regularly working in unsafe conditions, with their children often unprotected against child labour. The staggering lack of data on the topic shows how much they are in the shadow of our formal economy, how much they are excluded. All of them work in economic isolation, a huge factor contributing to the gender imbalances in the world economy. For them, millions of them, this is not a hobby, it is vital to their lives and that of their families. In many countries women feel unsafe working outside the home or are prohibited by written or unwritten rules in society to go outside. On top of this, in many countries there is no regulation in place to protect women and their children working from home. A catch-22 which needs to change. And Nest[93] does so.

Photo by game changer

There has been a large focus on production facilities, especially in the fashion, garment and textile sector in the last decades, tackling issues of healthy and safe working conditions, child labour, sustainable production practices and fair pay in those factories. Still, an estimated 40–60%[94] of the production of those factories is partly sourced from home-based workers. These home-based workers are paid less than their factory-based equivalents and they are invisible for formal measures, because they often work via middlemen. Pushing them into the factories is not a solution for them; at home they can take care of their family members and they feel safe. They often cannot afford spending on child care, and commuting to or moving closer to the factories is out of the question. We don't have to move, chase or push them into our formal system; we could link them in, hook up with them at home. Making working life at home worthwhile for them too, with rights, security, proper pay, protection, making sure they work safe, for themselves, for the environment and for their children. And that is exactly what Nest is doing, with a Standards, a Seal, while creating linkages between the informal home-based workers and the formal 'industry,' step-by-step including them. Nest has done so against the long-standing stereotyping of artisan's work and working from home not being able to scale. Mind you, this sector by sheer number of women producing hand made products from home is already huge in itself. According to Research and Markets, the global handicrafts market reached US$718 billion in 2020, and is expected to reach 985 billion in 2023.[95]

LINKING ALL PLAYERS IN EQUALITY

Nest has built and grown an open and global movement, called the Artisan Guild, with 1,000 artisan groups in over 100 countries, connecting over 197,000 handworkers. In this way Nest indirectly impacts close to a million lives. And they keep growing. To convince the last reader that many global supply chains start at their homes: 92% of total artisans are exporting.

In close collaboration with the artisan groups, continuously surveying them and capturing their needs, Nest has developed a Standard for Ethical Production in Homes and Small Workshops. Acceptance and adhering to the Standard is high, due to the fact that this was developed in close collaboration with the home-based artisans, as well as with the industry players such as big brands and so-called open factories too. Both, big brands and home-based artisans, are considered equality important. Over 10 global brands are committed to improve conditions with the Standards, brands like Patagonia, West Elm,[96] Eileen Fisher and Target.[97] As a brand, when you adopt the Standards, you are offered a Nest Seal of Ethical Handcraft, a symbol of assurance that the product your end-consumers buys is ethically handcrafted in a home or a small workshop. In this way, Nest is linking all players in the global chain.

COVERING THE CHAIN

The brands gain quite a lot from joining this Nest movement. Before, the fuzziness of data about the invisible workforce made it hard to build a more sustainable and responsible supply chain, and especially the last mile was always hard to connect with. Through this movement, connecting brands and big producers to the artisan, collecting data while doing so gives information about and visibility to this large part of their 'workforce.' It provides a good starting point to take actions to improve working conditions, proper wage, payment and quality control, to name a few. Most brands were using their own standards. This is what made it hard for artisans to comply to, because all brands came with their own standards. This practice also let to the fact that it was hard to control and measure, because it is hard (to impossible) to evaluate by any external, independent parties like auditors. Take, for example, how this worked for a factory: there was a lot of redundancy in compliance, performing many different audits for different brands. Imagine how this would look if the factory also has to include the home-based artisans supplying to them via middlemen, in their compliance. Nest's Ethical Handcraft programme is rooted in the Nest Standard for Homes and Small Workshops – a production regulatory framework that includes 100+ standards to ensure the wellbeing of workers in traditional working environments. In combination with the creation of an open movement, which makes it possible to tackle all of these issues. Resulting in supply-chain efficiency for the brands, transparency in the full chain, and inclusion of this last mile into the homes – the workplace – of the artisans.

PLACE IS AT THE DOORSTEP

The Nest programme is education focused and is partnering with artisan businesses and factories with home-based labour, jointly improving working conditions at home, growing understanding of child labour and healthy work environments. To illustrate, take the results of 2019, reaching over 40,000 artisans in 18 countries, with 20 brands participating:

- ninety per cent had workers' policies in place (up from 18%, baseline)
- ninety-four per cent had health and safety equipment and supplies in place (up from 44%, baseline)
- the gap between artisan wages and minimum wages was close to 7% (down from a gap of 28%, baseline), so the **pay flows** back **into the family**
- over 50% had age verification in place – a measure against child labour (up from 28%)

These figures demonstrate the power of transparency in the last mile of the global chain, for both the big brands as well as the artisans.

Photo by game changer

PEOPLE AT THE HEART OF IT

Training is a key element in the operating of Nest's Ethical Handcraft programme. It applies a training-first approach, in which the artisan or open factory is provided with a training to grow understanding of the Standard and ways to comply. Together with participating businesses, Nest is continuously piloting and implementing improvements for home-based working conditions.

Next to the training, continuous support is provided to develop sustainable growth paths and come up with corrective action plans to increase compliance with the Standard. In addition to the Nest Ethical Handcraft programme, the organization offers an annual application-based Accelerator programme for 10 artisan business, supporting the growth of their enterprise and leadership. As a result, their revenue increases on average with a little over 8%.[98] Parallel to this, Nest has co-created a digital learning centre, where any artisan business globally can join the Guild and receive access to a range of learning tools (webinars, templates, etc.) as well as access to a volunteer matchmaking programme with industry professionals for pro-bono consulting projects. Many larger companies participate by creating employee engagement opportunities where staff can offer hands-on support and mentor artisans, with specific requests coming from the artisan community. This is a powerful tool to provide and receive expertise and exclusive pro-bono support, because it opens up a direct communication channel between the brand and artisan. This element of Nest's approach aims to grow inclusiveness through engaging the employees of large companies, creating a **learning loop** between the visible and (previously) invisible parts of the global supply chain. The trainings, the learning centre and the communication platform is centred around the people and connecting them.

PLAY AS A GROUP

Nest has become an authority – based on the data coming through on their platform – on this previously invisible part of the economy. Whereas the stereotype picture of the home-based artisan being a mom of three making nice products for tourist and local use, the data collected by Nest show a different picture. Through widespread use of telephone, email and social media the interconnectedness is immense. This allows them to take part of international trade: over 90% of the artisan business in the Nest movement are engaged in export,[99] most of them indicate it's not the local market but the international wholesale they are utilizing. From a survey Nest conducted with the Council of Fashion Designers of America (CFDA), also most designers report they source from one to five artisans around the world, 75% indicate they would like to *expand* their sourcing from artisans.[100] Another study from Nest, in close collaboration with the Gerson Lehrman Group, shows that only 4% of brands are in the habit of conducting home visits assessing work and working conditions.[101] So, brands and home-based artisans are already heavily interconnected; there is a need to grow this even more, but there is very little insight in how to and little access to formalize this last mile into the homes. Formalizing meaning: getting insight, assessing wrong-doings of labour conditions or environmental issues, solving it together, agreeing on deals, fair pricing, committing to payments, tracking and tracing to avoid misunderstandings and exploitation, and so on. Through the Guild, home-based artisans can now **play** as a **group**. And in this way, as a group, with the Standard and Seal, Nest is allowing for equality between the home-based artisans and the large companies.

COLLABORATIVE

What's unique to Nest's approach is the full supply chain angle to it, in combination with the collaborative way it came into being, and continues to be further developed. The supply chain integration include artisan, big brands and their consumers in equality. They continue building, piloting and adapting the Standard in close collaboration. Both processes, the development process – and therefore the acceptance – as well as the compliance process of the Nest Ethical Handcraft Program is done in close collaboration between artisans and big brands. It is based upon trust, transparency and acceptance of not knowing, aiming to find solutions together. The fact that big brands joined in shaping the new Standard builds trust and momentum in the fashion and textile industry. It facilitates an easy access for other industry players to join.

Take, for example, H&M, matched by Nest with an artisan group 'All Across Africa,' agreeing to weave baskets. Partly through this H&M order, 497 jobs were created in Rwanda and Uganda in areas far away from their factories, reaching 2,852 people, 92% of the women report they used the increased income primarily for education for their children.[102] Nest's surveys[103] of worker wellbeing indicate that this holds true for many more: 40% of women primarily use the income they earn from craft-work for their children's education. This is demonstrating the long-term impact of financial inclusion. The orders from larger international brands such as H&M have allowed 'All Across Africa' to grow their revenue between 60–70%. However, bear in mind, this result did not happen overnight. The participation of All Across Africa in Nest's Artisan Accelerator – a business incubator programme – helped to set up the business and scale in Rwanda and Uganda. Clear signs of financial inclusion as a result of this Accelerator and collaboration with brands are, for example, that 80% of the artisans of All Across Africa use saving accounts, 94% bought health insurance, and all of them say they are proud of their crafts work.[104]

A **BLENDED MODEL** IS AN ENABLING FACTOR ...

The services to the artisans, their businesses and homeworkers are offered for free. Nest covers the cost through a mechanism of cross-subsidization. Partly the revenues come from fee-for-service from partners and partly the revenue is generated by grants from philanthropy, including foundations and individual supporters. Nest demonstrates a blended business model, and is as an organization leading by example when it comes to entrepreneurial collaboration. Most cost for operation and growing the Guild are covered by revenues coming from fees for ethical sourcing services to their corporate partners, and some are recovered through corporate philanthropy. Costs for research and advocacy are also recovered by a mix of funding from foundations, as well as done in paid partnerships with partners like Bloomberg Philanthropies. An enormous value of pro-bono services is generated by Nest and channelled to the artisans and their businesses, in close partnership with the large multinationals. Nest works with pro-bono partnerships, for example for legal support, to assure their operation is lean. To some partners, big brands in particular, they offer services to perform coaching on the job. On-the-job coaching to be inclusive of home-based workers, in the corporate business is an empowering tool; jointly identifying processes, policies and systems that hinder inclusion of small batch manufactory and home-based workers that can be re-created together. The Nest 'consultant' is insourced and sits next to the corporate team. These examples show how a blended business model looks like in a social enterprise aiming for financial inclusion.

At the Nest they are keen on keeping the ratio of fees for services from big brands, less than 50% as to ensure the work stays mission centric.[105] Nest values this independence, to avoid mission drift, and assure they keep the home-based artisan and their inclusive mission as the core of their organization.

COMMITTED

Closing the loop between the big brands and the home-based artisan small business requires a strong ability to build the bridge between the two. One lesson Nest has learned is to always **start small**. Convincing big brands to join is done by providing the proof that it works for a singular site of a partners. The Nest always connects the small business of the artisan with the big brand. Commitment to their inclusive mission stems from connection between the people, which is why Nest encourages **direct dialogue** between brands and artisan by organizing regular meet-ups.

At Nest, the hardest position to fill is the one who works with the corporate partners; it requires a lot of thorough vetting at the recruitment process. Apart from that, the whole team at Nest is **divers** and **roles** have a **fluid** nature. They build as an organization on the skills and expertise available in the full team, so there are no fixed roles. Roles evolve while people performing the role develop. This means that there is a **lot of conversation** happing at their work space, which is not always easy for staff members who like to organize their tasks and activities in a fixed working schedule. Part of what they aim for is that brands transition to a new working culture, another attitude, more inclusive toward home-based workers and consider them to be a formal part of their workforce. This is therefore, too, what Nest applies to themselves at the office. A diverse team, with many skills and expertise, is **constantly evolving, absorbing and learning** from collaborating with small artisan businesses and big brands. They reflect openly about the fact that they are in a continuous process of trying, testing and applying it, and also about how they struggle with it at their own offices.

Nest is actively seeking the participation of brands by opening up seats in their advisory board for brands. They are inviting brands into steering committee and board meetings. All of the above is infused with a very **agile** way of working.

According to Rebecca, founder of Nest: *"I like to be concrete; these are the 10 things to solve, what are the best next steps. The big vision is helpful, but I want the team to break down things into manageable steps, moving forward in small steps that collectively, and over time, create larger impact. No talk and theory only. We iterate as we go."*[106] It's in this entrepreneurial way of collaboration with the different stakeholders, that Nest is successful. By doing it while actively involving all the stakeholders in every step down the road, making sure all partners stay engaged. To quote Rebecca: *"We're hyper on action and iteration."*[107]

CHANGING THE RULES OF THE GAME

The pandemic crisis was a moment for Nest to seize recognition and deepen the understanding of home-work in itself. The COVID-19 pandemic provided an impulse for a fundamental revolution of working from home. The production of hundreds of thousands of masks in less than three weeks, by home-workers, set aside, supported them to showcase the power and resilience of this home-based workforce. According to Nest, it's time for a next step towards inclusion of home-based workers; it's time for others to follow suit.

Photo by game changer

Acknowledging the ambition that others need to join in, too, infusing change into the whole system to progress full inclusion, Nest is aiming for two objectives; one is more partners doing the same, for which they need more evidence to convince. Firstly, Nest is expanding their reach by empowering partners to train and use the Standard and methodology, a train-the-trainer model. And, they want auditing firms to join too. Nest is developing and testing a training to accredit external auditors through a licensing-formula. It requires more configuration, since the training-first approach does not fit well with the traditional way of working of auditors. There are two challenges to overcome with this objective. How to get to a new way of working in which auditors can audit at home, which is radically different from 'surveying' factories. It requires a lot of **trust**-building, **equality** and a different way of **communicating**. It also comes with the challenge of how to close the loop with the training that has to be provided up-front, which is not something auditors are skilled to do. Perhaps training companies are better suited for this, although they are not into auditing. The second objective Nest has, is to grow their early evidence into a tool for advocacy.

COLLECTIVE

By 2019 Nest launched their first State of the Handworker Economy report with the support of Bloomberg Philanthropies, revealing data and information about artisans, their small and medium enterprises, homeworkers and complex supply chains in which they operate. A unique tool that aims to set-off a large ripple of change through the whole system, made from complex, intertwined supply chains of textile, fashion and home furniture and accessories.

Both objectives – transforming auditing to a training-first approach at home, as well as the advocacy to fully financially include home-based artisans – aim to fuel the empowerment of other industry players to join, contribute and progress. This system-change approach has a collective action, at its core, in Nest's case this: jointly complying to the Standard that was developed together. Moving away from one telling the other what and how to do it, toward jointly agreeing on what is a good practice, and auditing afterward closely linked to the up-front training. This can only be done together, collectively including the huge number of home-based artisans in our formal economy, step-by-step. Mostly women – 74% of all artisans in the Nest Guild[108] – but many immigrants, refugees and rural community members too. Resulting in a world in which **everybody plays**.

CHAPTER 4

DAILY LIFE AS THE PLAYGROUND

One of the flaws entrenched in the current formal financial system is due to being centred around global banks, insurers, giant players in global markets. Most processes and procedures are designed to make these institutions efficient, as a result of which we have created a unique, global and powerful formal financial system. Being able to buy your airplane ticket or new laptop online, get it insured, and refunded when it's cancelled or out of stock is a miracle in itself. However, aiming for finance for all, this has become a flaw too. This flaw stems from the fact that financial services are disconnected from basic needs. Basic needs are the first and foremost reason to transact and exchange, this is especially true for the low-income families. The majority in the world, those living with little income, need money to get their basic needs fulfilled on a daily basis. Delivery of financial services is needed at the place where and at the moment when basic needs are fulfilled.

For those families living in remote and underserved parts of the world, there are two sides to money: the making of it – income – and the living expenditure side. Financial inclusion needs to happen there where they put in their hard work, buy their food, purchase input for their home-based business, where and when they need energy for cooking, when they marry off their children, when they build an additional room to their home, when they need the doctor's advice or medicine, when they get a gig.

On the street, when a passerby hails for a ride and the taxi driver gets paid, that's where gojek delivers the financial services. Supporting millions of drivers, gojek has a model evolving around the humongous number of gigs in daily life, as a mean to step-by-step financially include low-income people. Gojek is incorporating existing 'informal associations,' traditional ways of saving, at the core of their solution. They are adding health advise, insurance, work guarantee, credits, mobile wallets and transaction history to their offering, becoming a trusted partner in the daily life of the low-income people delivering the gigs.

In a rural village there is no pharmacy, no health centre nor hospital within the vicinity of an hour walking. That is the place where healthy entrepreneurs are providing health education, health-related products and preventive services, by empowering rural based micro-health-entrepreneurs. Healthy Entrepreneurs offers a health business concept for income generation and prefinancing facilities, which goes hand in hand with the fulfilment of basic needs of the rural villagers: knowledge about healthy living, over-the-counter medicines, soap, condoms and diagnostic screenings. Realizing access to health while simultaneously growing financial inclusion.

Let's have a look.

4.1 GOJEK – IT'S ALL ABOUT JOBS, JOBS, JOBS

Gojek is demonstrating a pathway to financial inclusion through formalizing the local gig economies, step-by-step. Perhaps a no-brainer, but nevertheless true, financial inclusion is also about jobs, jobs, jobs. Many of the countries where the financially excluded live have huge informal economies, with many informal jobs. By nature, since they are informal, income from those jobs is not taxed, but also those jobs are not protected. Not protected by labour law, no contracts or guarantees, the work is not insured, there's no protection against non-payment, working conditions are often unsafe and not healthy, and social security and pension are out of the question. What if we would take those informal jobs and step-by-step include them in our formal financial system? Let's for a change start with the benefits for the families and not with the taxes for the government. How do we get the hard-working people protected? Could we add benefits from being registered? For example, by provision of financial services, like being able to save, or perhaps getting a loan, by providing an insurance or work guarantee, and protection against non-payment.

This is exactly what gojek[109] is doing for 2 million so-called gig jobs, in a country with one of largest and vibrant informal sectors in the world, Indonesia. According to ILO,[110] the informal jobs account for a little over 60% of the total workforce in Indonesia. According to the Asian Development Bank[111] and the OECD,[112] this is even closer to 70%. Most of those informal jobs are done by independent professionals such as drivers, cleaners, and so-called mom-and-pop shops and other micro-enterprises (with fewer than five employees). The OECD found that 96% of the micro-enterprises offer informal jobs. Mind you, micro-enterprises make up the vast majority of all enterprises and employment in Indonesia, with close to 99% of all enterprises being micro-enterprise, according to the OECD.

DAILY LIFE AS THE PLAYGROUND

Ojek, in Indonesian, means "motorbike taxi" and is a popular way of transportation. Gojek started with an app to hail such a motorbike taxi, aiming to reduce the waiting time for a ride for both customer as well as for the motorbike taxi driver. Fast forward: anno 2020 gojek has close to two million motor bike drivers who've increased their income substantially via this app. On average, a driver reports an increase of income of 44%.[113] Next to offering motorbike taxi services, gojek launched other hailing services over the years, such as gocar for hailing a regular taxi ride by car; gofood for food delivery; gomart for having your shopping done at the market; gomed for buying and collecting prescriptions and medicines, connecting users with pharmacies; gotix for tickets; gomassage offering massage; and goclean offering cleaning services for your home and car, with an option to have it – the cleaning job – insured (against lost items) and with rework guaranteed. All of this is supported by several digital payments services, like gopay for online payment; gotagihan for payment of your electricity, water, tv and internet bills; gopulsa for buying your mobile telephone credits; and gosure for insurances. And, not to forget: paylater, offering the service to pay at the end of the month, and gopoints, a loyalty programme, very crucial in getting digital money accepted in a cash-based society.

Photo by Angie Siddharta

With over 2 million gojek drivers, and close to a million mom-and-pop shops for food, street vendors and other food merchants, their impact on society is enormous. As is the impact in daily life: increasing the orders for 93% of all those partners, with 3.3 million orders a day in 2020. That is 50 orders per second! Their total contribution to the total economy was over US$7 billion in 2019. By creation of new gig jobs, gojek reduced unemployment with an estimated 15% in Indonesia. A full 89% of the gojek app users indicate gojek has a positive impact on society in general.[114] An impressive boost of the gig-economy, but key here is that their success came from the fact that their services are delivered attached to daily life, not just for those buying the gig, but also for those delivering the gig!

PAY AND PERKS FLOW **BACK** IN THE FAMILY OR COMMUNITY

The increase of income flows directly back to the families of the ones delivering the gig. But also into the direct community, since those drivers did not only grow their income, they increased their spending with 31% too. Don't underestimate the trickle-down effect of 2 million drivers' increased spending! Of the other (non-driver) gojek partners, 85% have a wider audience to cater to.[115]

But it's not just about more gigs and more income. Imagine for instance cleaners having the option to protect their work through gojek with a work guarantee. All those drivers and food merchants having a track record of their income and some of their spending through the online payment platform. That's unprecedented. Having access to additional financial services such as, for example, access to credits or a health insurance. Not to forget, for all of them: protection against non-payment through the app. But there are other perks too: subsidized health support for parents, free counselling (mental health), free courses for personal development and in-house mentoring. As you can see, the uniqueness of the way gojek is tackling financial inclusion is a holistic approach, aiming to generate benefits that flow back to the supplying families and community.

PEOPLE AT THE **HEART** OF IT

Key to gojek's success is an acquisition of Mapan, which is on a mission to provide access to services and products for low-income people. Although it was actually a triple acquisition, next to Mapan, gojek acquired the biggest online payment gateway and Indonesia's largest offline payment processing company.[116] However, I believe the big success factor was Mapan, with an approach that integrates seamlessly with local tradition and local informal systems.

From the start Mapan aimed to deliver to the daily needs of the local village people. Let's take a snapshot of their daily life. Firstly, a pot you need for cooking in an average small Indonesian village will costs twice as much as it will in the city, and has a lot of unnecessary handles and add-ons you don't need. Costs for distribution and transportation of one pot to the village are high. And on top of that, as a villager you often pay exorbitant high cost for a loan you need to be able to buy the pot. The village head is still one of the most trusted persons in such a village. And, in Indonesia, the practice of 'arisan' is widespread. It is an old system of rotating savings and loans, traditionally used by groups of women. Mapan offers the pot and all other kinds of products, for half the price – reducing the cost through whole-sale. Mapan adapts the pot to the needs of the villager – through redesign – while bundling it with online financial services to the *arisan* groups in the villages via the village heads. According to Aldi Haryopratomo, founder of Mapan, the challenge is to know how to change financial habits: *"Financial education should be relevant to the needs of its audience. Arisan, which has been underestimated, is actually a strong and capable support group to encourage change for its members."*[117] Mapan taps into the daily basic needs and uses existing local informal systems rooted in strong tradition, via trusted local persons, and took it online. And therefore, with this magic mix, Mapan took off. After only 2.5 years into being, Mapan served a million families. Just because it kept the village people at the heart of their service delivery.

PLACE IS AT THE DOORSTEP

Then gojek and Mapan joined forces in a pilot to see what would happen when you offer both services in one family. What would happen if you offer the wife of a gojek driver to become a Mapan *arisan* leader, partly based upon the increased income of her husband, a gojek driver? That was the working hypothesis. The family would get an opportunity to buy a pan for cooking to start a home-based business and grow their household income, using the Mapan services and the gojek app. Some of the families joining this pilot went from poverty into middle class within a few months! It helps families, because it delivers all the financial services – income, protection, saving and loans – bundled with the input for a home based micro-business, at their doorstep. No wonder that this pilot resulted in the acquisition of Mapan by gojek.

Both companies and their founders share an inclusive mission: Mapan and gojek both aim to serve the society at large and specifically serve the needs of low-income families. According to Aldi, who became CEO of gopay after the acquisition: "One of our secret sauces is: we are closer to the user than to the investors. This bottom-up approach is better than any other model that I've seen."[118] A bottom-up approach and an inclusive mission with at the heart of it: the people, serving them at their doorsteps.

LINKING ALL PLAYERS IN EQUALITY

It's fascinating to see the **equality** in their perception of who the customer is. Services offered to the paying customer are directly channelled back to the ones delivering the service, the informal job owner. Through this mechanism, the integrated approach to financial inclusion is broadened and deepened step-by-step. When a paying customer gets a ride, the gojek app protects the driver against non-payment. The one who wants a car cleaned gets the service to insure the car cleaning job by gojek, against theft or a guarantee that the job is done well. But, at the same time, also the cleaners are protected against non-payment, they build a track record of good cleaning jobs delivered and are thus protected against false claims. On top of this, the cleaner can actually deliver an insurance and job guarantee to the customer, previously impossible. Looping benefits for the paying customer back to the delivering supplier of the gig is an integral part and core to the business of gojek. Through which they actually manage to financially include low-income families. The growth, the scale of its impact, could never have happened with this link broken. It's a matter of linking all players, but key to success is to infuse equality in the linkage between buying and delivery. Not putting the paying customer above the one that delivers.

Mind you, old-school business-as-usual models would increase profit margins, not changing the fact that it is ok to exploit the gig-delivery man. *"It's the industry that sees business as what you are selling. But we see it as who are you serving,"*[119] according to Aldi Haryopratomo. In their own view, gojek – and Mapan under its umbrella – they serve the low-income families. Digital money is just the glue for all of this, which allows for transparency, tracking and tracing. The financial technology behind this is important: what is core to its success is not the technology, but the acceptance of it by the local communities. This happened due to gojek's active role fuelling the linkages in this chain with equality.

CONNECTED

According to founder of Mapan and CEO of gopay, Aldi, it is both the sincerity to work via the trusted village head of a community, as well as the connecting and integrating services through the gojek platform that helps the community thrive economically. Tradition has it that the formal financial system is characterized by the fact that services are delivered separately: banks for money (transaction, saving and loans), insurers for insurance, shops for pans or furniture, telecom providers for mobile telephone credits. At the village level this looks different; the people need them integrated.[120] And that's why gojek offers these services integrated, with Mapan as a part of them. Mapan and gopay connect existing informal saving and loan practices in the communities with technology, through which a huge number of track records is built of these informal dealings. Through their platform, the track record of these dealing becomes formalized, they get protection, guarantees, credit, insurances, etc. Step-by-step formalizing and financially including them. In my view it's just a matter of time before formal banks, insurers and telecom providers step in, and regulation opens up to allow banks, insurers and telegiants to step into this space. Partnership with Mapan and gopay would serve as trusted partners for full financial inclusion. The fact that Nadiem Makarim, founder of gojek, stepped down as CEO early 2020 to join the government could be taken as a positive omen for regulatory reforms required for this to happen. At this moment, this connectedness allows for the first steps toward formally including millions of people.

COLLABORATIVE

Moving a hard-core cash society to digital money is not easy. Let's see how gopay, from gojek ,is nowadays considered to be the Southeast Asia's biggest mobile payment platform, based upon its success in Indonesia. Indonesia is a cash society, according to McKinsey; still, an estimated 99% of all transactions are cash based.[121] In Indonesia, around 80% is "underbanked" – without access to credit cards or long-term savings product – or "unbanked" – without access to a basic bank account[122]. How do you get millions of Indonesians to use digital money? At gopay it was not an easy ride, no pun intended.

The first steps to digital money is offering financial benefits like discounts and cash backs, to start using it. Again, gojek focused on the customer – which explicitly includes the gojek drivers. Asking, what do you like? Bubble tea, a popular drink. So, gojek closed a partnership with a very popular bubble tea joint where gojek customers could get their favourite drinks with loyalty points from gopay. This made them familiar with digital money. Following this, more partnerships were built with convenient stores and drug stores, and thus more and more cash backs and discounts opportunities were offered. More and more customers started to use gopay, opening digital accounts and using digital money.

However, when you're financially excluded and financially less literate, it takes a few more steps to get yourself familiarized with digital money. So, a few of the next steps gopay took were to make it as easy as possible for the gojek drivers and the other food merchants, mom-and-pop shop owners, to follow suit. From the feedback, gojek learned that drivers struggled with uploading their account at an ATM or bank. Hence, staff at convenience stores was mobilized to support gojek drivers to top-up their accounts. In this collaborative way, more and more drivers were also starting to save their earnings from a day's work on their gopay accounts. And they started to use the digital service to buy groceries, bubble tea, insurance or pay bills. By 2019, close to 70% of gojek's transactions used gopay.[123] An impressive accomplishment in a hard-core cash society. And most of this was realized in close collaboration with those partners that already transact with the gojek driver in their daily life, like bubble tea joints and convenience stores.

In addition to the fact that Indonesia is a cash society, millions of the small and midsize enterprises (SMEs) face large funding gaps.[124] This usually is even worse for the self-employed and micro-enterprises, such as the gojek driver, the food merchants, mom-and-pop shops, cleaners, and hair and nail salon owners. In mid-2018, gojek agreed with BTN,

Indonesia's largest housing finance bank, to provide access to subsidized housing. Through a governmental scheme for subsidized loans for entrepreneurs, all gojek drivers could get access to these housing loans through BTN.[125] Yet another step toward linking the people with informal jobs into the formal economy, in close collaboration with formal financial players.

PACKAGED ATTACHED TO DAILY LIFE

Other steps to grow the usage of digital money, for sake of financial inclusion, is to increase the moments in a day one can use gopay. As well as to increasing the ways to get money into your digital wallet. Nowadays it's possible to just upload your wallet with every gojek driver and payments are possible at all the merchants and partners.[126] Mind you, there are close to a million food merchants. Gojek also redesigned gopay, to be simple enough to use for the less digitally savvy.[127] Step-by-step, the previously informal, financially less literate gig suppliers are seeing the benefits of digital money and understanding the non-monetary benefits, like building a track record of income and spending. Just by packaging it to products and services relevant in their daily lives. And don't forget, in this way they get access to financial services. This is huge if you consider we're talking about over 3 million people. All of them can use digital money for their daily transportation, drinks, food, tickets, medicines, to pay their monthly bills for their electricity, water, internet and gas, and to get access to health insurance. This goes way beyond 'just' payment.

What makes gojek a success story -with USD12 billion in transactions in 2020[128] – is that the delivery of financial services is integrated with the fulfilment of the daily basic needs of the drivers. Take, for example, gojek's partnership with Doctor Anywhere. In close collaboration with them, gojek offers offline and online medical consultations for their drivers. Through a subscription fee, paid by gojek, each gojek driver has access to healthcare services for common illness.[129] Financial inclusion is a multifacetted issue; one aspect of it is that in order to being able to generate a decent income, one needs to be healthy, healthy to work. It is generally known that mainly the poor are excluded from healthcare. So, offering remote medical consultation adjoining informal gigs to the ones who do not have a health insurance is huge.

Meanwhile, gojek has successfully spread and replicated into Vietnam, Singapore, Thailand and Philippines. How come they also succeed in growing gojek's impact across South and Southeast Asia region? Because they stay true to a few of their key success factors while spreading. Firstly, getting close to unique needs and use cases – **daily life** – in a specific country, **putting the people at the heart**. In Indonesia this was the gojek driver and the *arisan* groups, for example. Looking for these is key to replicating into other countries. Secondly, *"Our strategy for expansion has always been working with local teams and local partners,"*[130] according to gopay CEO Aldi. Again, through **collaboration**, linking in with local systems, hooking up with traditions and trusted persons in the communities. Packaging financial services attached to daily life.

COMMITTED

The true face of a company often shows when the going gets tough. During the COVID-19 crisis, gojek stayed true to its inclusive mission. In early 2020, gojek provided income support to their drivers infected with the virus, even though they are not formally employed by gojek. Gojek also offered motorcycle purchase loans for them, until they could return to work.[131] This was possible due to a generous donation of a quarter of a year's salary from gojek's management, and gojek employees' salary increases for a year, in full consent of the employees.[132]

How did gojek – as an organization– manage all of this, keeping the people at the heart of it, as well as pulling off this immense growth? If you are such a growing organization, tackling all things new, you need all of your people to contribute in an **entrepreneurial** way, to solve issues the best they can with the means you have at your hands. *"Hiring for a growth mindset"*[133] is what founder Nadiem Makarim calls this. The most important matter discussed during recruitment interviews at gojek is the scale of the **growth mindset**, how much a person is willing to be and get better at something. *"Growth-mindset people believe that they can, and therefore they will,"* according to Nadiem. If you are here and just want to follow instructions, you will leave soon, and that is ok, according to Nadiem: *"... being always **willing to experiment and fail**, and **learn** from those failures, is something that is extremely critical as a guiding principle. You have to understand what you do NOT know. People who think that they have already become an expert will quickly close themselves off to new opportunities and new situations, and become very biased."*[134]

When you are working toward a 'new normal,' you need to come up with new solutions, new thinking, and you need to challenge the underlying assumptions. This is what is key to success. And no one can do so alone; it needs to be in each and every person in your organization, and with your partners, suppliers and sales networks. It requires an organizational culture, a mission and commitment that is so **contagious** others are willing to join and follow.

At gojek the philosophy behind how to stay focused is not to do everything you can do. It is to stay true to what the customers need. *"And to try everything we can, and then* *do what you do best ... and the way to do that is to create autonomous units, literally different organizations within an entity. It's their job to stay focused ... the method that keeps me focused the most is actually **using the product myself** ... I'm a super para-user myself,*"[135] according to Nadiem. Mind you, by customer they mean the gojek driver, too, not just the paying user of the app. Staying close to the driver needs to be a customer obsession and is important to uphold as a value. All of the above goes for the employees but also for the top management; "*being fearless*" is what Nadiem calls this, being the believer, the leader who knows that every obstacle is just one that can be overcome. That's the intangible value of gojek management: "*We firmly believe ... that if you help a lot of people out, the world will show a way.*"[136]

COLLECTIVELY GROWING TOWARD AN IRREVERSIBLE CHANGE

We're witnessing a massive replication and rise of similar kinds of this platform model, like gojek's, all over the world. Although many of them are more focused on the 'delivery app' than on actual financial inclusion of the gig suppliers. Take, for instance, Rappi in Latin America, Grab in South East Asia and Ping An's – leader in life and general insurances in China – 'do-it-at-home' app. This Chinese app reached 11 million financial and non-financial transactions, in two weeks during the COVID crisis. Non-financial transactions including, but not limited to online medical counselling.[137] The exciting part starts when the impact of these apps and platforms trickles down to lower-income people. Like Rappi's app, that more accidentally than baked into the mission as it is with gojek, turned out to be a golden job opportunity for many Venezuelan migrants in Colombia, Peru, Argentina and Chile.[138] The potential inclusion for lower-income groups will likely show when the collaborations between Visa and Rappi starts delivering results. Even if Rappi is more dedicated to the middle class and SME, less on the informal worker and the micro-entrepreneur, it will trickle down and provide new links and ways for low-income people to get access to financial services. Which happened, too, for example at Alibaba's grocery delivery, Freshippo, that was hiring workers from shuttered restaurants and retail shops during the COVID crisis.[139] And let's not forget about the many additional financial services Grab is adding in the recent years, next to the online payments and rewards attached to the usage, like insurance and lending for the millions of micro-entrepreneurs, drivers, restaurants and the likes. Bear in mind that the trickle-down effect for the millions they reach, even when unintended, is impacting the low-income people massively. Consider the fact that 21% of Grab's drivers did not have a job prior to becoming a Grab driver, and 31% of their merchants and agents had no income prior to joining Grab. Although we all know that opening a bank account does not imply you are included financially, just to demonstrate the power of these 'apps' provide: Grab is supporting 1.7 million micro-entrepreneurs opening their first bank account,[140] which is an incredible force for financial inclusion.

4.2 HEALTHY ENTREPRENEURS – BUILDING RURAL MARKETS FOR HEALTH PRODUCTS AND SERVICES

Living in a remote village in Uganda means that you can't go to the pharmacy when you're having a headache or ask a doctor why your baby is constantly crying. At least not within the vicinity of your home. It means that it's hard to buy sanitary napkins, let alone condoms as a teenager when you start having sex. Don't even think about trustworthy advice regarding birth control or contraception, or correct health information about less taboo and very preventable diseases like diabetes or pneumonia. Most of the time, if available, medicine is counterfeit, advice is not trustworthy and prices are skyrocketing. All these pills, health info, health-related products are a prerequisite for a healthy life, for being able to work. What if you could bring these products to fulfil basic needs to the remote areas, while creating local income-generating opportunities too? Basically, building the market in remote areas, and thus creating a local health economy. Bear in mind: over an estimated 2 billion people live in remote rural communities lacking access to essential basic health services, according to the WHO.

PAY AND PERKS FLOW BACK IN THE FAMILY OR COMMUNITY

This is exactly what Healthy Entrepreneurs[141] is doing: providing basic health education, health-related products and service in areas where no one else goes through micro-entrepreneurs. They train community health workers to become Healthy Entrepreneurs, sell healthcare products and educate their customers from their own mini-pharmacies, supported with solar-powered tablets. Thanks to the efforts of these passionate Healthy Entrepreneurs, people living in isolated villages in Uganda, Tanzania, Kenya and Ghana can stay healthy and be well-informed about health issues. Through nearly 5,000 community Healthy Entrepreneurs – of which 85% are women – over 4.5 million customers received basic healthcare products and services, 16 million health-related products were distributed, impacting the lives of 6 million people living in remote villages. This resulted not just in a doubling of the income of their community health entrepreneurs – it also realized a 55% cost savings on basic health services for these rural families. The **savings flow back** in the pockets of the families and **pay flows back** to the community health entrepreneurs, and all people living in those villages get the additional 'perk' of being able to live healthy lives.

Photo by game changer

COVERING THE CHAIN

Healthy Entrepreneurs manages a fully integrated end-to-end supply chain. They buy reliable health products – wholesale – at an affordable price and deliver them directly to the local Healthy Entrepreneurs based in rural areas. The existing range of products and health education targets the health of children under five years with products like anti-malaria medications, zinc and oral rehydration salts (ORS), as well as sexual and reproductive health products for women and adolescent girls with items such as sanitary pads, condoms, and contraception.

Each community health entrepreneur invests US$40 and receives a micro-business concept, including a starter kit with basic medical products worth US$70 on credit. This mini-pharmacy, the basket of health-related products, includes over-the-counter (OTC) medicines, and health-related products such as mosquito repellent, soap, tooth paste, water-filters and specific nutrition like vitamins. The health micro-entrepreneur repays the initial loan within one year, from the income she makes. Next to the income-generating, and the credit, the health micro-entrepreneurs receives business and financial management education. The health entrepreneur also receives a solar-powered tablet, used for tracking inventory and other basic business administration. Next to that, the tablet is used to provide health education to the rural villagers. Over 125 informational videos and tools for screening and consultation – guided questionnaires – are available to support the health micro-entrepreneurs to educate customers on topics such as nutrition, hygiene, immunizations, malnutrition of young children, pregnancy, breastfeeding, family planning, common diseases, gender-based violence, sexually transmitted diseases (STDs). Many of those videos and screening tools are coming from the WHO, all of them in the local language. Since all Healthy Entrepreneurs are community health workers, they are well-placed to do the health education and detect the need for further care, and refer to the right place. Healthy Entrepreneurs offers a Doctors@ Distance service with the tablet, a teleconsultation service to deliver tests and screenings results, diagnostics, referrals and health advice. Healthy Entrepreneurs brings the whole chain together, integrates the financial services in the offering of health products and services fulfilling the basic needs of the rural villagers.

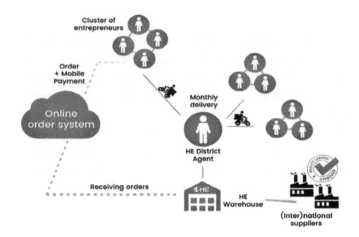

DAILY LIFE AS THE PLAYGROUND

This approach is bringing healthy living into the houses of rural families. The Healthy Entrepreneur is a community member, which assures a trusted point of contact in the village, and by doing so, assuring sustainability. The latter, sustainability, means that the offering of health services won't stop when the development programme (read: funding) stops. It is immune for corruption related to the government because it builds an independent market end-to-end. The 'basket' is broad and flexible, to allow the community health entrepreneurs to offer products that the people actually need and buy, which assures the earning of a proper income. As well as reduction of living expenses for the already small purses of the rural villagers. The solution is centred in the daily life of the villagers.

COMMITTED

More micro-entrepreneurship and consignment models at the base-of-the-pyramid have failed than succeeded, so why has this one become a success? A couple of reasons can be uncovered, all of them rooted in **trust**. Firstly, trust from the end consumer. To gain trust of the rural based family, you need to deliver good quality, affordable prices and always be there when needed. Healthy Entrepreneurs as an organization recognized this from the early start and invested heavily in supporting their health micro-entrepreneurs to establish this trust in their local communities. Being from the local community, speaking the same language, living around the corner alone, is not sufficient. Branding, safe (sealed) packaging and reliable information, consultations and good quality products are required too. Not just once, but all the time. This brings us to the second factor building **trust** with the micro-entrepreneur. The micro-enterprise's business model has to provide sufficient income over the years – not just in the beginning – so the community health workers can sustain their offering. They are the market. This requires profitability for their micro-health business. Healthy Entrepreneurs as an organization is committed to all of the above, organizing all that is needed to build this trust.

IT TOOK YEARS ... TO **REVERSE ENGINEER IT TO MEET THE NEEDS**

Several years were used to get the offering in the health basket to such a level that the sales of products and services resulted in sufficient revenue to the micro-entrepreneur. This included adding products with higher profit-margin to their basket. Compared to other micro-entrepreneurship models, the rate of discontinuing the micro-business is really low: after two years in operation, 90% of the health micro-entrepreneurs is still active.[142] This is related to another important factor for building trust: reliability. The health micro-entrepreneur must be able to trust both the products and the health educational information she gives to her customers. Only then will she grow her trustworthiness in the community. That's why Healthy Entrepreneurs takes the accountability for the full supply chain, building partnerships to buy reliable and **affordable** medicines in large quantities, as well as with the WHO, for example, to make sure the health education is trustworthy. Healthy Entrepreneurs walks the extra mile, no pun intended, to absolutely make sure they gain and keep the trust of the health micro-entrepreneurs and the villagers.

For this a third layer of trust is required: a reliable supply chain, from ordering to supply. The full health supply chain is facilitated by Healthy Entrepreneurs as an organization, as to never fail on the micro-entrepreneur, and the villagers they serve. Way too often, national medicine warehouses are found not open for business or out of stock, forcing local pharmacies to go to the black market. This is why Healthy Entrepreneurs organizes their own local warehouses, offers support with ordering, does the inventory management and also delivers to the health micro-entrepreneurs. All three levels – the chain, the micro-entrepreneur and the low-income customer – determine the trustworthiness of this local health market. Healthy Entrepreneurs is committed to tweak this full basic health chain, while growing financial inclusion too.

PEOPLE AT THE HEART OF IT

Healthy Entrepreneurs changes health-seeking behaviour in the communities. A research in 25 villages shows that families had higher odds on using modern contraceptives in those villages where community health entrepreneurs are active.[143] At the heart of this are the health workers who become health micro-entrepreneurs; they are the extended 'circles of change.' Take, for example, what drives Charlie, one of the community-based health entrepreneurs: *"I'm very happy to be a Healthy Entrepreneur. Now I can help my community with products they value and make a living for myself."*[144] The health entrepreneurs bring structural and healthy change to their own communities and inspire others to take steps to self-reliance for their villages into their own hands too. Joost van Engen, founder and CEO of Healthy Entrepreneurs, shares proudly how he has seen micro-entrepreneurs showing health educational videos to their peers after sunset, sharing tips about safe sex or about nutrition.[145] Each one of them is a social entrepreneur and passionate about improving village life for the better. An empowering force for growth toward thriving communities.

EVERYBODY PLAYS

"We have started our business by only building the supply chain," according to Joost, *"but by offering access to healthcare products only, we don't solve the issue. ... there is a need to provide health knowledge and expertise."*[146] One key success factor to bring this health education is through the network of micro-entrepreneurs, but how did the micro-entrepreneur network become so strong? It's partly due to the business-from-a-bag concept that is accessible for all enterprising community health workers, since Healthy Entrepreneurs offers loans, tools and training on business and financial management. But there is more to it. It turns out that mainly women, mothers actually, are well-established in their community and are the most successful community health-entrepreneurs. These women are the trusted point-person villagers go to for asking advice, which helps incredibly when sharing sensitive health issues. The female entrepreneurs stay connected to the people in their network of villages they serve. Like Joost has shared, the health education goes on after sunset. The female health-entrepreneurs get credited for their knowledge and support, for preventing people from getting sick, or preventing sickness from getting worse. Healthy Entrepreneurs supports the community health worker to take an active role in starting treatment or continuing, encouraging repeat check-ups, etc. It's word of mouth that travels faster than any campaign. The health entrepreneurs gain an income, and the villagers gain access to medicines, screenings and reduce their cost for both medicines and not having to travel to the nearest town. Everybody plays, and they all win.

A **BLENDED MODEL** IS AN ENABLING FACTOR ...

How come Healthy Entrepreneurs can do all of this, affordably and reliably? Next to the power of the network of community health entrepreneurs, unique is the combination of two elements. It's the accountability for the full health supply chain, in combination with the blended structure of Healthy Entrepreneurs' business model. Healthy Entrepreneurs delivers several steps in the full supply chain: wholesale purchasing, international contracting of medicines, sourcing of health education, branding, packaging, storage and warehouse management, new product and services development, local team management for order management and local delivery, training and empowerment of health micro-entrepreneurs. If the rural family that buys the paracetamol would have to pay for all the costs to keep the organization afloat, the prices would not have been affordable for them. Business-as-usual would not have worked to reach the last mile. Healthy Entrepreneurs has several different sources of revenue that cover for the full operation. Two thirds of the revenue of the sales through micro-entrepreneurs covers for the regular business: from purchase, to training the micro-health entrepreneurs, to order processing and delivery. One third is in the shape of programme grants, philanthropic funds and impact investments, which covers costs to develop new business, enter new markets, and other activities such as IT development, telehealth service development expanding the basket of the micro-entrepreneur.[147] Last but not least, Healthy Entrepreneurs mobilizes quite a lot of pro-bono support and expertise from partners too, which keeps their business as lean as possible.

PRICED TO WHAT THE PEOPLE CAN AFFORD

This blended business model allows Healthy Entrepreneurs to keep the prices for the consumers affordable. According to Joost, the premises where it all starts from and comes back to is two-fold: *"How much can the rural family afford?"* and *"How can the health micro-entrepreneur earn a proper income?"* All the costs for activities that cannot be covered with income from sales of health-related products and services requires other income streams.

Healthy Entrepreneurs has a deep understanding of family budgets, and carefully computes what they can afford. The families they reach live at least five kilometres away from a point of care facility, those families spend at least 15% of their income on acquiring basic health. This is, on average, a US$100 per rural family a year. Of which 55% is spent on transportation to get to the care facility or the place where they can buy the medicine.[148] These are the numbers of their daily budgets, for which Healthy Entrepreneurs develops their offerings. No diagnostic tool, medicine, or health-related product will get into the basket of their community health workers' micro-business that the rural household cannot afford. As a result of this importance of affordability, the millions of families Healthy Entrepreneurs serves realize up to 63% of savings on their annual costs for healthcare. What's even more, just due to the fact a healthy entrepreneur is active in their village, (black) market prices drop 17–25%, according to a study of the Erasmus University.[149]

COLLABORATIVE

The way to keep the prices affordable is to cover the 'remaining' cost from other income. And these are generated in partnership. Let's have a look at some examples. Many community health workers in the first few years, who started as health micro-entrepreneurs in Uganda, were empowered and trained in close collaboration with Simavi, a foundation aiming a healthy life for all in Africa and Asia. In collaboration with both Aidsfonds, a foundation aiming for a world without Aids, and Sawa World, on a mission to tackle poverty with local solutions, and funded partly by PEPFAR, an American government facility, thousands of young girls and women were trained to become entrepreneurs in Uganda.

Through this collaboration hundreds of Ugandan female Healthy Entrepreneurs were empowered, in areas where many more also received health information on aids, as well as other local micro-business opportunities. This multipartner collaboration was fully geared toward closing the loop between healthy living and making a living.

In partnership with Boehringer Ingelheim – one of world's largest pharmaceutical companies – Healthy Entrepreneurs developed a new business concept: how to offer health screening services and create awareness through a combination of telemedicine and in-person doctor visits, accessible and affordable. Jointly they created insights on a new business for Healthy Entrepreneurs, which solved an issue that is very relevant for people in remote areas: preventing and diagnosing hypertension and diabetes, which require a recurring service like monthly screening. This was done in partnership with Boehringer Ingelheim, with financial support and with their expertise. Basically, the pre-runner of the Doctors@Distance service came into being through this partnership. Through this collaboration, Healthy Entrepreneurs gained insights on how to break down access barriers for the villagers and reduce costs[150] for the delivery of the service. In the design for this new health service they made sure that there was a clear business opportunity for their health micro-entrepreneurs, by attracting recurring customers for repeat visits.

With the Philips Foundation, on a mission to accelerate healthcare access in underserved parts of the world, newly recruited Healthy Entrepreneurs in Uganda were trained and empowered. At the same time the new Doctors@Distance service was further developed and piloted, offering teleconsultation with a doctor. Healthy Entrepreneurs was financially supported by the Philips Foundation for this pilot and received diagnostic devices, hands-on support and expertise coming from Royal Philips, world leader in health tech.[151]

Another part of this collaboration was to explore and test different diagnostic and screening tools that could potentially be added to the basket of the community health worker. Interestingly, during the COVID-19 crisis their Doctors@Distance model became a top priority, and thanks to the volunteering advisory support of Philips, Healthy Entrepreneurs was able to create a dedicated call line and recruit doctors to provide consultations.[152] This illustrates how partnerships grow Healthy Entrepreneurs resilience.

A digital trainings module was developed, tested and implemented in local farmer communities in Uganda, targeting female farmers, in close collaboration with Cordaid, a foundation aiming to end poverty and exclusion, funded by the Dutch Postcode Lottery. In a Going for Gold programme, in collaboration with Solidaridad, on a mission to transition to a sustainable and inclusive economy, and Simavi, Healthy Entrepreneurs empowered women to become community health entrepreneurs in Ghana and Tanzania servicing artisan and small-scale gold mining communities. Bringing both health as well as economic opportunities in these communities. The programme was funded by the Dutch Ministry of Foreign Affairs.

Last but not least, Healthy Entrepreneurs is expanding and entering new markets with the support of Philips Foundation in joint forces with a funding facility of the Dutch government.[153] This allows for expand the business to enter and build three new markets in Uganda, Burundi and potentially Zambia. In this collaboration with even more partners, VSO, on a mission to create lasting change through volunteering, and Randstad, a global leader in HR services, VSO will support Healthy Entrepreneurs with technical assistance to strengthen their empowerment of female microhealth entrepreneurs. And Randstad will support Healthy Entrepreneurs with the recruitment of a sort of franchisees who could replicate the Healthy Entrepreneurs model into new geographical areas, as well as strengthen the recruitment capacity to select the best micro-health entrepreneurs.

Healthy Entrepreneurs clearly shows a strong capability to grow to an inclusive model, through partnerships that bring the basic health supply chain into being. Joost says about his collaborative approach, "*I find it incredibly powerful how the national government, private investors and the business community work together to take innovation in developing countries to a higher level. This is how we initiate truly sustainable change.*"[154]

CONNECTED

The joined value created in all these partnerships make that the boundaries of Healthy Entrepreneurs as an organization blur. Healthy Entrepreneurs operates as a network. On the one hand, there are all these strategic partners, on the other hand there's the network of micro-entrepreneurs spreading into the last mile. This connectedness enables them to cross-subsidize the basic health service offering of the micro-entrepreneurs to the villagers. It's this connectedness that makes Healthy Entrepreneurs **agile**, with small local teams, resilient and obviously intrinsically inclusive; their life line, the network of the micro-entrepreneurs, are the same people they serve.

COMMITTED

This connectedness is in the DNA of Healthy Entrepreneurs; it cannot be done by a few account managers. How does Healthy Entrepreneurs organize to execute on their inclusive mission? According to Joost: "*Healthy Entrepreneurs is just one big learning adventure.*" At Healthy Entrepreneurs. the international office, based in The Netherlands, is a supporting office to the local offices. "*Leadership and staff should always be local*" is a strong belief of Joost. When it comes to talent development, it's important to point out that learning objectives are a big part of the annual performance cycle. Each member of the team at Healthy Entrepreneurs has four personal development goals that relate one-on-one to learning. Several times a year, the members themselves reflect on their own performance and review this related to these learning objectives. A raise in salary is, for a large extent, dependent on these personal development goals. For local teams in Uganda, for example, this goes against mainstream opinion, where the local mindset is not much focused on learning and development. *"It goes without saying all staff members have a lot of freedom,"*[155] is what Joost adds, staff turnover is very low at Healthy Entrepreneurs. To learn and to be **local**, appear to be key elements of their success.

COLLECTIVE

Collaboration is key, according to Joost: *"The most efficient way to improve basic health services in hard-to-reach-areas is to work together with the existing community based organizations that know the way out in the fields. This new way of working is based upon a joint mission, a journey we are all part off. We need everybody to meet our joint objectives"* of universal health coverage and therefore an inclusive society. *"I believe the new way of working is one where we bundle, to give anything you have, put it on the table and try to align. We are part of a movement where we inspire each other, where we are complementary to each other, we are not conflicting, that is the new way of working, where anyone is invited to join."*[156] Joost clearly views his inclusive mission as a collective action of many stakeholders.

CHANGING THE RULES OF THE GAME

The dominant notion to push health products downstream is challenged by Healthy Entrepreneurs. Instead of pushing products and services down, once upon a time designed for the top-segment of the market (the Western world), Healthy Entrepreneur carefully watches over, and specifically adapts, redesigns and bundles those health-related products and services, offering loans and income attached to them. Healthy Entrepreneurs is applying new ways of delivery, through micro-entrepreneurship, and in a franchisee-ish model to expanding to other countries. They 'package' products and services with so much needed health education, reverse engineering it to the daily needs of the people living in remote areas. What Healthy Entrepreneurs offers is focused on prevention and inclusion. It is focused on local income-generation (jobs) of the micro-health entrepreneurs, and savings and affordability for the family. Their new way of delivering healthcare services, education and healthy products to the rural poor has opened new pathways of funding and financing of health education, community care and financial inclusion in rural Africa.

The way Joost sees it: "Simple and straightforward self-care and community based care play a key role in the functioning of a health system. Prevention and early detection of diseases are the key to avoid high expenses on healthcare. At the same time, these categories of care are in most of the countries around the world paid for out of pocket. For which financial inclusion, in terms of income generation opportunities, and thus building a local health market, are extremely important. Contrary to what traditional public health experts (still) believe, donor and tax money will never finance self and community based care. In the future, primary health care services in remote and hard to reach areas are more offered using telehealth solutions instead of physical movements to health centers. Therefore, it is key to empower rural communities with financial services like digital payment services. On the long term, this will help to open health insurance schemes for more vulnerable people too."[157]

CHAPTER 5

LINKING ALL PLAYERS IN EQUALITY

One of the strengths of global supply chains and what makes them unique is the fact that consumption and production are disconnected. Each partner in the value chain adds value, is well-placed to do so, and made this added value its core business. None of the parties in a chain would be able to make a laptop, jeans or perform an air flight all by themselves. This is what makes our current economy and financial system supporting it a miracle in itself. While this holds true, we also see some cracks in this system, that make finance for all hard to happen. On a global level, we see that where the money is made, where the consumer pays, that's not where the ingredients grow, the mining is done or the production is happening. We know that the global balance is off, since we exclude such large parts of the world population – the hard working, producing, mining and ingredient growing people. So, the core question for all of us to answer is: how do we reestablish missing or broken links and introduce new mechanisms as ways to find a new and better balance? A rebalancing act after which each partner gets its fair share, and all of us are included. That's our dot on the horizon, where we want to go with financial inclusion. Let's look at the three directions these game changers are taking us.

Firstly, transparency makes the mechanisms in our diffuse and complex global chains more visible, after which corrective actions can be taken. As we have seen with BanQu, who developed a system in which global brands gain transparency in their supply chain, while simultaneously the refugee factory workers and migrant miners are getting economic passports that can be used as a proof for their hard-work and open up financial services to them. Nest is demonstrating another solution based upon transparency too, 'closing the loop,' so to say, by directly connecting the big brands with the home-based artisans, providing protection and financially including them. These new solutions create unique levels of transparency and traceability, both-ways, which is simultaneously empowering the people who were previously invisible and excluded. Linking all players, and infusing equality in this linkage, is core to this lever, which is demonstrated beautifully by both examples of gojek and Healthy Entrepreneurs, described in the previous chapter too. In this chapter, BIMA will be featured. BIMA provides protection at your phone, against accidents, for health and hospitalization, anticipating high funeral expenditures. From policy to claim, fees are paid through mobile air time or monthly fees. BIMA is familiarizing millions of lower-income people with protection through prevention and insurances, just one click away from their couches. BIMA is also harnessing the power of technology to track, trace and monitor, while connecting multiple partners. BIMA links global leaders in insurance as well as mobile phone network operators to serve lower-income families using their phones. A model revolutionizing both access to preventive healthcare as well as financial inclusion, spot on the families' daily needs and usage of their phone as a lifeline, linking in new players in the playground of financial inclusion.

Like with BIMA and Healthy Entrepreneurs, the second direction many game changers take to financial inclusion is having others contribute to reach, therefore shouldering the costs of reaching the previously excluded together. In this way, the beneficiaries – the unbanked or underbanked – do not necessarily pay for the full costs of the financial services themselves. Revised cost recovery mechanisms enable cross-subsidization schemes or, in old-school terminology: new business models for financial service delivery to low-income families. Linking all players in a chain offers the opportunity to reorganize in such a way that a hybrid value chain is jointly built to reach the last mile. This then allows for a blended business model, like Root Capital has done, financially empowering our food farmers with a blended funding model. Like Solar Sister does, bringing solar solutions to the families living in remote villages, with a blended model. In this chapter, Tienda Pago will be featured, linking in Fast Moving Consumer Good (FMCG) companies. Tienda Pago is tweaking the supply chain, as to offer millions of street stalls and mom-and-pop shops an opportunity to increase their income. Tienda Pago is delivering financial services such as inventory pre-financing loans and electronic payments to them, through the distributers of the FMCG companies. Mom-and-pop shops are financially included, empowered, and increase their sales, because Tienda Pago managed to connect these players, delicately balancing the benefits for both.

Lastly, there's the direction of closing the loop between consumption and production locally. As demonstrated by Healthy Entrepreneurs, bringing health education, products and services to the rural areas while providing for income-generating options too. Building a market at the so-called bottom of the pyramid. Or gojek, closing the loop between consumption and production of local 'gigs,' while offering a diverse set of financial services on the go for the informal workers. Both of them demonstrating the power of linking players in a chain, allowing for value creation locally. In this chapter, ACRE Africa is featured, offering agricultural guarantees and micro-insurances to farmers. ACRE Africa demonstrates how this unserved farmers' market can be protected against agricultural risks, by bundling, adapting, and repackaging financial products and services of several partners in the local agricultural value chain. ACRE Africa is reorganizing existing and forging new linkages in the local value chain, between different players, firstly and foremost speaking to the daily needs of low-income families, resulting in sustainable financial service delivery to this previously un(der)served market.

Let's have a look.

5.1 BIMA – PROTECTION THROUGH YOUR PHONE

One thing the majority of us have in common is our cell phones, our lifelines – that's what binds us. The phone is a powerful tool as an equalizing measure. What if you could protect yourself against life's biggest financial and health risks through your phone in every corner in the world? That is what exactly what BIMA[158] does. BIMA is fuelling inclusion through a mobile platform offering life and health insurances and mobile health services to lower to mid-income, financially underserved people in nine countries across Africa and Asia. Within a few minutes of registration, through minimal number of simple questions, customers can insure their families against a loss, disability, income disruption and large funeral expenditure. You don't need a smartphone for this. BIMA customers can also get access to teleconsults with qualified doctors, personal health records and hospitalization insurance coverage through their phones. They pay via deduction of prepaid airtime credit, via their monthly bills or with a mobile wallet.

In the past decade, BIMA has reached 37 million people, 75% accessing an insurance for the first time in their life! They are providing 575,000 new policies a month. Claims are handled easy and quickly, payment is within three working days. Mobile health services reached 2.2 million customers, providing 800,000 teledoctor consultations a year, with a large proportion of their customers living on less than US$10 a day. Perhaps not the lowest income class, but for sure the lower-income group[159] that is so far being financially underserved.

Photo by game changer

DAILY LIFE AS THE PLAYGROUND

BIMA offers the services at their **doorsteps**, through their phones, adapted to the lower-income **families' needs**, in their own language, addressing all their questions through a hands-on call centre service and a physical network of on-the-ground agents. This is what BIMA calls the key factor to their success, the *"human touch."* BIMA has built network of more than 2,000 sales agents that are out there in the communities to offer *"education and build **trust** around our product,"* according to Gustaf, founder of BIMA.[160] BIMA has numerous on-the-ground awareness raising campaigns in the communities. Their clients can pick up the phone or visit a nearby office to get support, either on how to register or clarify questions they have on an insurance product previously unavailable to them. BIMA is out there, in their clients' daily lives.

PEOPLE AT THE HEART OF IT

All BIMA's services are designed to support the customer's in the different life phases. A life insurance when you get married; a text message service with health informa-tion when you become pregnant; an option for a hospital insurance when you fall ill. BIMA is encouraging cus-tomer engagement as to become a trusted partner in their life. Making it easy and simple for the customer is core to BIMA's business. According to Gustaf, from the start they were aiming to design a product portfolio that is useful for their users, lower income-people. They were not going to limit their product portfolio to what is technically or legally defined as an insurance. They always look at it from the customer perspective. *"What we learned from the feedback from customers was that they wanted access to doctors. We could provide it through an insurance policy and cover it. But what we discovered was that a cheaper way of doing it, and a way that is more convenient for the customers, was to say, 'you buy an insurance from us and you'll get unlimited access to a doctor on a phone.' And then we bundled these two products,"*[161] according to Gustaf.

In the past few years, BIMA took several bold steps acknowledging the power of prevention to their insurance services. BIMA aims to be inclusive and affordable, which has led them to add preventive services to their offering. Staying healthy is way cheaper than (paying for) curing peo-ple. When you bundle a health insurance with preventive care through the phone, it appeared not just to be a *"cheaper way of providing access to doctors for the customers. It was also creating an opportunity for us to offer a more engaging product portfolio,"* according to Gustaf. *"Thanks to that, we provide access to doctors, over time we found out that people can stay healthy and we have less claims as a result of that."*[162] BIMA puts the family at the heart of it, making sure the whole family is covered, even if it is the husband who buys the insurance and pays for it.

LINKING ALL PLAYERS

BIMA does so in a highly networked organization model, through partnerships with mobile network operators, insurers and doctors. Each time BIMA enters a new market they do so in partnership with a mobile network or mobile money operator. They started in Ghana, for example, bringing family care insurance with Tigo, a leading global mobile network provider. Each time BIMA develops a new products or services, it's done in close collaboration with an insurer. They entered Bangladesh in partnership with Robi Axiata and Pragati Life Insurance, reaching over 5 million customers, doubling the insurance penetration within three years. BIMA got into Sri Lanka with Dialog, part of Axiata, and the largest Sri Lankan mobile network operator. Together with Axiata's subsidiary Smart, BIMA became the largest provider of life insurance in Cambodia, within a year after entrance. And so on.

COVERING THE CHAIN

BIMA recognizes that insurances fall outside of mobile telephone operators' core business and strategized to bring all insurance and mobile health services through these mobile networks. In partnership with insurers, BIMA manages everything from product design to distribution and sales. BIMA provides the technological platform to run the insurance service all the way from awareness raising and education, to sales, up to claims administration and payment.[163] In addition to that, partnering with doctors too, and offering mobile health services as well. BIMA bundles their offering, health services and insurances on the phone. Like with Tigo in Senegal several years ago, BIMA offered a 'freemium' micro-insurance service. Those customers spending over US$3 a month on mobile phone service are eligible for a life insurance covering between US$125 and US$630. But customers can opt to pay a small fee, less than a dollar, deducted incrementally month by month from their airtime account, to double their coverage. Tigo experienced direct revenue as well as brand strengthening.[164] In such a way, BIMA can bundle their service and offer it in the daily lives of their clients, and links new players into the arena of financial inclusion.

BIMA has built a last-mile infrastructure by differently tying together these partners. Playing the role of value chain coordinator, creating a win-win-win for all partners. Mobile network operators being able to add value with financial services, insurers being able to enter new markets, and the customers getting access to products previously not available to them.

COLLABORATIVE

It's with their partners that BIMA develops new insurance products. For instance, BIMA supported Tigo Tanzania to launch their first life and hospitalization cover insurance product available via mobile phone. In Pakistan they launched their low-cost accident insurance service with Warid Telecom and Alfalah Insurance. *"The average person simply can't afford to pay traditional insurance premiums. By partnering with Warid and Alfalah Insurance to deliver insurance through a mobile phone, we are lowering costs for our valuable customers and making it possible for every family to access insurance,"*[165] said a spokesperson for BIMA Pakistan. Even though BIMA only offered it to Warid customers, it registered over 100,000 subscribers in less than seven months of operations, showcasing that the new service is spot-on the consumer need. BIMA demonstrates relentless drive to launch new products in collaboration, redesigning and adapting it to the needs of the lower-income consumer. A life and health product in partnership with bKash in Bangladesh, an accident insurance with Jazz, Pakistan's largest mobile operator. And so on.

CONNECTED

BIMA is an organization operating as a network with their strategic partners on one side, and the network of sales agents in the communities of lower-income people on the other side. *"BIMA's success has been based on our mobile technology as much as our on-the-ground agents, who are dedicated to educating customers about the role and importance of insurance. They have been essential in raising awareness about our services and building trust with our customer base,"*[166] according to Gustaf. *"We have discovered that it works best for sales agents to educate customers about the products, so they understand what they're buying."*[167] Mind you, the majority of BIMA's customers have never bought an insurance product before. These first-time customers prefer to speak with a **local** person, before they buy. BIMA's client-centred network of highly trained, product-savvy agents, is focused on achieving high levels of customer product awareness, trust and satisfaction. Calls from the agents and perhaps a visit to the office is what helps building **trust**. BIMA's agents support thousands of people a day with registration and questions about the products.

PRICED TO WHAT THE PEOPLE CAN AFFORD

Through the collaborations, BIMA is reengineering the financial services back to the needs of their customers, while keeping the prices affordable. *"Some people think there's a cultural reason why these people don't get insurance but it's really because people haven't been able to profitably offer insurance to the mass market,"* according to BIMA's Deputy CEO Mathilda Strom. She adds: *"The reason we can do this profitably is the physical network .... The most important thing is distribution."*[168]

Next to educating first-time buyers, selling and distributing to them, collecting premiums on a recurring basis is key to offering insurances affordable to the lower-income segment as well. *"We solved this through going into partnerships* with *mobile operators*,"[169] according to Gustaf. In partnerships BIMA develops new services, enters into new markets, and builds and strengthen local promotion networks. This collaborative approach and therefore the connectedness is what enables them to keep the price affordable. Due to their redesign of service, and the fact that they integrated parts of the value chains, they spread cost differently across the value chains. And jointly they become more efficient than each one of them alone could have been. This is the magic mix that enables BIMA to keep their services affordable and speaking to the customer's needs.

IT TOOK YEARS ... TO **REVERSE ENGINEER IT TO MEET THE NEEDS**

This magic mix did not come to them overnight. A continuous drive to include the vulnerable people with an end-to-end solution to protect themselves and their families for their daily life risks means constant **learning**, **innovation**, **testing and piloting** new products, pricing and promotion models. For instance, in the test and learn phase in Ghana, offering teledoctors for a US$1 monthly fee, BIMA hosted 'doctors camps' offering free screenings for blood pressure, eyesight and other diagnostic tests. In partnership with banks, cooperatives, church groups and transportation authorities, BIMA has put in the effort to distribute the service targeting the more vulnerable groups among traders, taxi drivers, carriers.[170] In Bangladesh too, to raise awareness of the service, BIMA holds free health camps in collaboration with their partner Robi.[171] According to BIMA, *"There's a lot of work that has to be done in terms of understanding what the barriers that customers are facing are, and developing strong **empathy** with them. ... We spend quite a lot of time engaging with local regulators to try and put the right ecosystem in place to enable us to do what we do."*[172]

COMMITTED

BIMA's strategic partnership approach is deeply rooted in the DNA of the company. The commitment to their inclusive mission sits with their people. But how do you nurture the power to innovate, and how do you empower a whole team to engage with partners, while staying focused on inclusion? According to Gustaf, one of the biggest challenges to overcome are the constantly changing business dynamics. He stresses it's the **human touch** that makes the difference, not the mobile technology. It's crucial to select the right people, to put in place a strong team and review your teams continuously. *"Give them the opportunity to take on tasks where they can make the most impact. Building a committed and supportive team will be key to driving company growth."*[173]

At BIMA, an ideal team member is someone who enjoys **creative problem solving**, dares to **think big and start small**. Most of the talent at BIMA does not come from the insurance industry; they all come from different walks of life,[174] making **diversity** a key driver of their success. 'BIMA's got Talent' – an internal annual challenge, showcasing talent outside of the workspace like singing and dancing – is an example how they cultivate diversity in the company, explicitly celebrating differences, igniting **empathy** and understanding. RUN is BIMA's global diversity programme focused to empower women and changing the gender bias, within BIMA as well as in their customer base.

EVERYBODY PLAYS

The network of sales agents supports their inclusive mission also in another way. BIMA is deliberately aiming for **gender balance** in their agent network, with 51% of female agents. Because it is easier for women sell to other women, independent of whether it is over the phone or out there in the field."[175] This helps to serve everybody, to knock on all doors.

Next to that, BIMA is a leading example of how to engage other partners: mobile phone operators turn out to be great partners in financial inclusion.

COLLECTIVE

By mid-2018, BIMA got their very first telemedicine license attributed by the Health Facility Regulatory Agency in cooperation with the Ministry of Health in Ghana. BIMA's licensed mobile health service is a big step in recognizing the importance of bringing prevention in the mix with insurance. BIMA doctor subscribers can make unlimited calls to a medical practitioner to seek advice and medical consultations over the phone, before their condition gets worse, for a small monthly fee. The mobile health service is also offering discounts at laboratories and home medicine delivery too, and through the BIMA platform apps, wellness tips and inexpensive medical tests are accessible. This sweet spot – offering services to stay healthy – is where the system change kicks in. It's now a matter of a joint collective effort to make this the new normal.

COLLECTIVELY CHANGING THE RULES OF THE GAME

If Gustaf could ask one thing from the industry as a whole, it would be: *"To work together on developing regulation, striking the right balance between having controls in place while at the same time enabling for innovation, within insurance as well as within telemedicines."*[176]

5.2 TIENDA PAGO – INVENTORY LOANS FOR PETTY SHOPS BY FMCG COMPANIES

Most people in the world buy their coffee or tea, detergent or toothpaste, pre-packaged seasoning or soap at a petty shop. Nearly half of the world lives on less than US$5 a day, and they do their daily groceries at Lakhsmi's place or Josefina's shop. Lakhsmi holds 50 different items on stock in her shop of barely two square meters in the front space of her home, buying her inventory from three different vendors. Josefina keeps close to 160 items in her 10 square meter shop, while living upstairs. She puts the cash in two different boxes: one to replenish her stock, the other as 'profit,' her salary. Everybody in the street knows Lakhsmi or Josefina, as do the handful of suppliers, who deliver their stock weekly. But nobody in the formal financial system has ever heard of her. Imagine, 3 billion people buy their daily stuff in a mom-or-pop shop like theirs, and we don't care to financially include them?

Photo by game changer

171

Josefina pays her suppliers in cash, coming directly from her sales. Expansion of her business is therefore not easy for her. The delivery man regularly visits her petty shop, often twice a week, solely to collect the money for the deliveries. If Lakhsmi's sales were bad last week or she had unexpected health or educational expenditure, this immediately reflects in lower sales the week after, since she can purchase less inventory for her business to sell. It's not easy to manage weekly fluctuations, let alone seasonal ones or overcome other hurdles in business. In Peru, 70% of those merchants are female, like in most other countries. And 75% of these mom-and-pop shops do not have a bank account. In Mexico alone, there are around one million of those petty shops. How would the world look if we offered them financial support to grow their business and to overcome risks?

COVERING THE CHAIN

Tienda Pago[177] does exactly that. They link 'tiendras' and 'bodegas,' small mom-and-pop shops in our formal system through their suppliers. Tienda Pago offers these petty shop owners, and their suppliers, electronic payments and inventory loans, in joint effort with large Fast Moving Consumer Good (FMCG) companies. Josefina in Peru or Mexico can pay electronically for her supplies on delivery, using her phone, through a closed payment system of Tienda Pago. She can get a loan to pre-finance her inventory, which she can repay from her sales revenue the week thereafter. In this way Josefina has more flexibility, and she can expand her stock with new items. Basically, Tienda Pago is providing inventory loans and cashless payment to petty shop owners, offering the opportunity to increase income and to build formal credit history on the go. Tienda Pago does so while also offering cashless collection services to the suppliers of the petty shops and the large FMCG companies, such as Coca-Cola and Nestlé, and their distributor networks, allowing them to build more efficient distribution networks. Tienda Pago is covering the chain, integrating financial services to low-income micro-merchants at the corner, with the supplies of their shops.

EVERYBODY PLAYS

Tienda Pago supports over 27,000 petty shops, steadily growing since its launch in Peru and Mexico. These micro-merchants in Peru take on average a loan of US\$332; in Mexico the average loan amount is US\$224. Active merchants use it around three times a month.[178] Tienda Pago provides on average 1,000 loans a day, which empowers the petty shops to increase their revenue.[179] This financial inclusion of mom-and-pop shop owners happens in the last mile of the chain, piggybacking upon the products and processes of FMCG companies and their distributors supplying them. A beautiful demonstration of how to get everybody to play. Tienda Pago empowering 'partners' to knock on the door, capacitating them to deliver financial services, and Tienda Pago makes sure they knock on all doors: 60% of Tienda Pago's customers are women.

PLACE IS AT THE DOORSTEP

Mom-and-pop shops can get credit to purchase inventory, for a week – till the next delivery – for a fixed fee (2.5% in Mexico, 1.5% in Peru) from Tienda Pago, with their phone. No need to leave their home. After an initial call of the petty shop owner, Tienda Pago visits the shop to sign off the agreement as well as to provide some training. After which the cashless payment and delivery is realized through their electronic payment platform with the distributors of the fast-moving consumer good companies where the petty shop owners already buy their inventory. Both Josefina and the delivery man connect and exchange by phone, with simple text messages, which is safe and efficient. Josefina does not need to have a bank account. Tienda Pago assesses her creditworthiness based upon past purchase of inventory, in collaboration with the FMCG company. Credit lines for petty shop owners are increased by 20% after four consecutive on-time payments. Repayments are done through banks or agents like convenience stores and pharmacies. Which means that the mom-and-pop shop owners can take a loan and get their weekly supplies delivered at home, and repay around the corner. The financial service is bundled with their shop's supplies and delivered at their doorsteps.

Photo by game changer

PAY AND PERKS FLOW BACK IN THE FAMILY OR COMMUNITY

To waive transaction costs for the petty shop owners at the banks, Tienda Pago has bank accounts with several banks in Mexico and Peru. On average, petty shops that regularly use Tienda Pago increase their sales 20%, according to a study from IFC -International Finance Company,[180] a sister organization of the World Bank. This inclusive approach ensures that the micro-merchants can actually use promotional offers from their FMCG suppliers and jump on the opportunity to increase their revenue. Tienda Pago's pre-finance facility offers the shop owners an opportunity to invest in higher-margin product items and to add new products in their petty shops. This is what makes the mom-and-pop shops more resilient, having a credit line available for times of seasonal fluctuation or emergencies. Tienda Pago maintains a low default rate. Why? Firstly, because petty shop owners value the **affordable** credit, obviously. But secondly, Tienda Pago is tied to their suppliers, which is incredibly important to the mom-and-pop shops. This approach to integration of the supply chain, holds value for both ends. There are clear benefits for the informal shop owners: the pay and perks flow back in their family and home-based business.

IT TOOK YEARS ... TO **REVERSE ENGINEER IT TO MEET THE NEEDS**

The first couple of years were filled with going to the streets, their shops, doing pilots. Each pilot was testing another assumption, testing different pricing models. At the start, close to 40% of shop owners did not continue to use Tienda Pago after the first usage, 45% of registered merchants never used it after registration.[181] Tienda Pago, continuously adapted the offering to the needs of the mom-and-pop shops, **asking for feedback** in each and every pilot. They found out that pricing is not the key determining factor for usage, it's all about easy access and growing the understanding of the intuitive usage of the phone for payment and loans.

Tienda Pago found out that the four following factors are crucial to get micro-merchants to accept and use electronic payments and credits by phone:

1. No additional cost for usage. At Tienda Pago, there are no costs to set-up the mom-and-pop shops, no cost for sending text messages to Tienda Pago, no cost for repayment at the banks or agents.
2. Easy, simple and intuitive ways to use. The truck driver does the heavy work in terms of electronic payment. The credit and electronic payment is only used for buying inventory.
3. Manage the whole experience of the petty shop owner. At Tienda Pago, processes are in place how to navigate the shop owner through the welcome journey: when you become a client, when to call, how to talk, what to convey, when to ask for additional address of home or school, where to repay and when to providing bank branch details. The 'customer experience' is designed to the **daily needs** of the petty shop owners. Tienda Pago only considers them a client after four times using it, because only then the behaviour changes.
4. Actively involving the FMCG companies. At Tienda Pago, they jointly orchestrate the customer journey. FMCG companies are given the time to witness that this inclusive approach is actually (also) resulting in more sales through the mom-and-pop shops that use Tienda Pago.

And all those years of testing and piloting, taking it to the shops in the streets, is bearing fruit. Tienda Pago managed to bump up retention rate to 72%.[182]

PEOPLE AT THE HEART OF IT

Tienda Pago aims for financial inclusion, not necessarily facilitating higher sales of FMCG products, that only comes as a result of it. Take, for example, the explicit decision to keep the cost for usage of Tienda Pago – the app, text messaging, repayment at bank and agent –for free for the mom-and-pop shop owners. At Tienda Pago, they learned a very important lesson, now ingrained in their full organization: *"Each time we got an idea behind our desk, and tested it, it failed. Ideas come bottom-up, from the street,"*[183] according to Dan Cohen, founder and CEO of Tienda Pago. As a result, their service delivery is spot-on the needs of the micro-merchants, it solves their problems, and only due to that, the adoption of electronic payment is realized. And as an additional result: sales and income of their clients increases. Obviously, this delivers value to the FMCG companies and its distributors too. But mind you: it happened in this order.

COMMITMENT

"We're a mission driven company," according to Dan. *"**Innovation**, helping, being accountable, are the core values in our teams."*[184] They give **a lot of independence** to their teams. *"I only constantly repeat to everybody at Tienda, whatever we do behind our desk is not working, we have to go to the streets."* When new staff is recruited, and regularly afterwards, they are encouraged to go out and **listen** to the calls in the call centres, and absorb the questions they get from the owners of petty shops and street stalls.

"In those years we have become strong in rapid testing of new ideas," according to Dan, *"how to develop pilots quickly."* Going to the mom-and-pop shops, **getting the insights and feedback** from the client base is ingrained in the organization. It reflects in the staffing, people like it and stay a long time, or they are gone quickly. It is the mission that sticks in your heart, and going out there is what you like. If you want to stay behind your desk, Tienda Pago is not the place to be. It's all about the people, people to connect with. Tienda Pago has learned to take the time to recruit and hire. According to Dan, *"We hire slow, fire fast."*[185]

LINKING ALL PLAYERS IN EQUALITY

At the core of Tienda Pago's approach are the solid and strategic partnerships with the FMCG companies: Coca-Cola, AB-inBev, Gepp (Pepsico), Kimberly-Clark, Gloria, and their distributor networks in Peru and Mexico. The FMCG companies and their distributor networks gain quite some benefits. Obviously, there is the increased sales from micro-merchants using Tienda Pago. In addition, the FMCG companies can organize their distribution more efficiently: less sales and cash collection visits are needed, payment handling is safe and secure and invoice reconciliation is automated. Of course, Tienda Pago holds a promise, continuing this growth, to acquire more customers for the FMCG companies.

It sounds so easy – why did this not happen already? Well, one of the lessons learned in this segment is that teaming up in the last mile works better than trying to do it all yourself. Most FMCG company have tried electronic payments, invoicing and credit provision to micro-merchants, each in their own way. This led to the current dominant situation in which it is extremely hard to impossible for the petty shops to deal with all the different demands, processes and systems from different suppliers of their inventory. Tienda Pago is solving this from the perspective of the micro-merchants: offering one solution for the mom-and-pop shop owner, bringing together multiple distributors and FMCG companies. Tienda Pago has reengineered the service back to the reality to meet the needs of the mom-and-pop shops. Convenient, and therefore convincing for the petty shop owner. Simultaneously taking some work – cash collection and pre-financing – off the plates of the FMCG companies and their distributors, which was not their core business anyway. The solution Tienda Pago offers is empowering for the mom-and-pop shop owners, without increasing their dependency of the FMCG companies.

And while simultaneously allowing FMCG companies to focus on their core business too. It's linking petty shop owners with the FMCG companies and their distributors in a very equal manner.

Tienda Pago is successful in this extremely delicate balancing act between the big and powerful FMCG companies and numerous micro-merchants, infusing equality in the linkages. It's quite daring to embrace the required complexity that comes with this; just think of the long term you need for building strategic partnerships with FMCG companies, and the extreme short-term of micro-merchant loans. But they did it and proved it is possible, Tienda Pago is linking all players, while tweaking the chain in the last-mile to financially include the mom-and-pop shops.

COLLABORATIVE

When you talk to the distributors and explain the model, the value is immediately clear to them. *"The hardest part is to convince the higher structures of the FMCG companies,"* according to Dan. But, it is exactly this, the integration with the multinational FMCG companies that enables them to change the delivery and distribution chain and include this last-mile segment. The inclusive services Tienda Pago offers could not be delivered without the collaboration with the FMCG companies and their distributors. For example, the benefits of Tienda Pago's service and encouragement to actively use it among petty shop owners, is done by the distributors. It's through training the distributors and integrating services support with the delivery of the distributors, that the micro-merchants are familiarized with Tienda Pago's financial service. It's through the support helpline of the FMCG companies that adoption of mobile payment, wallet, pre-finance facility, among the mom-and-pop shops is increased. It's in joint effort with FMCG companies, that creditworthiness is assessed based upon past purchase records of the FMCG company. It is the distributor that brings the message that the street stall is pre-accepted; it's the delivery men that helps them to set-up and start using it. None of this could have happened in isolation – all of it is done in close collaboration. They jointly carry the efforts for customer acquisition and adoption of mobile payments, wallets, loans and other financial services in the future.

How did Tienda Pago succeed in building those partnerships with FMCG companies and their distributors? The approach of building the collaboration has two distinct features. Firstly, they start a partnership with a small proof of concept. In most cases the convincing becomes much easier after seeing the results of the test. Following the spirit of **'think big, act small.'** Secondly, Tienda Pago always looks for a champion in the company, acknowledging that it's all about interpersonal relationships. Collaboration with those large FMCG companies and their distributors is a unique part of their strategy, offering them the opportunity to build a hybrid value chain to serve the last mile.

CONNECTED

As an organization Tienda Pago is networked on both sides. On one side, they maintain multiple relationships with distributors and FMCG companies, connecting them with many processes and systems. On the other side, there's the huge network of mom-and-pop shops, tea stalls, petty shops, micro-merchants, street food stalls and so on.

A **BLENDED MODEL** IS AN ENABLING FACTOR ...

Through this connectedness Tienda Pago can apply different cost sharing mechanisms. They have relative low cost of capital, partly due to impact investments, partly due to the fact that their loans are actually inventory from the FMCG companies. Another cost sharing mechanism comes into being by leveraging client acquisition with their partners, the FMCG companies. Same goes for the cost of client education, which is also leveraged with the FMCG companies and their distributors. The same goes for awareness raising and after sales support. Apart from being lean, they apply a blended business model too. Revenues come from fees from the mom-and-pop shops, as well as from fees from FMCG companies for cashless services. This blended model is what enables Tienda Pago to keep the prices affordable for the petty shop owners.

COLLECTIVE

The focus on partnerships and building an ecosystem was deliberate from the start, according to Dan Cohen: *"To serve the micro-business market, you cannot do it alone. You need cooperation from multiple parties. Governments, telcos, big brands, old banks, and new solutions providers. Everyone needs to come together and be prepared to work together over the long-term – because big changes don't come overnight."*[186]

5.3 ACRE AFRICA – EMPOWERING FARMERS TO MANAGE RISKS

Financial inclusion of the small-scale farmer is a prerequisite for sustainable production of our food and ingredients. Modest estimates indicate that 30% of our food is produced by smallholder farmers – with less than 2 hectare.[187] And what small-scale farmers need are financial services: access to loans to grow their business, and insurances to protect them against risks. The risks for a family farmer are mainly to overcome occasional events like drought, storms, flood and erratic rains, or other production risks related to crop and livestock. This is especially true for those living in places that are prone to such events. However, globally less than 20% of smallholder farmers are estimated to have agricultural insurance coverage.[188] A CGAP study reveals that across Mozambique, Tanzania and Pakistan 61%, 36% and 72% of farmers indicate their crops have been destroyed by weather at least once in the past five years.[189] Even though a billion people have been taken out of poverty over the last 15 years, according to the World Bank, in the same period, natural disasters pushed 400 million people (back) into poverty.[190] Managing risks for their crop and livestock, for their agricultural business, is not a nice-to-have, it is a must-have. Not only to grow out of poverty, but also because our food production is depending on it. So, apart from just being humane, it is in all of our interest that our financial system gears up to include and support smallholder farmers. Not just with loans and savings, with insurances of all kinds too, as to manage risks.

Photo by game changer

COVERING THE CHAIN

And this is exactly what Agriculture and Climate Risk Enterprise (ACRE) Africa[191] is doing: linking smallholder farmers to agricultural insurance products in Kenya, Tanzania and Rwanda. ACRE Africa is not an insurer; it's a service provider linking and collaborating with local insurers, farmer aggregators, agricultural input companies, development partners, finance institutions, and other stakeholders in the insurance and agricultural value chain. By connecting the players in the chain, ACRE Africa manages to offer affordable micro-insurance to small-scale food farmers adapted to their needs. ACRE Africa undertakes the risk assessment, the product development of tailored micro-insurance and risk monitoring. They play a role of value chain orchestrator.

One of their products is, for example, a replanting guarantee in close collaboration with a seed company, UAP Insurance and mobile network operator Safaricom. This replanting guarantee protects the farmers against drought during the germination phase of their crop. Farmers get a card with a unique code when they buy a bag of seed at the shop for all their farm input. The card explains how they can register location, planting date and when the cover period starts on

183

a mobile platform.[192] Weather conditions and crop conditions are monitored using satellite imagery, and pictures taken by champion farmers in the village. If drought or excess rainfall affects the crop, the farmer receives a mobile money transfer.

EVERYBODY PLAYS

ACRE Africa protected 8.5 million beneficiaries, reached 2.1 million smallholder farmers,[193] insuring them against agricultural risks – underwritten by several different local insurers – for crops like maize, coffee, wheat, cashew nuts and potatoes, but for livestock too. ACRE Africa's typical farmer is a woman who cultivates 1.7 acres of land and runs a household of six family members. Up to 89% of their clients are accessing crop insurance for the first time. And 54% of their farmers live on less than US$3.20 a day.[194] Insured farmers produce more, earn on average 16% more than the uninsured, and invest 20% more in their farms. A clear and convincing case of what financial inclusion means for small-scale farmers, and therefore for our food production too.

COLLABORATIVE

In Tanzania, ACRE Africa bundles insurance – at the start of the planting season – with loans from credit institutions, the premium payment of the insurance is pre-financed by the credit institution and the farmer pays it back as a part of the loan instalments. Through the integrated delivery with the credit institution, farmers are protected against widespread default when severe weather event happen, like storms. This shows that there's not just value for the farmer, but that there's added value for the credit institution too. Like with the replanting guarantee, ACRE Africa offers this insurance in joint forces, in collaboration with insurers and credit institutions.

In Rwanda, ACRE Africa offers livestock insurance for dairy cows. An insured farmer is required to keep to a so-called Care Calendar, performing routine animal health practices and vaccines. If they do so, and the insured dairy cow dies of a range of accidental causes, the farmer receives compensation to buy a new one or repay the outstanding loan. This insurance product supports the animal health policy of the Ministry of Agriculture and Animal Resources. ACRE Africa is adapting their insurance service to the agricultural reality the family farmer is in, always in partnership.

These examples illustrate that ACRE is leading and collaborating with partners to bundle and adapt the micro-insurance product, and offers an integrated delivery. *"Getting partners to work with you is very, very important,"*[195] according to George Kuria, CEO of ACRE Africa. The key insight from years of piloting and testing with the smallholder farmers, according to George, is that *"insurances need to be firstly commoditized and secondly bundled, especially since it is not seen as a primary input for farming,"* you need to bundle it with the products that the farmers consider to be primary, *"you need partners selling products to bundle the insurance with."*[196] Bundling assures that the insurance has strings attached to daily life, like for example with the seeds; this is what makes the insurance tangible, which allows it to be put it on the shelf next to the fertilizer. Or, for example, having it comply with animal health policy of the local government. Collaboration with partners is what makes it possible to make insurances tangible and package insurances to daily life.

PACKAGED ATTACHED TO DAILY LIFE

ACRE Africa launched Bima Pima, a new insurance product in Kenya, protecting farmers for climate-related risk to their crops. The insurance is affordable for a small-scale farmer and packaged as a scratch card and bundled with other farm inputs in such a way that it suits a farmer's needs. It can be bought off the shelf where the farmer buys farm input like fertilizer. It's convenient, there is no signing of policies required, and payments of premiums can be done in small amounts over a period of time. ACRE Africa automated the full insurance process, from sales and satellite monitoring of the farm, to payouts that are triggered by no or low rainfall in a specific area. Due to this, the administration costs are kept as low as possible, which is keeping the premium affordable. Distribution is done through agro-dealers and the use of trained village champions who are fellow farmers and relate to the challenges these farmers face. ACRE Africa has over 500 village champions in Kenya who train farmers on good agronomic practices and can offer support next to insurance.

Photo by game changer

PRICED TO WHAT THE PEOPLE CAN AFFORD

ACRE Africa **continuously evaluates** and improves their insurance products and services. When evaluation and tests showed that timely payout after bad weather events contributed to 30% insurance policy renewal, ACRE Africa started exploring block chain solutions enabling payouts in seconds. This required involvement of new partners for smart contracting and a digital insurance platform.[197] The pilots look promising: reduction of costs to issue policies could reduce by 40%. What's interesting is that ACRE Africa indicates that this could result in a deduction of premium prices of 30% for the farmers.[198] This illustrates ACRE Africa's drive to **price** to what family farmers can **afford**.

PEOPLE AT THE HEART OF IT

The process to adapt to customer's needs never stops. Just recently, an 'old' challenge surfaced again. Using George's words, *"Insurance is an intangible product that needs some believability."*[199] ACRE Africa started to add pictures taken with mobile phones by champion farmers in the village to monitor the growth of crops, in addition to satellite images. This was adapted after finding out that farmers felt they did not feel part of the entire process. *"It made them feel it was now real, as opposed to when they only monitored with satellite images,"* according to George.

Partly due to some disrupting development in the Rwandan market, ACRE Africa started another learning loop, ordering an independent 3-D client value assessment for their livestock and maize insurance products and services. It's not just indicating an internal organization culture of **continuous learning**; it underlines that the people are at the heart of their service delivery. The study identified behavioural aspects that are key to understanding how their product is perceived, in order to improve it to better suit the needs of the famers.[200]

Another study gave ACRE Africa the insight that impact in the lives of the farmer is higher when insurance comes with complementary agricultural services to the farmers, like Good Agricultural Practices (GAP) advice or soil testing.[201] Like with health insurances, in the case of BIMA, offering it in combination with preventive health services makes a lasting impact in the lives of lower-income people – healthier living, with fewer claims as a result. Likewise, agricultural insurances have deeper impact when they come with complementary agricultural services. Because ACRE Africa keeps the people at the heart of their service delivery, they go out, and dare to ask the right questions.

IT TOOK YEARS ... TO **REVERSE ENGINEER IT TO MEET THE NEEDS**

ACRE Africa started as a project by Syngenta Foundation for Sustainable Agriculture (SFSA), called Kilimo Salama (Safe Farming), in Kenya. This was five years before the inception of ACRE Africa as an independent social enterprise. The micro-insurance was developed to insure farm inputs (seeds, fertilizer, chemicals) against drought or excess rain. It was jointly developed with partners, UAP Insurance, MEA as fertilizer distributor and mobile phone provider, Safaricom. The project took care of awareness raising and education, with field days, farmer group trainings, radio shows and a helpline. They learned to distribute through agro-vet shops, to reach the farmers in a convenient way. They learned to make registration and payout paperless, through the mobile phone. They learned how to grow the credibility of weather data, and eliminate conflict between insurer and insured.[202] With each step, new challenges were identified and solved, and new assumptions tested. Nowadays ACRE Africa is credited for its strengths that the indexes they use are based on several data sources, such as solar powered automated weather stations, satellite rainfall measurements, and government area yield statistics. Each index was experimented with, since the project started, and this continues all the way up till today, it's a continuous process of reversely engineering that never stops.

"It's pilots, it's testing, it's going to the ground, it's sitting down with the farmers, finding what is important for them,"[203] according to George.

CONNECTED

One of the challenges with insurance is the lack of trust from local communities, partly because it is not a tangible product in itself. That's why ACRE Africa applies a *"hybridized approach through high-touch (in-person) approaches and low-touch (digital) means."*[204] This means that ACRE Africa relies heavily on automated processes, as well as on a peer-to-peer network, the Village Champion Model. This is a network of farmers who are considered to be the rural change agents, called champions. The farmer champions are trained on good agricultural practices, financial literacy and insurance. They get compensated for each insurance cover sold, and gain recognition from their farmer peers as the 'go-to' point.[205] This Village Champion model supports ACRE Africa to better understand the needs of small-scale farmers and their communities, and to educate them on insurance. This network helps in transferring knowledge both ways, and leverages trusted social (informal) structures in the village. It is key for increasing **trust**.

This so-called hybrid value chain that ACRE Africa has built makes their organization operate as a network. On the one side, ACRE Africa is connected with the strategic partners in the chain, like insurers and reinsurers, farmers associations, finance institutes, mobile network providers and agricultural input providers, to jointly overcoming some area specific challenges related to the localized insurance product and market in development. On the other side, there is this network of village champions in the villages where the smallholder food farmers live. ACRE Africa operates as a network integrator and coordinator.

It's through this connectedness that ACRE Africa is able to run a low-margin, high-volume sustainable business serving rural African smallholder farmer communities.

A **BLENDED MODEL** IS AN ENABLING FACTOR ...

It's only fair to point out that most of the costs invested up-front by Syngenta Foundation will never return through revenue from the micro-insurances sold to low-income farmers. If ACRE Africa would have taken all these costs for building the market and the last-mile infrastructure and had to recover it from the insurances they sell, the prices would never have been affordable for the farmers. After Syngenta Foundation carried most of the development cost for bringing the market into existence and developing the insurance service, ACRE Africa can now run as a financially sustainable business, delivering agricultural micro-insurances to some of the poorest farmers of Kenya, Rwanda and Tanzania.

Since its inception as an independent social enterprise, ACRE Africa is covering their organization costs with revenue from sales of their micro-insurance services, and with revenue coming from advisory and training services. ACRE Africa actively pursues entrepreneurial collaborations to develop, deliver and distribute micro-insurances in joint efforts, which contributes to being able to carrying the cost together. It's this blended model that enables ACRE Africa to continue to innovate to de-risk smallholder farmer production and improve rural livelihoods, growing financial inclusion.

The above is prone to the misconception, a long-living myth, that there is no business model for insurance for the poor. Let me quote George here, *"It's wrong to say that there is no market ... we have found a route to market ... the point is: you have to be in the place where the farmers are."*[206]

Last-mile channels need to be built to be able to be in the place where the farmer is, and the costs for this channel can be recovered partly by collaborations with partners. There is no question that the need, and thus a market, for these insurances is omnipresent, just take the fact that nearly all farmers indicate that their community faced a climate shock in the last two years.[207] A blended model is an enabler to deliver a solution that speaks to this need.

COLLECTIVE ... TRIGGERING AN IRREVERSIBLE CHANGE

Recently another phase started, by the end of 2020 when ZEP-RE (a regional PTA reinsurance company) became the majority shareholder of ACRE Africa, with Syngenta Foundation no longer being the main shareholder.[208] In this phase ACRE Africa will scale their insurance services, Syngenta Foundation will aim to replicate the system change approach toward building new markets for agricultural micro-insurances for the smallholder farmers. After the inception of ACRE Africa, Syngenta Foundation has been kick-starting innovative and affordable agricultural insurance schemes for the small-scale farmers in other parts of the world too. Their approach is one that usually combines:

- weather and yield indices to keep the premiums low
- implementation through a local enterprise, working in partnership with several local partners in the chain, like credit unions, microfinance institutions, farmers' associations, input providers, mobile network operators
- insurance in a bag concept, attaching insurance to the farming input, linking it into the farmers' daily reality
- financial education and awareness raising about insurances for the small-scale farmers
- and a mobile technology as a means to reach scale

Syngenta Foundation is launching Dana PANDAN in Indonesia, with ACA insurance as the insurer and CU Rahayu as the credit union providing the farmers with cash and input loans. Assessments are done through satellite. They build the non-existing market in collaboration with Indonesian partners. It takes them an estimated three years to develop the exact right mix of the insurance product, collaboration partners, and designing the product to speak to the specific needs and circumstances of the farmers and unique situation in East Java in Indonesia. They actively reengineer the insurance product back to the needs, creating an enabling environment – an ecosystem of trusted partners – that embeds education in their service. And they jointly built trust through a local network of champion farmers. All of this is key to have in place before being able to launch a micro-insurance product.

Same in Bangladesh, Syngenta Foundation kick-started the Surokkha project. Partnerships with insurer Green Delta Insurance Company (GDIC), reinsurer Swiss Re, farmers' aggregators, microfinance institutions and several Farmers' Hubs are facilitated. They are jointly distributing a weather index insurance in five districts. They are piloting, modifying and redesigning it to the needs of the smallholder farmers as to manage weather-related risks on crops. Partners get capacity building support and farmers are educated. The big challenge for weather index-based insurance is the lack of awareness about the concept, trust in the entire local insurance market and lack of weather data. The project is going through continuous learning loops, developing and testing the product, while building a last-mile distribution channel.[209]

These examples demonstrate a clear replication strategy, eyeing for a system change at country level, bringing similar micro-insurance markets into being, one after another. Syngenta Foundation and ACRE Africa are on a joint mission to show that this group of smallholder farmers is an untapped market and deserves to be served and financially included. They both acknowledge that these markets are hyper local, and that they cannot be served 'alone.' The question of 'how' is answered; we only need more players to join.

Simon Winter, Executive Director of Syngenta Foundation, stresses that it's important to do *"that more"* on top of public private partnerships and the innovations from social enterprises such as Root Capital among others. He elaborates: *"... Further improving how collectively we can learn about innovation practices and technologies that work best, and influence positively policy and incentives frameworks to encourage replication and scaling ... the key here is multi-stakeholder initiatives ... such umbrella initiatives need to be strengthened and integrated at a country level ... we need to focus on systems level delivery and adoption."*[210]

CHAPTER 6

PLAY AS A GROUP

One of the dominant elements in our current systems is the individual; however, each one of us relates to and engages with others. Humans are social creatures by nature. And if COVID has taught us anything, it's the power of the community: food kitchens and group responses, taking care of each other and a global effort to develop a vaccine were all around. But also in regular life, each of us has experienced deeply moving acts of groups without which we would find life less meaningful, be it in school, at work or in the mosque, at the soccer field or making music together. We move through life from one group to another, moving from your educational group (school, vocational training class or university) to your group of colleagues at your company, being part of artisans, or being one of many farmers growing crops watered by the same canal, becoming a father, or joining the group of backpackers, you'll join a group on social media, or be part of a committee at the city council or at your child's school; later in life you become part of a home for elderly, or join the group of elders in your village. All of us are part of a family, a village; all of us have a sense of belonging to neighbours in the block we live in, or the book readers' club, the miners working the same mine, friends of people in the same address book, living along the banks of the same river, vegetarians and so on.

Some unique characteristics of a group are: cohesion, knowledge and understanding of the context, solidarity, speaking the same language, social capital. Many of these are actually the same elements considered to be the strengths of the so-called 'informal' economy: knowing each other, understanding the surroundings and slang we speak, vouching for each other, reciprocity, giving and taking at different moments in time, protecting your neighbours and neighbourhood together, caring for communal ground – farm land, forest, river or mine – sharing the same values, putting in a helping hand in times of needs at school

REIMAGINING FINANCIAL INCLUSION

or maintaining the local road, water well or playground. That's why there is an opportunity to be found here for financially inclusion.

There is a reason why all over the world – not just in developing countries – you can find groups that manage money together. Like Mapan (from gojek) is incorporating the informal saving groups in the village, called *arisan*, a widespread practice in Indonesia to save and take a loan among groups of women. Village Saving and Loan Associations (VSLA) and Rotating Savings and Credit Associations (ROSCAs) are everywhere, and were coined the poor man's bank for a reason: they've proved to contribute hugely to financial inclusion. The Village Saving and Loans Association states that there are 20 million active participants in 77 countries worldwide,[211] so not a small movement. But we should not leave it at this; there is way more to be done, for which we can follow the same line of reasoning that is behind the *arisan*, VSLAs and ROSCAs. We should untap the power of the group to manage our money and organize financial service delivery.

Like many of the game changers in this book they developed their inclusive solution by taking the group as a premise. They have incorporated a sense of community in their innovative solution, and by doing so, the solution becomes intrinsically inclusive. The Nest is supporting and empowering the group of home-based artisans, identifying them and making them visible, which allows them to play as a group. BanQu and Tala both engage the group their client is part of, in their solution. BanQu incorporates the (overseas) family as an alternative way to identification. Tala's solution spreads through the friends and family in the address book of their client. ACRE Africa's model is based upon a network of village champion farmers tapping into a trusted social and informal village structure. They show that incorporating relatively simple features of a group is a powerful tool to drive inclusion. Can you imagine what happens if you embrace the full potential to play as a group?

SOLshare offers each person in a village the opportunity to consume solar power, but also to produce it, or both consume and produce it. By connecting their solar home systems, a village grid comes into being. By facilitating trade of solar energy at the SOLbazaar, SOLshare empowers the villagers, individually but as a village too. SOLshare links consumption and production locally, between individuals in one village, as well as between village grids. With all the villages connected to trade solar power, 'the villagers' as a group become a serious actor in the national power production, while simultaneously driving financial inclusion in those remote villages, with the SOLbox as a mean for income-generation, transactions and saving.

Uplift Mutuals is incorporating the strongpoints of a community in its solution to healthy living. Uplift offers preventive care in combination with health insurance, for and by the community members. The representatives of the community members themselves run the Uplift Mutuals health insurance scheme. As a group, they decide about and determine the rules. When the group plays, it's about staying well – and not 'just' about curing when sick – a reason prevention works in combination with a health insurance. The key to sustainability and affordability.

Let's have a look.

6.1 SOLSHARE – EMPOWERING SOLAR POWER PROSUMERS

Let's for a moment imagine a family living in a sunny off-the-grid village in Bangladesh, using a solar home system. Not too hard to imagine the benefits of solar power, with the sun being for free: this family saves costs on diesel or saves time on collecting wood, their children do not burn themselves and there is no smoke from the open fire, while there is light in the evening to study or work. It's not hard to imagine that this family could earn some additional money with the power now available to them, or even by selling their excess solar energy. The family feels good about supporting their neighbours, supplying them with renewable energy when they need it, for their solar flour miller, for example.

Photo by game changer

Their neighbours can enjoy the same benefits of having access to energy in their village, and the family earns some additional income. Sharing solar energy in a rural and sunny off-the-grid village is a no-brainer. Actually, the whole village benefits from a local renewable energy market, selling and buying from each other. Simultaneously, the whole village benefits from less pollution. Apply all the peer-to-peer sharing platform principles to solar energy in sunny rural villages – the biggest taxi company in the world not owning any taxi, the biggest hotel chain in the world not owning one single bed – and voila: the biggest solar energy provider without an energy plant. And the brilliance of it is: all the production is done by, and income goes to, the poor people!

This is what SOLshare[212] does, hosting a network of village solar-power-grids to share affordable solar electricity in Bangladesh. With the support of a box, an app and a web, SOLshare grows a solar electricity trading platform: SOLbazaar. Low-income families can turn their excess solar electricity into income, without hassle. Simultaneously, it provides families with micro-enterprises an option to purchase more solar power when needed. Exactly at the place where they need it and when they need it. Rural families in sunny villages can now invest in solar power generation, knowing they can trade it and make an additional income for the family, from the free sun, with minimal risk.

PLAY AS A GROUP

SOLbazaar is SOLshare's peer-to-peer network that is a solar energy marketplace too, where solar-home-system users can buy and sell excess energy from each other. SOLshare enables one family to connect to another family's house, using internet technology, and so on, to make a village solar power gird, connecting the houses producing and consuming solar energy in a village. Each village solar grid connects with another village's solar grid, connecting hundreds of households. Individual village households and villages as a group truly and literally empowered.

Photo by game changer

What is good to know is that in Bangladesh alone there are over 5 million solar-home-systems, touching the lives of 20 million people.[213] On average, they produce 30% of excess solar energy. While at the same time, still only 37% of the poorest population of Bangladesh lacks access to energy.[214] Against this backdrop, SOLshare has installed over 50 micro-grids across remote and rural Bangladesh and two pilot micro-grids in India, connecting 1,500 families, touching the lives of 5,000 beneficiaries. Most of their customers are farmers who earn less than US$5 a day.[215] By empowering the villagers and the villages to play as a group, SOLshare is building an alternative solar-power production facility for and by the rural villages.

LINKING ALL PLAYERS IN EQUALITY

Let me bring you back to the rural household in a sunny village. When the solar-power generated on their rooftop is more than they use as a family, the amount of taka on their solar-power meter –the SOLbox – goes up. When a family needs solar power because their solar electricity of that day is used, the amount of *taka* on their meter goes down. Easy does it. Even the families that do not produce solar power on their roof can still benefit from the solar electricity available in the village through the SOLbox. Neighbours swap solar electricity through their connected meters. It's this simple. It's linking local solar-power producers and consumers in a village, and between villages into a network. SOLshare is gearing up the transition to renewable energy from the bottom up as well as acceleration of financial inclusion since SOLshare brings income, trade, transactions, savings and investment opportunities to the villagers, just by linking all players in equality.

Photo by game changer

EVERYBODY PLAYS

Let's elaborate a little on a core and unique value of SOLshare's solution: the so-called prosumer. The empowering force fuelling the transition to solar power, and this creation of a local solar energy market, is the option to become a prosumer, a person who does not only consume energy but also produces some. It has never been this easy to become an entrepreneur and generate some income, from the free sun. Through an interface with a mobile wallet, users can start easily. And when you are a user, a consumer, it's also easy to become a prosumer. For this a rural villager only needs to buy a SOLbox. This can be done by paying at once, or repaying with instalments. When a family invests in such a SOLbox, they can generate a profit within a month! By doing so, the family takes the power into their own hands, getting the agency to become self-sustainable, as a family first, and then as a village. And SOLshare makes this available to each villager and each village, closing the loop between production and consumption locally.

PAY AND PERKS FLOW BACK IN THE FAMILY OR COMMUNITY

The pay and other benefits, like all tools to start your own income-generating activity – internet, mobile money, access to energy – all flow back into the family and community. Even without becoming a solar-power producer yourself, you can benefit from the solar electricity in your village, and start using the solar energy to start a micro-business. Or with the light, the internet and the mobile money that SOLshare prosumers bring into your village. Or with your mobile phone, since charging your mobile phone is suddenly possible in this previously off-the-grid village. Through this solar-power production and trade, locally in the village, all the other benefits of inclusion kick in too: a healthier home without smoke, less pollution on village level. It comes with the light, the internet, the mobile money, bundled in the SOLshare offering, that realizes an increased wellbeing. All prerequisites for thriving communities.

When we talk about inclusion, specifically financial inclusion, apart from the income-generating opportunities that SOLshare offers, it is interesting to see that many villagers use SOLshare's box as a savings account. They keep an eye out for an opportunity to increase or start their solar production when they have saved sufficient money to invest. This holistic way of financial inclusion, bundled with solar energy, is offering many opportunities for income generation, to reduced costs of living, and access to mobile money, internet, and an alternative saving account.

COLLABORATIVE

To get to this envisioned country-wide network of villages – with connected solar-powered grids – partnerships are key for SOLshare. First of all, partners for implementing the solar-home systems, like with Grameen Shakti, the not-for-profit wing of Grameen Bank founded by Professor Yunus, supplying renewable energy solutions through microfinance schemes to unelectrified villages in Bangladesh. Grameen Shakti has close to 2 million solar-home systems in their network. In collaboration with Grameen Shakti, SOLshare is interconnecting those solar-home-systems, financially supported by a grant from UNDESA.

Another type of partner is supporting SOLshare to innovate, like for instance the partnership with TTP, a leading technology company from the UK. SOLshare is jointly developing the next-gen trading platform, insourcing unique technological expertise. SOLshare is, for example, also developing and implementing rural-based e-rickshaw charging points in largely off-grid areas with support of GIZ's EnDev Program, German Development Cooperation's Energizing Development.[216] These partnerships support both distribution as well as a lean research and development at SOLshare. It's SOLshare's way to innovate delivery and distribution to the last-mile villages. According to Dr. Sebastian Groh, founder and CEO of SOLshare, *"We piggyback on them."*[217] These collaborations are of strategic importance to SOLshare, because SOLshare does not wish to sell, own or implement any of the solar-system assets, like the cables, the batteries, solar-home-systems, nor all the solar-powered devices, like lamps, cook stoves and solar-powered cow-milking machines, fans or fridges. SOLshare operates in the business-to-business segment, partnering with many (solar solution) implementers, training thousands of their field staff to be able to deliver the SOLbox, to start purchasing solar energy or distributing and selling the solar power. Guess what, entering a new country, piloting the solar-sharing solution in Assam, India, is done in close collaboration too, with CYGNI, provider of solar solutions for homes and offices. These partnerships are all contributing to the inclusive innovation, since the innovation lies in a unique way of distribution.

PACKAGED ATTACHED TO DAILY LIFE

On top of the collaborations required to innovate and innovate distribution, SOLshare has partnerships more focused to bundle the financial service offering. For example, the entire transaction system, payments, exchange and settlement is done via a mobile money platform that is fully integrated into SOLshare's trading network. This is realized in close collaboration with the giant bKash, a mobile money transfer service – Bangladesh' equivalent to MPesa. This partnership offers SOLshare the opportunity to integrate financial service delivery in daily life, allowing all transactions to be done in taka and in Bangla. It makes it possible to transact with a mobile phone – no need of a smartphone. SOLshare has an integrated offering, bundling solar power and financial services, jointly distributed; this is only possible in close collaboration with partners.

A **BLENDED MODEL** IS AN ENABLING FACTOR ...

SOLshare takes a trading fee from every transaction done through the platform, and generates a relatively small revenue from the sales of the meters to connect to the SOLbazaar. Through leveraging strategic partnerships – their products, services and infrastructure – as well as with grants and match funding, SOLshare manages to cover the remainder of organizational costs for distribution, customer education, research and development, as well as staff costs.[218] Of course, other partnerships are key to cover organizational costs too, for example with TTP and GIZ; these partnerships help to keep R&D lean. SOLshare is not applying a model in which the end user pays for the full costs of the organization. SOLshare clearly demonstrates a blended business model, in which costs are shouldered jointly, with a mix of sales revenue, fee for service, fee for development, impact investments and philanthropic funding. The mission to serve the rural poor to transition to solar power comes first, which requires taking a long-term view. The shorter-term profitability and how to get the right mix (blending) of cost recovery for the organizational model follows.

CONNECTED

Partnerships are the lungs of SOLshare, while the solar-powered network of villages is the beating heart. SOLshare's boundaries blend on all sides into a network of solar-producing villages, and the enabling environment of their partners. An important rationale behind building the partnerships for SOLshare, for growing this network, is the intelligence that is required to fuel the transition to solar. The transition to renewable energy can go fast, as long as it follows the needs of the villagers – the producers, consumers and prosumers. In simple terms, like any regular electricity grid, also this peer-to-peer solar network is required to manage power load. This means: a continuously matching of supply and demand during the day and night times, with peaks of storage in the middle of the day and peaks of demand during twilight and at night. Growth of the network follows supply and demand; both supply and demand should grow roughly in equal measure. But how do you know when you need more solar energy supply (batteries, for example) and when do you need more solar demand (solar cook stoves, for example)? To determine this, all partners are provided with the data coming from SOLshare's platform database. In this way, solar device-implementing partners can adapt their sales and implementation of solar devices stimulating either production, like solar-home systems, or they can stimulate consumption, like the lamps, cook stoves, solar-powered irrigation pumps, e-rickshaws and charging points, and the likes. SOLshare takes the role of connector, coordinator and orchestrator in this network of supply- and demand.

Like with all networks, the network effect kicks in with new partner joining, in this case a village grid, then the value of the network multiplies. With SOLshare's solution, this goes far beyond access to energy; it is accelerating financial inclusion by bringing connectivity, mobile money, income generation, reduction of living costs and the means to transact, save and invest, too.

PRICED TO WHAT THE PEOPLE CAN AFFORD

One influencing factor to fuel the transition to solar power is, of course, the price. Currently, the impact of price on trading is studied by SOLshare with a series of pilots, with different price settings. The pilots are performed to grow the insights in the relation between price, consumption and production. In a world of only solar power, there's still so much unknown. It might not make sense to offer the same price at night, when all batteries are empty, as at noon when all batteries are full and the sun is burning. The pilots serve to learn how exactly they should set the price, *"We have to be careful because we don't know how people will take it. And our goal is still to end energy poverty,"*[219] according to Sebastian. *"Of course, the price will be set to what people can afford,"*[220] clearly showing this is a prerequisite.

PEOPLE AT THE HEART OF IT

A golden rule building a pro-poor business culture is to stay true to keeping the customers out of the cold wind, according to Sebastian: *"First of all, you need to realize that if you are in the social impact space, your customers are in a very vulnerable position, so the Silicon Valley fail-fast-and-improve mantra only works if you learn a lot: fail-fast-learn-a-lot, and that ONLY applies while NOT impacting your customers negatively!"*[221]

Keeping the focus on serving the poor is a *raison d'être* for SOLshare, which clearly shows from their approach to **reverse engineer** the peer-to-peer solution **back to meet the needs of the customers**. Through **open feedback loops** the customers play the biggest part in the development of the technology. Take, for example, how SOLshare has diversified their service offerings explicitly following the needs of the people in their local context. Knowing there are over a million electrical rickshaws in Bangladesh,

SOLshare started to offer an alternative pay-as-you-go service for solar energy consumption on the go. SOLshare is
expanding to the electric three-wheeler market; currently
over 1.5 million of those electric vehicles are ploughing
the streets without a sustainable way to charge them. This
offering is designed for plug-and-play usage, like charging
your electrical rickshaw at the local market. Putting the
people at the heart, taking the local reality of the rural
villagers and developing your service from there is core to
SOLshare's enterprise.

COMMITTED

Not surprisingly, a factor contributing to the success is
rooted in **trust**. Maintaining the solar energy grid is done
by the people in the village. Once people enjoy the benefits of the local solar power market in their own village,
the sense of 'ownership' is high – much higher compared
to the national electricity grid. Theft of solar electricity
shows to be much lower compared to theft of the national
electricity grid.[222] People don't steal from the homes of
their neighbours.

The other side of the same coin called trust is an organizational one. SOLshare deliberately instils trust as one of
their core values in their organizational culture. To do so,
employees are encouraged to solve issues themselves as if it
is their own start-up. Only when your organizational culture is rooted in trust will you succeed in gaining the trust
of the people you serve. Trust is fertile soil for **constant
innovation** too. Only when employees feel trusted, do they
dare to come up with new ideas, dare to speak up when
they disagree and dare to **challenge the status quo**. Other
aspects feeding full commitment of the workforce to the
inclusive mission SOLshare has, are inspiring, coaxing and
encouraging employees to **learn**, to **control their own time**

and to give **authority to act** on their expertise. Building a social enterprise, with impact maximization while balancing financial sustainability, Sebastian tried many different new ways of organizing. The one thing he recommends is: *"You will only find out what is for you the golden middle path if you bounce back and forth. You have to try."*[223]

Maintaining a workforce that is pro-poor, innovative and building toward a fundamentally new system is a challenge. How do you do this? If you wish to grow to a new normal, no one knows exactly what it will look like. To cope with this, you need **diverse** team members. First of all, you need to *"keep the right balance, going against the mainstream, but still being able to work together with it,"* for which *"I recommend **having a team with complementary personalities** in order to be able to stick through,"*[224] according to Sebastian. At SOLshare they deliberately make strategic hires to cultivate a **diverse** work place, coming from a strong belief that a social enterprise thrives from friction, discussing and debating challenges. At SOLshare, an explicit approach to transform work-culture stereotypes is in place. When a new employee joins, the first month is used as a 'cushion period.' It's meant to be a time without specific tasks and an explicit encouragement to look into different departments, allowing the new hire to gravitate toward tasks that naturally beckon the person. This indicates that **roles** get their shape in a **fluid** manner. But how do you manage to work toward the same dot on the horizon, with fluid roles and a diverse team, without knowing exactly how to get there? At SOLshare they focus by jointly agreeing to work toward one key performance indicator (KPI): trade volume. This indicator was defined by the whole team, and the target is set and progress is monitored jointly by the whole team too.

COLLECTIVE

SOLshare triggered Bangladesh's villages to join this solar-power-grid network on a shoe string. They've built a decentralized structure, growing a movement bottom-up, with a unique approach in which the rural family gets the agency and keeps their autonomy. The families can grow their own village solar market. What's next? *"Bangladesh has been leading the revolution on solar and we are about to pivot to the revolution of utilities,"*[225] Sebastian shares, by connecting the decentralized solar-power network to the national centralized grid. SOLshare envisions a future in which both power networks blend. The timing is perfect, with Bangladesh' strong declaration of climate action in place. And in a highly conducive context with high adoption of solar-home systems, an estimated 65 million people still lack access to sustainable energy, and 35 million people live below the national poverty line.

It is the relentless drive and strong future-forward thinking power that brings SOLshare to lead and explore the next steps toward full inclusion, which can only be taken collectively. Just recently, after bringing together the full set of stakeholders, government, donors, academia, development organizations and the private sector players, a pilot was kicked off, aiming to advance a model to allow for joint energy planning between the public and the private sector.[226] This joint exploration of such an integration of grids shows a strong capacity to **think out of the box**, as well as an ability to design and lead collective actions. This jointly co-created regulatory sandbox was launched and will support regulators to investigate what happens when you relax the rules on a small-scale solar energy production. It offers an opportunity to build early evidence to convince others, and for others to learn and follow suit.

CHANGING THE RULES OF THE GAME

One of the regulatory reforms that is required to scale SOLshare's model is to relax the rules for home production of solar power. SOLshare is stepping into advocacy, partly by creating and sharing the early evidence. Partly by demonstrating how-to '**think big, act small**' to get to a point where the excluded rural ones will be fully included in the future. Partly by envisioning a world in which they are linked in and hooked up with the national system, while generating their own income, growing their own local rural solar economy. The stakes are high, the discussion is tough and time consuming. Why? Sebastian is a strong advocate that the prices for which the poor sell their solar-power should be higher than the price for which they buy from the national grid. He argues that this is rightfully so, because:

- it is solar and thus renewable and better for the environment
- the value add is in the fact that it is stored
- it is available in the remote places, where the national grid is not[227]

This is not an easy message to take in for some stakeholders. SOLshare has realized an alternative pathway to inclusion; it's in these advocacy efforts and through collective actions such as the regulatory sandbox, that SOLshare is changing the rules of the game.

6.2 UPLIFT MUTUALS – A COMMUNITY INSURANCE MODEL TO HEALTHY LIVING

India is a huge country with roughly 1.4 billion people. Over 88% of the workforce is in informal employment, according to ILO,[228] and 65% of the population has no health insurance.[229] An Indian family of four earns on average an income of US$2–6 a day. Nationwide, 64% of all health expenses are out-of-pocket.[230] Out-of-pocket expenditure is what an average family spends on medicines, diagnostic and so-called outpatient care. Outpatient care is made up of medical procedures, diagnostic tests, screening and other health services that can be provided to the patient in a setting that does not involve an overnight hospital stay. The remainder, 36% of the other healthcare expenses of an average Indian family, goes to hospitalization. However, most of the commercial health insurances available in India, as well as most of the government schemes offered, are focused on the hospitalization. This leaves the Indian family of four with a few dollars a day, empty-handed, without an option to insure the largest burden of their expenditure on health. And this is how an estimated 40 to 60 million people in India become financially vulnerable due to the burden of healthcare costs, every year.

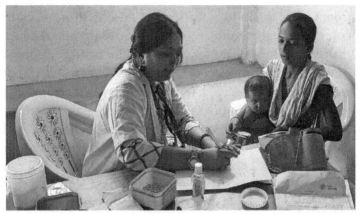

Photo by game changer

So, for an average Indian low-income family, the only option remaining is to stay healthy. What's keeping such a family living with a few dollars a day from healthy living? The reasons can roughly be tied to the following three issues, generally referred to as lack of access to healthcare:

1. Not knowing. This means an average low-income family has little awareness and knowledge of healthy living. Does not know how to tackle unhealthy behaviour. Does not know where to go if one of them is not feeling well. Does not know which medicines, tests, scans to take. Does not know what to pay for those medicines and diagnostic services. Does not know the quality of the medicine or the health service.

2. No access. Bear in mind those families do not have a family doctor around the corner. This means an average low-income family has to travel a long distance to see a doctor, or to visit a medical expert, a health centre, or a hospital in case they need them. Or, they cannot go there due to other reasons, like not having an identification card, or not having the time or money for transportation to go there.

3. Not affordable. This means an average low-income family cannot afford the medicines, diagnostic tests or any other healthcare service.

Combining these two facts – no health insurances to cover your biggest burden of healthcare cost, and the lack of access to healthcare for a low-income family – brought Kumar Shailabh, founder of Uplift Mutuals, to wonder what would happen if you go back to the unity in a community to share and manage risks related to bad health together. What if you just take care of yourself and your family, and have access to a doctor around the corner who helps to stay as healthy as possible, and when shit hits the fan, you can carry the burden together, as a community? Knowing that the majority of the existing insurance schemes "*incentivize sickness*," Shailabh got convinced he needed to try it differently. "*In the long run, nobody will be able to fund this current model, it's a reactive model. We should focus on prevention.*"[231] And that's the reasoning behind Uplift Mutuals' Biradaree model, which means community model.

PLACE IS AT THE DOORSTEP

Uplift Mutuals' Biradaree model[232] is solving exactly the three main issues, sharing and reducing health risks as a community by:[233]

1. Sharing information. Through helpline services 24/7 to provide medical help over the phone. Through women-centric (peer) health coaching, offering health education and information related to nutrition, reproductive health, seasonal health issues, as well as about diseases specific to women. With awareness raising and health education through health talks, health camps and offering screenings delivered at the doorsteps of the community.

2. Providing access. By putting medical professionals around the corner, offering referral services and tools to identify each community members that joins. All these measures facilitate access to the right and closest healthcare service. Healthcare services are delivered by

a network of preferred Biradaree hospitals, health centres, community clinics and pharmacies. Some preventive and diagnostic health services are also delivered by nearby medical professionals. To assure that members go and visit these medical professionals, Uplift Mutuals made them cashless. This preventive care is delivered at their doorsteps and truly accessible.

3. Carrying the risks and cost together. The health services delivered by the preferred Biradaree hospitals, health centre and community clinics are offered with member prices, which are negotiated down for all members by Uplift Mutuals. Uplift Mutuals puts doctors and medical professionals in the communities, and offers affordable medicine and other health tools, like scans and tests. In this way, Uplift Mutuals facilitates to carry costs collectively. Because Uplift Mutuals can get the wholesale prices, the costs go down. With periodic fees from members, they can carry risk and cost together. In addition to that, the member fees allow for building a buffer: disconnecting when you pay your membership fee and when you need the (money for) medicine or healthcare services, like diagnostic check-ups or hospitalization.

PLAY AS A GROUP

Sounds like a health insurance, no? But the differences are:
- it's fully focused on prevention
- it's owned and managed by the community themselves, mainly women

According to Shailabh, founder and CEO of Uplift Mutuals: *"When women drive insurance, it's for wellness, not illness."*[234] The health insurance is embedded in an environment geared toward prevention. This speaks to the needs of low-income people in these communities, who just want to stay healthy. Unique to Uplift Mutuals solution is the fact that the community members own the fund, they make the rules attached to the fund, and ultimately decide who gets the money and how much. The community is taught to govern the insurance scheme together. According to Shailabh: *"We give the community the platform, over which they can own and run their health Mutuals scheme."*[235] Uplift Mutuals empowers the community to play as a group.

IT TOOK YEARS ... TO **REVERSE ENGINEER IT TO MEET THE NEEDS**

"Insurance is a social product, it's not a financial product. Insurance works on social cohesion," according to Shailabh. Uplift Mutuals has dedicated over a decade to develop the right mix of products and services in multiple low-income communities in India to get to the current community-led and managed mutual health micro-insurance model. Their approach aims to give the community (back) the **agency** and autonomy to manage their own health, to ignite health seeking behaviour. Many risk-sharing principles were explored, and tested how best to put them into practice. The whole design of the Uplift Mutuals health insurance is based upon *"how to strategically design a model where people are part of the health insurance,"*[236] according Shailabh.

In the first few years of pilots and revisions, the following questions were answered through on the ground testing in and with the communities. How to exclude certain ailments, validated by the community members? How to enrol the full family, to ensure girls are not excluded? How to cover for no exclusions based upon age? How to design new products and processes, keeping the members as decision makers? All of this was developed and incorporated in a management information system. Data and **feedback** from the families were collected and on a regular basis and – most importantly

– shared back with the communities, which supported Uplift and the communities to refine interventions.

Photo by game changer

Those years of reversely engineering to meet the needs of low-income families and their whole community provided the deep understanding that in India, *"People don't take early treatment"* and *"people don't get the value of the existing insurances, people don't understand how it is done. There is no transparency in decision-making. And it does not help them with their daily needs. It will only help them when they fall ill,"* according to Shailabh, *"and the question is: what happens when I don't fall ill?"*[237]

EVERYBODY PLAYS

Nowadays, the Uplift Mutuals community model is assuring that everybody can join, and everybody is empowered. The inclusiveness comes from the fact that the insurance scheme is owned and managed by the members. Community member are trained by Uplift Mutuals, empowering them to make their own decisions, and this goes far beyond creating transparency. Community members elect representatives for every 2,000 policies, for a year. Representatives decide on product rules, premium amounts, coverage of ailments, sub-limits and exclusions. And they take seat in a claims committee. Representatives are trained to empower them to make decisions on claims handling and running the scheme according to a set guidelines and rules, as well as dealing with grievances.

Uplift's management information system enables the communities to make responsible and rational decisions based upon data. With the help of state-of-the-art technology, providing a mobile channel, in multiple languages, Uplift Mutuals collects data, which flows back to the community representatives regularly, fuelling decision-making by the communities themselves.

PAY AND PERKS FLOW **BACK** INTO THE FAMILIES AND COMMUNITY

The premium is around US$22 for a family for a year. On average, 60% of all the premiums go into a risk pool, 30% goes into the value-added and preventive services such as the help desk, medical professionals, health camps, regular check-ups and medicines.[238] The remaining 10% is to cover costs of the organization and platform. Uplift Mutuals' platform enables a swift reimbursement to patients, several hours compared to the standard market time of 35 to 40 days.[239] This model led to a very sustainable claim ratio, around 2% of its members file (mainly) hospitalization claims. Due to the focus on preventive health services, members are prevented to fall seriously ill, with 70%[240] of people using the healthcare out-patient services around the corner. This is what keeps them healthy. So, it's not just affordable health insurance that speaks to their needs; it's actual doctors around the corner, and health education, affordable medicines and diagnostic tools. All for an affordable premium. What's more, other perks such as agency, decision power and cost savings on not having to travel to see a medical profession all flow back into the family and community.

COLLABORATIVE

How come Uplift Mutuals is able to do something that seems impossible for the industry? Well, it's clear that partnerships have been key. Partnerships to reach out to the families in the communities, for example. Through many partnerships with microfinance institutions, Self-Help-Groups (SHGs) and cooperatives, nine communities – in rural, urban and tribal settings – were catered to their needs. Nine different health Mutuals communities are today serving over 450,000 low-income people and is growing.

Uplift Mutuals also has had partnerships with the largest mutual insurance companies in Canada, Sweden and The Netherlands. The support of these partners has been invaluable for testing different assumptions and interventions in joint pilots. Other partners shared their expertise, with which Uplift Mutuals could develop products and its organization. For example, the partnership to develop a renewed marketing strategy with Achmea and its Foundation. Or, for instance, the partnership with Tieto,[241] the largest public ICT company from the Nordics, to develop a web-based platform, including an app for Uplift Mutuals Biradaree members for claims settling. Not to forget about the partnership (between 2016 to 2018) with the International Cooperative and Mutual Insurance Federation (ICMIF), through which the annual contribution for members has been kept low.

A **BLENDED MODEL** IS AN ENABLING FACTOR ...

The costs for the platform, the health insurance and all the preventive health services brought to their communities are covered from the revenues from the premiums. But partners jointly carry additional organizational costs. Some partners jointly shoulder cost for development – like IT and apps – others sponsor pilots to test assumptions or support the roll-out in new communities; other partners offer pro-bono activities and expertise, which helps Uplift Mutuals to keep its organization **lean**. And another group of partners offers cross-subsidization. This is by no means to say Uplift Mutuals does not have a sustainable business model. Keep in mind, in the part of the world where the included ones live, cost for (access to) healthcare is usually covered by the government. We cannot expect the other half of our population usually living in countries with governments with smaller pockets to cover all these costs – for doctors around the corner and health education – all by themselves. Uplift Mutuals is doing the impossible here. Facilitating other partners to chip in creates an alternative pathway to inclusion – with a new business model, a blended one.

CONNECTED

Uplift Mutuals envisions inclusion to happen by building a movement of connected communities, jointly carrying the costs for Uplift Mutuals Birdaree model of prevention plus insurance through the platform. It's through this connectedness that Uplift Mutuals can accelerate healthy living – like with all insurances, for jointly carrying the risks and costs, economies of scale matter, a lot. With more communities connected, the network effect grows. Not just for economies of scale of the platform, also for health and claims data. But most importantly, for scaling the impact of prevention: having access to health education, a doctor and affordable medicines and tests. Having this is massive in the lives of low-income families! So yes, we talk about financial inclusion, even more specifically about health insurance, but essentially we're getting a much more holistic form of inclusion.

Uplift Mutuals has developed a unique capacity to train, both the community, as well as the partners. They host two end-to-end lab-kind of training modules. These trainings get the partner and the community up and running in a certain period, educate the newly elected representatives, and supports in setting up the governance of the scheme in and with the community. This training approach allows Uplift Mutuals to replicate to other communities. This replication goes through their community-facing partnerships. Uplift Mutuals is also reaching groups of people through companies as partners, such as Naaz group of hotels, for example, to become a host of primary healthcare services and mutual health protection for its employees. Another example is in two localities in Mumbai with a Muslim majority. Uplift's model by design itself is ethical and hence Shariah compliant and offers a solution to insuring one of the larger parts of population in India – of people who don't buy insurance – which is over 170 million people.[242]

Community by community, Uplift Mutuals grows its network, and so does the data flowing through the platform, which is available for the communities. These data will grow into a larger body of evidence that is envisioned to help to convince government, partners and investors to start joining. Ultimately, igniting an empowering force for healthy living.

PEOPLE AT THE HEART OF IT

This empowering force from the Uplift Mutuals Biradaree stems from the dedication to put the power of information back in the hands of the community members, in combination with the fundamental democratic member participation.

When Uplift Mutuals piloted the practice to put a doctor in the slums, it taught them two things. Firstly, it made the insurance a tangible product to the people. It resulted in a direct reduction of risk, and it worked out well to nudge health-seeking behaviour. Secondly, they witnessed that it developed in a gate keeping mechanism. It encourages members to live healthy and take action to prevent falling ill or getting a more serious condition. Similarly, for the 24/7 help desk and health screenings. At the same time, Uplift Mutuals found out that the same preventive services were powerful mechanisms for renewal too. "*Our stickiness went up, our trust went up,*"[243] according to Shailabh. The second part of this same gate-keeping mechanism is related to the claims "*women come together and decide on these claims ... that creates a level of the ownership,*" contributing to sustainable claim rates. Uplift Mutuals' Biradaree model allows for high levels of **agency** and self-management, which is what makes it cost-efficient. But it is the power to the people that comes first.

Photo by game changer

COMMITTED

Uplift Mutuals mission is big and ambitious, but their approach to get there is so full of connections with daily life of the families they serve. How do they manage to balance the two, to stay on course, with this grand mission, taking steps to deliver on their promise to the people living in poverty? At Uplift Mutuals they *"really **listen** to women,"*[244] according to Shailabh. This is not just talk; you can see it back in their teams, close to 80% of their teams is female, as is the board. Their organization is far from hierarchical; it's a flat model. Shailabh has seen a trend in their new-hires *"either they last six months or 10 years, there is no in between. For those who stay, their sense of **commitment** is very high."* Looking at the way they organize, it is **devoid of policing** and managing. After six months into your role, there will be **no supervisor** any more. They are building an organizational culture with the people, based upon **self-responsibility** and appreciation. This culture is to make **everybody feel safe, secure** and **at home**. Because, only then, when you feel safe and secure, can you become a community and build something as a community.

All their development, trainings and standard operating processes are tested in the community, adapted and taken back into the community again. Every training goes back and forth with and to the community. At Uplift Mutuals, *"Everything has to be measured by the community,"* according to Shailabh, and this goes both ways. *"It's not just from our side, it is also at the community side, they also get measured. When you take the responsibility to be on this committee, you cannot not be there for three times in a row; we measure them too. Claim handling is serious, IF you take up the responsibility you are measured that you take it seriously."*[245] Their culture, systems and processes are rooted in mutually carried expectation, **trust** and **reciprocity**. *"If you use ropes, not everybody will climb; it is important to check the rope, who starts to climb,* *why others don't,"* Shailabh explains. You can't do this without being **open**, **transparent** and **honest**, both ways.

COLLECTIVELY

Uplift Mutuals shows a relentless drive to continuously seek new pathways to accelerate healthy living and inclusion. Furthering the vision to transform health seeking behaviour on the long term, focusing fully on prevention, Uplift Mutuals is taking the next bold step. The next addition to the network of communities are Mutuals for children. Uplift Mutuals is bringing awareness, health education and actual health protection at schools where the children of low-income families go. They offer doctors, preventive health services and health status baseline capturing at schools, through which a medical history is built, and health-seeking behaviour is inculcated at a young age. Again, this service is bundled with education to parents and teachers. Again, it is offered around the corner, at schools. Again, it is incorporated in the daily lives of low-income people. This bold step is designed in such a way that it allows action taken collectively at schools. And again, it's done in a collaborative spirit, with the corporate social responsibility (CSR) budgets of companies. Bear in mind the backdrop in India, where it's legally mandated that companies contribute to society through their CSR arms. It's a very conducive environment to grow this collective action, in which health protection is provided to the children in government or aided schools.

CHANGING THE RULES OF THE GAME

Acknowledging that Uplift Mutuals cannot include all the low-income communities alone, they invest considerable time and efforts in changing the regulatory framework too, which is required to accelerate inclusion through this community health model. Mutuals in India are currently unregulated by the Insurance Regulatory and Development Authority of India (IRDAI) and do not come under the purview of the law, so there is currently very little scope for other organizations to adopt this Mutuals model. Partly as a result of this, many potential investors are reluctant to invest for the longer term. Another related issue is that currently nobody publishes their data, unfortunately. So, when it comes to communities, health insurances and data on claims and healthy living, little is known. To convince the government, there is a lot of data needed. Even though the early evidence Uplift Mutuals has created looks very promising, much more is required. In collaboration with the International Cooperative Mutual Insurance Federation (ICMIF) and a consortium of like-minded leaders in the space of micro-insurance, Uplift Mutuals consciously contributes to the building the larger body of evidence that is required to convince the Insurance Regulatory and Development Authority of India (IRDAI) to get Mutuals and cooperatives covered by the regulations. Even though we all know insurance is about numbers, it's hard to convince partners to invest for the longer run to get to those big numbers. This is aggravated due to this regulatory gap. It's what we call a crystal clear systems failure, or in normal language: a catch-22. A dilemma Uplift Mutuals aims to solve by working toward an enabling environment for partners to start doing the same, ultimately changing the rules of the games.

'CHANGING FORTUNE'

After drowning you with the details on the *why* of all these amazing game changers, *what* their inclusive solutions look like and *how* they do this, just because the devil is in the details, it's now time to surface what their new models show us.

At the end of the last century a movement started to take shape aiming to bring prosperity to the so-called base of the pyramid (BoP), with C.K. Prahalad[246] spearheading it. From a bird's-eye view, this base of the pyramid is roughly the same part of the population as the financially excluded ones, the ones the game changers in this book are keen to include. The movement at end of the 1990s was convinced that so-called BoP ventures could 'find a fortune' at the base of the pyramid, summarizing it very unnuanced and cutting some corners here. This movement identified business as a force for good, believing that there were huge markets to be found in this excluded part of the world. Early this century, Prahalad and his followers adapted their ideas somewhat based upon the first wave of BoP ventures. They found out that these huge markets were not just there to be tapped. A decade full of BoP ventures, research and studies brought new insights. We gained a better understanding that these markets were not simply there, ready-made, but these markets ought to be created and developed. Ted London, Stuart Hart and their peers progressed these insights with next-gen businesses strategies to untap the BoP as a market[247] by first creating the market explicitly *with* the BoP. They continued to be convinced that so-called BoP ventures offered the prospect of helping to alleviate poverty. Their findings and guidance was less on 'finding a fortune' at the BoP, but more on 'creating a fortune' *with* the BoP. Their seven guiding principles, a road map for ventures to 'create a fortune' *with* the BoP are telling and you will recognize some of them.

1. creating market opportunities
2. crafting solutions with the BoP
3. orchestrating effective experiments
4. managing failures
5. establishing co-mingled competitive advantage
6. leveraging and transferring social embeddedness, ultimately
7. enhancing mutual value

Stuart et al. also offered an important recommendation: to strive for collaborative interdependence. *"Business managers and donor community professionals must break away from their traditional paradigm of working independently,"* but they also noted *"collaborative interdependence remains difficult to establish."*[248]

Yet another decade down the road, we see that the game changes featured in this book have taken many of their guidelines at heart and applied them, financially including the people at the base of the pyramid. You recognize that they are indeed crafting their solutions *with* the BoP; this gets very close to what I have coined reverse engineering to meet the needs of the family, a feature we have seen by many of these game changers' practices. But you can also note a difference when it comes to this guideline, since these game changers do more than just that; they also promote, educate, deliver and sometimes produce *with* the people at the BoP. You also recognize that the innovators in this book are orchestrating effective experiments; this is what I've described as going to the streets and doing tests and pilots. However, the game changers add a few significant elements, which is the continuity of the experiments, pilots and tests, after their social venture came into being, resulting in continuous learning loops. As well as the need to be based locally. The learning loops relate to the guideline of managing failures, but the difference is that they are much more interactive, learning loops go both ways and they continue. And the learning loops are not just with the BoP families, the beneficiaries; they are with strategic partners too. These loops of learning are not just meant to develop the product or service; the game changers also integrate loops of learning to educate the people they serve and the partners they work with. Learning by these innovators is often taken as a route to scaling, replicating, to progress the system change, to convince the larger industry to join in spreading the change – inclusion – in the system. Where I notice an even bigger difference is in the guideline of establishing co-mingled competitive advantage. Most of these game changers show a strong inclination and an explicit diversion from competition. On the contrary, they demonstrate a strong capability to collaborate. The game changers found new ways to act upon this recommendation of collaborative interdependence; as you have seen, collaborative and connected are key features of *how* they organize. While the guidelines of social embeddedness and mutual value creation can definitely be recognized in the systems change approach these game changers take, I want to underline a remarkable shift. These game changers have centred their solutions around social embeddedness and mutual value creation – these are not just a few features. Their *why*, *what* and *how* are evolving from this. For these social innovators, inclusion is equivalent to social embeddedness. And the only way to realize inclusion is by ways of mutual, joint value creation.

These game changers are not 'creating a fortune' *with* the BoP. Taking stock of their journeys to serve the BoP families, financially including them, I noticed that these social innovators apply a fundamentally different narrative. Instead of 'creating a fortune' *with* the BoP, they are missioned to '*changing fortune*' for families at the BoP, from bad (being excluded) to better (being included). That's why I dedicate this conclusion to this important transformation that seems to have happened in the past decade. These system-changing innovators, with their social ventures aiming for financial inclusion, have changed this narrative of connecting profit to poverty alleviation. Their social ventures are missioned to 'change fortune' for families at the BoP, and therefore they shifted to:

- the perspective of the BoP family – a sustainable venture is just a means to an end
- fortune in the sense of 'chance,' instead of fortune in the sense of 'wealth'
- allow for agency in the hands of the people

1. MOVING TOWARD THE PERSPECTIVE OF LOW-INCOME PEOPLE AND FAMILY

Key here is to take the perspective from the mom-and-pop shop owners, the refugee worker, the gojek driver, the family farmer, the home-based artisan. Taking that perspective, these game changers ask what does the low-income family need, how does it work on their end. From that starting point, they start to discover new grounds, develop products and services in joint effort, organize bottom-up, not just for product design, but for joint delivery, awareness raising, promotion and education, and sometimes joint production too. They incorporate – often traditional – informal associations, already existing in the lives of the BoP family, into their solutions. Almost all of them have built their last-mile infrastructures with two legs – one leg is the technology and the other is populated with the people they serve. This is one part of what is coined a *hybrid value chain*. The other part is the fact that they all deliver jointly with partners. As a result of the latter, their new networked way of organizing is likely to have a blended sort of business model. All of this is stemming from moving their perspective fully to the perspective and needs of the BoP family. Let's have a look at a few of those shifts.

SHIFTING TO DISCOVER NEW MARKETS WITH FAMILIAR TECHNOLOGIES AND FACES – HYBRID VALUE CHAINS

We're familiar with online payment, with platform systems, with solar solutions and telehealth. We're familiar with global chains, tracking and tracing mechanisms, being wired through internet technology and our mobile phones. Bringing these familiar matters to the streets, to the slums and the rural villages, taking them into the homes of the BoP families, speaking to the families' needs, these game changers are discovering new grounds. New grounds being: new markets to be created and developed. Most of these game changers are 'new kids on the block,' although many of them bring a track record within 'the industry.' It is often these new faces – not hindered by pre-conceptions and not constrained by preconceived ideas – finding the gems in our cluttered chains, inter-twined processes and multifaceted interfaces that are cur-rently often excluding low-income families. Like Tienda Pago, building a new ground where mom-and-pop shop owners get financially included with inventory pre-financ-ing facilities. This is partly done based upon the existing systems and processes of distributors and fast-moving consumer good companies, partly through phones with a closed loop cash system; nothing really new, just a matter of reorganizing in the chain, keeping an eye on delivering value for the BoP family. Likewise with BIMA and ACRE Africa, it's not just the new technology, it's actually the different way of organizing and doing so together with existing partners – mobile network or money providers, insurers, and in ACRE's case, agricultural input providers too – that brings this financial service for 'a new market,' the previously excluded, into being. Like with Tienda Pago, both models of BIMA and ACRE Africa have built a human-faced channel, a network of people connecting with their clients, integrated with their channel facilitated by IT. ACRE Africa has its Village Champion Model, BIMA it's agent network. What's key is the fact that they do this, to 'be there' in the lives of people they serve, around the corner. This is exactly what Healthy Entrepreneurs is doing too: empowering a network with micro-health entrepreneurs, with technology (including but not limited to solar powered tablets with supply chain software and educational videos) and a pharmacy business model with peers that bring health in the rural and remote villages.

SHIFTING TO INCORPORATE INFORMAL ASSOCIATIONS

Gojek is way more than just a technology platform matching demand and supply; one key success factor was Mapan that supports the family of the gojek driver, making it possible to grow household income by incorporating informal association – the Indonesian practice of *arisan* – in their solution. This is an example of how to incorporate existing informal mechanisms that are familiar to the family in an inclusive solution. Nest is taking the informal home as a workplace, and works from there with the big brands to financially include them, taking the informal workplace called home as a premise. BanQu, as well as Root Capital and Healthy Entrepreneurs, are not pushing people to cross over to the formal system; instead, they incorporate their informal reality, rooted in tradition and trusted social networks, in their inclusive models. BanQu takes identification with overseas family, as an alternative – often informal route – to inclusion. Root Capital is taking cooperatives of farmers with neighbouring fields, and SolShare is taking villagers, with all their informal associations and social structures, and works with them as a community. Healthy Entrepreneurs and Solar Sister both have distribution models that rely heavily on the informal association their village-based micro-entrepreneurs have with their communities. This incorporation of informal social structures represents a huge opportunity since it allows them to tap into strong existing social networks and assures the solution to fit with existing cultural context.

REIMAGINING FINANCIAL INCLUSION

In their models, management practices based upon bureaucratic controls are absent. This makes sense, since these practices are often mainly based upon static data. These new practices of the game changers show that next to static data, the informal associations offer alternative factors (data) to take into account. These alternative factors capture dynamic behavioural data, which are very important for facilitating financial transactions: they capture relationships, behaviour and the social context. BanQu, Tienda Pago, Tala, gojek, all of them use family and friends, and existing business relationships too, as a core feature for their inclusive practice. Solar Sister, Healthy Entrepreneur, Root Capital, Uplift Mutuals, ACRE Africa and Solshare base their model heavily on the community as the social context. They all take the social context and existing relationships as a decisive factor in their offering of financial service. Dynamic social data coming from the informal association, on top of static data, is what enables their inclusive solutions.

And by doing so, it helps to build trust and leverage social capital. Many of the game changers have pioneered how to incorporate these existing informal associations and social realities into their inclusive practices. Similar to what happened with microcredits a few decades ago, the self-help-groups are becoming a core organizing mechanism of many microfinance institutions. Likewise, this turns out to be an incredibly powerful tool to create new pathways to financial inclusion.

SHIFTING FROM EFFICIENCY AS A SERVICE TO INTEGRATED DELIVERY IN JOINT FORCES

These game changers are moving the focus out of the financial institute into the daily lives of the families. They do so by delivering the financial service attached to the fulfilment of daily basic needs. To be able to do this integrated delivery, they need partners. For the financial service to reach the playground of daily life, they all have teamed up with partners who play a role in the lives of the BoP family already. Tienda Pago has teamed up with the fast-moving consumer good companies and their distributors to deliver inventory loans and cashless payments attached to the supplies for their petty shops, with the purchase as collateral. Nest has joined forces with big brands to progress financial inclusion of home-based artisans. Healthy Entrepreneurs and Solar Sisters are teaming up with those who live around the corner, the village-based micro-entrepreneurs. BIMA and ACRE Africa partner with mobile phone network providers, insurers and have built a network of people (agents and champion farmers) to reach their clients, partly through their mobile phones. Like My Oraline Mobile is aiming to deliver numeracy skills training in a joint effort with the financial service providers. And SolShare is integrating financial service delivery with solar energy, in partnership with solar solution implementers and a mobile payment platform. Healthy Entrepreneurs integrates delivery with OTC medicines, SOLshare and Solar Sisters integrate delivery with solar solutions, ACRE Africa integrates insurances with seeds, and gojek does so attached to gigs. None of them delivers financial services stand-alone.

While it might be technology that is a fuelling force for financial product and service innovation, in aiming for financial inclusion the focus is shifting to innovation in delivery. In terms of delivery there is a long last mile still to overcome. None of the game changers aim for one efficient financial service alone; all of them offer bundled financial services that fulfil a basic need of the BoP family. And technology is often just a means to do so. It's often used to tweak the supply chain; their innovation essentially lies in the way they distribute and deliver. Joining forces to deliver financial services attached to medicines, airtime, doctor's advice, solar power, clean water, gigs, groceries, meals, transportation – everything is an opportunity to bundle it with, as long as it fulfils the basic needs of the families previously excluded.

SHIFTING TO SURF THE BLUE OCEANS TOGETHER

And to do so, integrated delivery, you need to partner up on both sides. All the game changers in this book have built last-mile infrastructures by differently tying together existing players. On the one hand, their inclusive solution was brought into existence with and spreads through the same people it serves. And on the other hand, it was made in close collaboration with the financial institutes, big brands, international development organizations, micro-finance institutions, insurers. There's nothing new. Like Amazon is not building new book stores, Uber is not own-ing new type of taxis, AirBnB is not building new hotels. Like the Blue Ocean strategies,[249] the system-changing strategy of these game changers is innovating customer value – usually in delivery, not in the product – putting the people they serve, the BoP family, at the heart. How-ever, unlike the Blue Ocean strategies, the strategies of the social ventures are not focused on cost reduction, but more on affordable pricing for the low-income family. As a result, putting the impact in the lives of lower-income people over profit, these game changers apply new cost-re-covery mechanisms in which all partners shoulder the cost for operation, resulting in blended business models and hybrid value chains.

Most of the time, this goes hand-in-hand with the actual shared value creation. Last-mile infrastructures are costly by nature, because the people live 'remotely,' far away from financial institutions and where big brands sell. The costs to reach them are too high for the end-beneficiaries to carry them fully. By restructuring the chain all partnerships are contributing to cost recovery, and revenues come from several players, not only from the end-beneficiary. In return, or on the other hand, the people served are also joining in, creating shared value. Root Capital is demonstrating a blended finance model, creating value with fair trade brands and impact funds to the farmers' communities. And the farmers join too, creating the value, putting farming practices in place that are more sustainable and more inclusive. Root Capital starts with the reality on the ground for the group of farmers, in the agricultural enterprise, not separating financial inclusion from sustainable use of soil and water, not separating it from women's and youth empowerment. The joint value creation is at the core of the approach, more income and growth of farmers' businesses on the one hand, and more sustainable farming practices, less depleting for our soil, respecting bio-diversity, for the fair trade brands (and the society at large) on the other hand. In this way, the financing partners can financially include this group that was previously excluded.

There's another key element to this. Many of the game changers illustrate that changing the system they are in can be realized through collective actions. They acknowledge that the impact of their innovation can accelerate and reach millions more of BoP families, if others replicate it, adopt the lessons, act upon the evidence created. That's why these innovators take a substantial share on their shoulders to infuse the change, i.e. inclusion, into the larger system, for 'others' to follow suit. They don't aim to become one Amazon, or one Uber or AirBnB to serve in each corner in the world. They aim for others to take the lessons learned, the evidence, the design principles, the innovation, the approach to inclusion and spread the change likewise. Like Root Capital's role in building a Council of Smallholder Agricultural Finance, or Tala's role in building the Digital Lenders Association. SolShare put in considerable efforts to connect the national grid with their network of solar village grids in a regulatory sandbox. The same goes for Uplifts' efforts to get Mutuals regulated, and My Oral Villages efforts to globally start measuring numeracy skills.

While I'm noting that business as usual does not work at the base of the pyramid, I am not arguing to get rid of 'business.' I'm just surfacing that these game changers suggest that we should organize differently, more in collaboration, less in competition. More as a network, less as one single organization. They give a signal that the capitalist definition of an organization as *the* entity to be profitable is obsolete when we aim for inclusion. These game changers are driving financial inclusion – and have thus build BoP ventures – with networked organizations. They work in collaborative interdependence, with blended business models and in hybrid value chains. Such a hybrid value chain is what brings financial inclusion. The networked structure, the diffused last mile, that is 'the entity' that should be considered to be sustainable. That's how we will (learn to) surf the big blue ocean together. That is how we should envision to financially include the base of the pyramid, together.

2. CHANGING FORTUNE FOR THE BETTER

Leaving the narrative of finding fortune or creating fortune behind, these game changers focus on changing fortune of BoP families for the better. It starts with accepting that we need more value creation at the base of the pyramid. Transparency in global supply chains is instrumental in taking corrective actions, to improve lives of the low-income people and ultimately include them. But it cannot be left unsaid: more value creation will have to stick at the BoP. Let's stop beating around the bush: more value is required to be created at the BoP to turn the fates and fortune of low-income people for the better. These game changers demonstrate how this can be done: joint value creation through integrating delivery and sometimes production; by closing the loops between income-generation and consumption locally, at least parts of it. That's one shift to changing the fortune for those families for the better. While the game changers do so, the people they include and serve become an important and integral part of the organization of these game changers, performing parts of the awareness raising, education, promotion, distribution, delivery and production. This often happens through self-organizing, another important and adjoining shift. Many of the models these game changers depend on cannot be done without this active participation of the people they serve and include, in their networked organization. This is the way how they managed to financially include them; teaching them how-to create the value at the BoP is an integral part of the way to change the fortune of those families.

SHIFTING FROM SILOED SINGLE SERVICE TO JOINT VALUE CREATION

BIMA is creating joint value, with mobile network or mobile money providors and insurers, which creates an opportunity for the lower-income people to actually have access to insurances. Uplift Mutuals is taking healthy living and health insurances into the community, for and by the community. Solar Sisters is creating income-generating opportunities by integrated financial service delivery with solar power devices. The latter is 'just' sales done by the rural-based micro-entrepreneurs, but we've seen the potential of SolShare, closing the loop with production of solar, allowing the rural villagers to become producers of their solar. That is where bad fortune is fully flipped to wealth creation for the BoP family. My Oral Village is changing the fortune of oral people and takes a long-term, systemic approach growing numeracy skills, aiming to shoulder this 'burden' with mobile financial service providers and other partners. This is another example of integrated service delivery: financial service providers are asked to jointly create this value of numeracy skills for the oral people, delivering it integrated with their services, benefitting both the industry as well as the BoP. These examples show that the joint value creation is sometimes done with other partners for the BoP families, sometimes it's done with the BoP families, and most of the times with both.

The 'technical' aspects of financial services are complex, but technology is rapidly becoming an enabler to facilitate partners to integrate financial services in their relationship with the rural families. More and more innovative financial solutions that drive up inclusion show a shift away from one-to-many to many-to-many. Like Tienda Pago is delivering inventory loans to many mom-and-pop shops, based upon purchases of multiple FMCG companies and their distributors. An example in which many FMCG companies deliver financial services to many petty shop owners as opposed to one bank offering loans to many clients. ACRE Africa, like BIMA, offers insurances to many families based upon the services of many insurers and many credit institutions, yet another illustration of this many-to-many shift. Or take Uplift Mutuals, offering health insurances and preventive health services in many communities, in collaboration with many partners. Only due to this many-to-many structure can they operate their platform approach and many other company resources like data. Uplift Mutuals is feeding back health and claim data to the communities they serve; SOLshare and Orali Mobile do so with data of usage. NEST does so likewise, but different too. Many big brands are together progressing financial inclusion of many ateliers of home-based artisans, in joint efforts through a Seal and a Standard, collecting data on the go of this 'invisible seg-ment' of the workforce. Like BanQu is in close collabora-tion with many large brands, shouldering costs to identity and build track records of hard work – i.e. economic pass-ports – for the producing people at the base of their chains: many-to-many again. All their inclusive solutions show a joint value creation and integrated delivery, stemming from a mission to change the fortune of the families at the base of the pyramid.

All of them taking the role of orchestrating the last-mile network, or hybrid value chain, as to include the poor. The game changers collaborate, not just with other partners, but also with the beneficiaries themselves. Healthy Entre-preneurs and Solar Sisters both walk the extra mile, to assure that their community health entrepreneurs or solar micro-entrepreneurs have a sustainable business and gen-erate a proper income. This is where and how more value sticks at the BoP. Likewise, with SolShare, producing solar energy is the additional value creation that stays at the BoP, while it also allows for financial inclusion – income, transactions, loans, savings and investment opportunities. With Uplift Mutuals there is a value created in the communities: access to healthcare. This cannot be separated from the health insurance, obviously, as the preventive healthcare services are an integral part of Uplift Mutuals' solution.

The point being that it is the joint value creation that makes them game changers and makes them intrinsically inclusive. Most of these game changers realize inclusion by building processes, platforms, mechanisms that facilitate joint value creation (many-to-many). They integrate financial services delivery by reorganizing the last mile of the chain. The speed in which we will reach the future of finance for all will depend on how easy we will make it for others to join in the financial service delivery, jointly creating value that changes the fortune of the BoP family for the better.

SHIFTING TO FACILITATING BOTTOM-UP SELF-ORGANIZING

After Uplift Mutuals trains the members how to govern an insurance scheme, the community owns and manages the insurance scheme themselves, as a group. It's through this health scheme that they are financially included (the insurance), but they get the opportunity to access preventive health services too, and that's why they take control of their health as well (protecting their health). When SolShare empowers a village and offers the opportunity to produce, consume or prosume solar energy in a village, the villagers take ownership of their energy production, and become protectors of the means to do so. It's through this energy production and consumption that they are financially included too, with the SOLbox being a way to save money, transact and make a living. When people become aware and are educated how to govern an insurance scheme, how to produce solar energy, they want to influence the outcome and take ownership. Likewise with Tala. Even though Tala offers unsecured loans based upon behavioural data on the phone, repayment rates are as high as with microcredits, which are secured by social capital. This is partly due to adjoining financial education that comes with Tala's solution, and partly also due to the trust Tala clients experience. When the clients feel trusted, they take ownership and feel accountable for repayment. Tala users not only have great repayment rates, but they promote this service too. Which in its turn builds trust and social capital, not just because the services comes recommended by your friend; repayments by friends is incentivized. Promotion done by the clients is the self-organizing part, but it is also where the inclusiveness stems from. Behaviour change does not come easy; looping the benefits back to the family or community is one of the strongest motivators.

There is a powerful result of inclusiveness in itself. By offering to change one's fortune – with medicines, access to health services, solar, numeracy, gigs or financial service support – the people feel included, take ownership and are likely to contribute. The community health micro-entrepreneurs of Healthy Entrepreneurs are raising awareness and taking health screenings remote. Healthy Entrepreneurs is facilitating them in such a way that the community health entrepreneurs self-organize part of this inclusive solution. Same with Solar Sisters. ACRE Africa's Village Champions operate as an incentivized but self-organizing network that educates, is out there for questions, support and advice, performs sales and monitoring services. Of course, ACRE Africa took the efforts and investment to educate and mobilise them. All these examples demonstrate self-organizing in and by a community. Many of the game changers show that this is apparently a great alternative for top-down organizing – which is expensive and labour-intense. It's what contributes to the lean models of many of these game changers. The self-organizing does not happen automatically; this is where the innovators play a key role. Many of the game changers take an active role in facilitating the self-organizing of the groups and communities they serve. It's not that their models just rely on cheap labour of the BoP families taking on some parts of the delivery or production. The game changers invest in awarenes raising, educating, teaching them to produce and govern. They empower the people to self-organize. Solar Sisters explicitly states that transition to solar at the base of the pyramid equals investment in female entrepreneurship and leadership. SOLshare and Uplift Mutuals have taken this to the extreme. SOLshare facilitates villagers to become their own, and perhaps even their nations' producers of solar energy. Uplift Mutuals facilitates communities to take control and self-organize so they can live healthy.

3. ALLOWING FOR AGENCY

This self-organizing is an extremely powerful way, too, to put agency in the hands of low-income people. Each and every game changer feels missioned and is merely acting on behalf of the people they serve. And there is a huge pearl in the oyster here: core to their beliefs and how they organize is their trust in the people to know best. This goes way beyond 'customer obsession' or redesigning to the needs of their clients. The networked ventures of these game changers have organized their teams and often reorganized the chain, to convene, empower and facilitate the people they serve to take agency. BanQu is putting the agency back in the hard-working hands of the people at the base of the big brands' chains. BanQu empowers the refugee factory worker and family farmer with an identity and a track record of their hard work. Same with Tala and Tienda Pago, trusting the enterprising people, putting the agency and control back in their hands, to take a loan to grow their business and income.

Putting agency back goes with trust, empowerment through awareness raising and training, and also important is sharing information. Putting the information back in the hands of the BoP people, like BanQu does with the economic passport, or like Uplift Mutuals does with health data, is important to empowering them to make their own decisions. Tala, BanQu, Root Capital, Solar Sisters, ACRE Africa, Healthy Entrepreneurs, Uplift Mutuals, and Nest all invest heavily in training. They all train the families they serve, and most of them train their partners often too. Convening the people they serve to self-organize. Like Uplift

Mutuals teaching them how to govern and run preventive health services and a health insurance scheme. Like Root Capital teaching communities of farmers how to produce more sustainable and more inclusive. Like Health Entrepreneurs and Solar Sister teaching them to run your own business, educate their clients, be agents of change themselves. Like Nest trains the home-based artisan how to improve their 'production facility,' while simultaneously as well as empowering them to ask for similar salaries, labour protection as their factory-based colleagues. Like SOLshare teaching them to produce and trade solar, to save and invest. Or on a very fundamental level, like My Oral Village, empowering them through numeracy skills, a very basic one to take agency, and therefore key to unlock the potential of the oral BoP people.

SHIFTING TO DISTRIBUTED DECISION-MAKING

And with this agency, comes joint decision-making. When people – the family farmers, the refugee factory workers, the migrant miners, the home-based artisans, the female entrepreneurs in villages – become visible, get a voice, are empowered and get organized, they can decide on behalf of themselves. The financial needs they have can be served more precisely, and in collaboration with them. Other players who 'deal' with low-income families in their daily lives already can deliver financial services to their needs. However, what is key for this to happen for the previously excluded people is to be empowered and get facilitated to speak up and make their own decision and voices heard. Like the big brands do in the case of Nest, step-by-step progressing financial inclusion of the home-based artisan, in dialogue with each other. Nest is putting the agency in the hands of the home-based artisan, firstly with a training-first approach. After this, Nest is progressing inclusion on the one hand by distributed decision-making or better: joint decision-making of big brands and home-based artisans. On the other hand, Nest is convening self-organizing of home-based artisans, empowering them to get in dialogue with the big brands and act on behalf of them as a group. Nest is making them part of their own protection, making them part of prevention against exploitation, in close collaboration with big brands, of course. The point here is: Nest invests in, convenes and facilitates the BoP people, the home-based artisans, to take agency to change their own fortune. Similarly, with Uplift Mutuals, SOLshare, Root Capital and Solar Sisters.

POWER SHIFTS TO THE FRONT LINES, AUTHORITY AND PROTECTION BY PEERS

Related to the distributed decision-making is the shifting in power, from the top to the front lines. When Solar Sisters sell and distribute solar devices, they ensure they do complete justice to the needs of their peers: mothers living in rural villages. Through an economic passport the hard-working people at the base of so many chains own their data and can decide where they take it. Before, many partners owned parts of their track record of their hard-working life, leaving the hard-working people empty-handed, nothing to show for their long history of hard work. With BanQu's solution, their track record is with them. Like the Nest's Seal came into being with the home-based workers themselves, Nest convenes and facilitates to makes them visible and get a voice. This is shifting power to the front lines.

Telling your child or student what to do often does not result in them doing so. But when their friends tell them, they'll most likely do it. Peers overpower authority. Likewise, this applies to financial products and services too, awareness raising to use them, advice when not to use them, works best when coming from peers. Unique for all the inclusive solutions of these game changers is that it is done – developed, delivered and distributed – with the people they serve. It's them, their peers who determine what norms, values, and rules are to be applied and complied with. It's them, their peers, who spread, promote and market. It's them, their peers, who raise awareness, educate and trigger behaviour change. With this, the power, the authority and protection shifts to their peers too. BanQu engages the family members to identify, Uplift Mutuals engages community members to determine the rules of coverage, Healthy Entrepreneurs engages the entrepreneurs to raise awareness and educate other community members, SOLshare empowers villagers to produce solar energy and get financially included, ACRE Africa includes farmers to monitor crop cultivation and provide farming advice. As a result, the community gets the ownership, takes accountability, which results in protection by the same people of that community. The community and the social venture have a mutual interest, with protection against malpractice as a result. At gojek it's the members of the traditional savings groups that check whether the pot or pan is bought from the loan provided to the wife of a gojek driver. Reconciliation is not done with a receipt by a person that does not know the client. At SOLshare the villagers protect their solar production means, and won't steal power from their neighbours. At Tala, the peer-to-peer community is becoming the first advisor (authority) in financial decision-making.

It's often protection that is at the heart of rules made by authorities. These game changers are indicating that putting agency back in the hands of the people they serve, provides fertile soil to perform a similar level of protection. This follows a similar logic as the development of self-regulation of the industry, which happened in more and more countries in the recent decade within the sector of microcredits. With the community health insurance scheme of Uplift Mutuals, when people take control to stay healthy and use the preventive health services instead of going to the doctor too late, it is actually protection of their own health. They do so, since they have determined the rules themselves, or at least, their peers have done so. This is why they protect their health and maintain low premiums – and therefore affordable health insurance. The agency, joint decision-making authority, and protection is with them. With SOLshare it's the same story, protection by peers. These game changers demonstrate a shift away from complying to rules set by an authority to protection by peers. It's with their peers we will offer finance for all.

CALL TO ACTION

Like Lao Tzu[250] is conveying in the Tao Te Ching:

Thirty spokes meet in the hub. Where the wheel isn't, is where it's useful.
Hollowed out, clay makes a pot. Where the pot's not is where it's useful.
Cut doors and windows to make a room. Where the room isn't, there's room for you.
So the profit in what is ... is in the use of what isn't.

This book too is meant to describe how all our lives are connected, even if we don't 'see' the financially excluded people. All those people financially being excluded are part of our lives too. If we can see this as a whole, then we can start to imagine how an inclusive world would look like. And we can start to work toward it. We're at a turning point in history, we all have witnessed that we cannot continue to go with our current excluding ways of operating. '#Metoo,' 'Black Lives Matters,' 'How dare you ...' all relate to issues of inclusion in general, and therefore in one way or the other to financial inclusion too. Or actually: financial exclusion. Women, black people and the young generation are excluded in one way or the other, by dominant elements in the systems we have built, and they demand change. The 2008 credit crisis, 9/11 and COVID also relate to this issue of exclusion, demonstrating the damaging consequences of the cracks in the system. I know this is so high-over, and all over the place, that it barely means anything anymore. But it does to this point: these matters are huge and interrelate. The grandness of these issues can make us feel too small to do anything about it. But just think of a night you tried to sleep with a mosquito: you're never too small to make a difference. So, how can you – albeit small – start changing the financial system so that all of our kids can live their lives to their potential?

Like the saying goes: through the cracks in the wall the light shines in. Therefore, the call to action of this book is to not ignore what is going on and to not look away. Just look into another direction, see what you can do and act upon it! Metaphorically speaking, you can wait a long time for the enormous metal bridge across the broad river to open for 'the excluded ones' to cross over. Alternatively, when you look the other way, you will see a small canoe peddling to the other side. There are alternative ways, without denying the huge bridge has its value. The time has come to complement the bridge with canoes and float to the other side too, so that the other half of this world can cross over too.

The game changers as described in this book and the way to look at them, their similarities in *why*, *what* and *how*, as well as their differences, feature with just one purpose: to show it can be done! It can be done in such a way that it has the potential to change the system. We have to start doing it differently. And each one of us can act upon that promise, right now, right here, from where you are, in your current role, with your resources, with your network and expertise. As a consumer, as a decision-maker, as a staff member, with your research, with your investments, with your team, your department or your company. The decision to contribute is yours.

Let these game changers inspire you and work as an eye-opener. More action is needed for financial inclusion. And you can take action, so please join. We don't need more of the same; we need to start doing it differently. Firstly, you can start to inquire if the products you buy the services your company provides, the investments you make, the ingredients your organization is sourcing, the programmes your foundation is supporting are made in an inclusive way. Are you contributing to one or more of the five levers? If you are a social entrepreneur or innovator, have a go and check if your venture helps everybody to play, if you could empower the previously excluded to play as a group. Banks, insurers, financial service providers, be appetized to explore and support new models for financial services in collaboration with partners 'out there': try linking with existing players. If you work with a team in a big business with global supply chains, go ahead and take action to take small steps toward ethical sourcing that aims to include the base of the pyramid. For fintechs and insurtechs, check if you could grow the impact of your technology by including the last mile in your reach, by linking with existing players out there. If you're in a research department, consider contributing to the creation of evidence that support new models like these. For funders and impact investors, grow your impact to invest in similar system-changing inclusive models, please focus less on the financial sustainability of the venture on the short- to mid-term; true system change takes time. Blended models and hybrid chains are the way to reach sustainable inclusion. If you are with a corporate venture arms, CSR or corporate foundations, collaborate with social entrepreneurs such as these or focus your development programmes to tackle one or more of the five levers. I hope you see you're all needed, and it is possible for you to make a difference and become partners in financial inclusion. Financial inclusion if for all of us to make it happen.

The key features the inclusive solutions of these game changers have in common, to *what* they do and *how* they do it, are meant for you to use, so we can jointly take the bull by the horns. As you have read, these inclusive solutions are designed in such a way that the more partners join, the more excluded people are served. They are yours to 'spread,' which means to include more low-income people. So, secondly, go ahead and use the five P features. How? Again, in many different ways you can act. The five P elements of an inclusive solution can serve as a sanity check. Don't sit idle, but use it to check the programme you fund, the solution you consider to invest in, the pilot you're planning to undertake, the service you aim to develop: does it have the people (previously excluded) at the heart of it? Is it delivered and distributed to the doorsteps? Is it packaged attached to the fulfilment of the basic needs in daily life, with an affordable price? Does the pay or do other benefits and perks flow back to the family or in the community? Feel free to incorporate them in the policies your CSR department or foundation is revisiting, in the goals the venture arm of your company sets, in the impact measurement of your investment portfolio. Step up and make sure that your sourcing department or supply chain solution is financially including the people as the base of the pyramid. You can use the five P elements to explore where improvements are needed. I welcome you to include them in your supply chain, improving on your ethical sourcing practice.

Last but not least, this goes for the five C features too, describing the ways these game changers organize. If you deem these five C features of *how* the inclusive solutions take root, to be true, go ahead and support the growth of this way of working. If you want to contribute to changing the financial system, please join in cultivating these skills and attitudes required to organize like that. Have a look at your organization and see where it 'meets' the base of the pyramid. In those departments you could grow the skills to collaborate instead of compete. Have a look in your supply chains and aim to grow transparency both ways, join and support your suppliers in learning how to organize more as a network. Grow the skills to work in partnership. As a social venture or innovator in financial inclusion, instil an organizational culture that motivates through commitment. Incentivize collaboration, as opposed to competition. Foundations and investors, consider investing and participating in creating spaces to spread these new ways of working. Invest time and energy to creating the place and space to connect and collaborate. Each one of us can participate and invest in building the evidence, while learning collectively. All of the above are means to grow financial inclusion. All of you can fund or share resources to build and grow collective actions. All of you can lead and join collective actions that ignite financial inclusion. Financial inclusion is not one-size-fits-all. It's more a way of weaving, weaving different patterns and types of cloth.

To make it easier for each one of us who wants to contribute to financial inclusion, I would like to conclude this call to action with the following matrix. The matrix is meant to help carve out your contribution. The beauty of the promising picture these game changers have given us is that they consider financial inclusion a collective journey and therefore welcome you to participate. And there are many more out there, social entrepreneurs and innovators alike, to join forces with. The matrix is quite self-explanatory and is based upon the practice in place with the game changers. The examples I've plotted in the matrix illustrate how a player like you could team up with social enterprises such as the game changers described in this book. May this overview spark your imagination about what you can do and where to contribute, and with whom to join forces. I hope it helps to work out your contribution – that's my call to action I would love to leave you with.

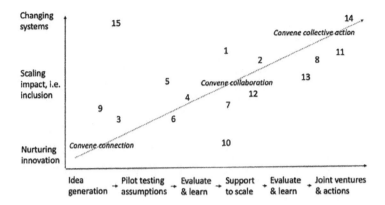

1. Like Shell New Energies (their venture arm) contributed to the three-year **study** by technology-enabled social impact company 60 Decibels, outlining the hurdles of the solar sector to reach the full potential, to reach the families in the world's least developed countries.

2. Like Axiata is **investing** in BIMA, entering new markets with mobile insurances.

3. Like Philips is sharing **expertise** and **network**, and Philips Foundation is **providing the spaces to connect** and work out collaborations with social entrepreneurs, aside from **funds** for a **pilot** to test a doctors-at-distance service, with Healthy Entrepreneurs.

4. Like Coca-Cola and Nestlé by **sharing** order **data** from **systems, network** and customer acquisition and helpline **processes**, and Oikocredits by sharing financial support with Tienda Pago.

5. Like H&M **ordering** from, **supporting** and **collaborating** with Nest, driving inclusion of home-based artisans.

6. Like Anheuser-Busch InBev (AB InBev) **partnering** with BanQu to provide transparency in the whole chain. In partnership with AB-InBev, BanQu ran a **pilot** to support casava farmers in Zambia, to grow from subsistence farming into commercial farming. Next to including community by community, also through **investment** with ZX Ventures, the company's global growth and innovation group.

7. Like the Clinton and Mastercard Foundation have worked to improve lives of farmers growing their agribusiness, providing **funds** for financial education and training for rural communities in close collaboration with Root Capital as their partner.

8. Like Starbucks (and other private partners), joined in contributing to the Root Capital **learning report** on "Financing Farm Renovation," together with other partners like USAID from the public sector, and the Ford and Skoll Foundation from the philanthropic sector, **building** a **collective action** together.

9. Like Palmetto CSR has **mobilized** their **customers** to support with a **financial contribution** from each sale they made to support female micro-entrepreneurs of Solar Sisters, bringing solar to remote villages in Africa.

10. Like the Achmea Foundation, who **seconded experts** from Achmea with Uplift Mutual to further their micro-insurance strategy, in close collaboration with ICMIF partly **subsidizing** some of Uplift Mutuals micro-insurances at an earlier phase too. Or like technology partner Tieto and Uplift **jointly developing software** to serve the community as a group for claims handling.

11. Like the smallholder farmers **programming** of Syngeta Foundation grew into ACRE Africa; receiving **investments** of the Lundin Foundation, Grameen Crédit Agricole Foundation and LGT Venture Philanthropy, to scale. Like Syngeta Foundation **kick-starting** many more farmers' insurance markets and **investing efforts** in **building** multistakeholder **partnerships** to serve these markets, at a country level.

12. Like gojek partnering with DBS, not only for jointly **expanding payment services** in Singapore, but also **improving the experience for driver-partners and** exploring **collaboration** (scaling) opportunities in Indonesia.

13. Like Philips with the Dutch government matching funds to **invest** in Healthy Entrepreneurs to **expand to other new markets**, while Randstad **joins forces with expertise** and **technical assistance** to improve recruitment skills.

14. Like Rabo Rural Fund, Root Capital, Oikocredit and other members of the Council of Smallholder Agricultural Finance taking **collective actions**, such as engaging other stakeholders to address barriers to agricultural market growth and impact.

15. Like Endeva and partners are **creating safe spaces**, with SOLshare, for ideation, generate **concept notes** and workshops to bring together stakeholders and work on **proof of concepts** to scale aiming for systems changing, connecting local solar grids to national power production.

ENDNOTES

1. Chaia, Alberto et al. "Half the World Is Unbanked." Financial Access Initiative, October 2009.

2. Sinek, Simon. (2009). *Start with Why*. London: Penguin Books.

3. Unicef. "1 in 4 children under the age of 5 do not officially exist." Unicef, June 2020. https://data.unicef.org/topic/child-protection/birth-registration/

4. United Nations. "Nearly two-thirds of global workforce in the 'informal' economy – UN study." *UN News*. 30 April 2018. https://news.un.org/en/story/2018/04/1008562

5. Demirgüç-Kunt, Asli et al. "Global Findex Database 2017: Measuring Financial Inclusion and the Fintech Revolution." World Bank, 2018. https://openknowledge.worldbank.org/

6. UN Global Compact. "Heads of state join CEOs and UN Chiefs at largest-ever UN convening of global business leaders." UN Global Compact. 16 June 2020. https://www.unglobalcompact.org/news/4578-06-16-2020

7. Demirgüç-Kunt, Asli et al. "Global Findex Database 2017."

8. Laloux, Frederic. "Reinventing Organisations." Brussels: Nelson Parker. 2014. 56.

9. Laloux. "Reinventing Organisations." 231–232.

10. Website of Tala: https://tala.co/

11. Siroya, Shivani. "Devex World 2018 talk." https://youtu.be/w1nBkqLoWO8

12. Siroya, Shivani. TEDxVictoria talk, "Empowering the Emerging Middle Class." November 2019. https://www.youtube.com/watch?v=oteXfrV2T1c

13. Tala. "Impact report 2018." https://tala.co/2018-impact-report/

14. Hempel, Jessi. "Give People Some (Micro) Credit—and Transform Their Lives." *Wired*. October 2018. https://www.wired.com/story/wired25-melinda-gates-shivani-siroya-credit-loans/

15. "The Mobile Gender Gap report 2020." GSM Association. March 2020. https://www.gsma.com/mobilefordevelopment/wp-content/uploads/2020/05/GSMA-The-Mobile-Gender-Gap-Report-2020.pdf

16. Tala. "Putting Education in the Palms of Customers' Hands." Tala. 12 September 2019. https://tala.co/blog/2019/09/12/enlighten-by-tala-putting-education-in-the-palms-of-customers-hands/

17. Oswere, Rene. "Digital Lenders Association says every customer has constitutional right to privacy." *Citizen Digital*, 5 March 2020. https://citizentv.co.ke/business/digital-lenders-association-says-every-customer-has-constitutional-right-to-privacy-325241/

18. Cheney, Catherine. "A look at digital credit in Kenya and why access alone is not enough." Devex. 2 November 2018. https://www.devex.com/news/a-look-at-digital-credit-in-kenya-and-why-access-alone-is-not-enough-93748

19. Siroya, Shivani. "Shivani Siroya Wants to Bring Credit Coverage to Every Corner of The Globe," Forbes. 18 July 2018. https://www.youtube.com/watch?v=CpJO1Zsqq7o

20. Website of Tala: https://tala.co/customer-stories/

21. "Shivani Siroya –Tala." TheLeapTV. April 2019. https://www.youtube.com/watch?v=ot15xzz0VvY&list=RDCMUC7lhMp7ftAmQp56_P2oaAfg&start_radio=1&t=300

22. Shivani Siroya's 's profile as an Ashoka Fellow: https://www.ashoka.org/en-nl/fellow/shivani-siroya

23. Ibid.

24. Siroya, Shivani. "Shivani Siroya, founder and CEO of Tala, shares her vision for a new model of financial services." Co-op THINK. 19 June 2018. https://www.youtube.com/watch?v=JeLfkuXxYdw

25. "Shivani Siroya – Tala." TheLeapTV.

26. McCormick, Meghan. "Leading Fintech Tala Looks to Develop New Products Designed for A Volatile World." Forbes. 17 September 2020. https://www.forbes.com/sites/meghanmccormick/2020/09/17/leading-fintech-tala-looks-to-develop-new-products-designed-for-a-volatile-world/

27. "Shivani Siroya, Founder and CEO of Tala, Shares Her Vision," Co-op THINK.

28. Siroya, Shivani. "Tala: How to build a startup that changes lives." Silicon Valley Bank video. 18 August 2017, https://www.youtube.com/watch?v=xzRaXAPx4f0

29. Siroya, Shivani. "Shivani Siroya, Founder and CEO of Tala, Shares Her Vision." Co-op THINK.

30. Website of Root Capital: https://rootcapital.org/

31. William Foote's profile as an Ashoka Fellow: https://www.ashoka.org/en-us/fellow/william-foote

32. Willy Footer, interview by author, March 2021.

33. Website of Council of Smallholder Agricultural Finance: https://csaf.org/

34. Price, Dennis and Bank, David. "Tough Love: How a dose of banking discipline strengthened financing for smallholder farmers." Stanford Social Innovation Review. Summer 2016. https://ssir.org/articles/entry/tough_love#

35. Foote, William. "Root Capital," Skoll, 14 November 2009. https://www.youtube.com/watch?v=UlQenGBQaf0

36. Willy Footer, interview by author, March 2021.

37. Willy Footer, interview by author, March 2021.

38. Foote, Willy. "Three Ways Mission-Driven Leaders Can Foster Social Intrapreneurship." Forbes. 30 May 2019.

39. Foote. "Foster Social Intrapreneurship."

40. Foote. "Foster Social Intrapreneurship."

41. Foote. "Foster Social Intrapreneurship."

42. Foote. "Foster Social Intrapreneurship."

43. Price and Bank. "Tough Love."

44. Price and Bank. "Tough Love."

45. Price and Bank. "Tough Love."

46. Daniels, Donna. "With Root Capital, RSF Doubles Down on Impact – and Impact Measurement." RSF Social Finance. 4 December 2019. https://rsfsocialfinance.org/2019/12/04/rsf-doubles-down-on-impact/

47. YPO. "How Willy Foote Took the Road Less Traveled and Became a Catalyst for Change." YPO. 17 January 2020. https://www.ypo.org/2020/01/how-willy-foote-took-the-road-less-traveled-and-became-a-catalyst-for-change/

48. Saldinger, Adva. "New impact fund could put smallholder finance on path to asset class." Devex. 22 January 2020. https://www.devex.com/news/new-impact-fund-could-put-smallholder-finance-on-path-to-asset-class-96399

49. Saldinger, Adva. "New impact fund."

50. Willy Foote, interview by author, March 2021.

51. Website of BanQu: https://banqu.co/

52. *The Kingdom*, Episode 7, Interview with Ashish Gadnis: "Blockchain Use Case to Fight Extreme Poverty." Soluna. 19 September 2018. https://www.youtube.com/watch?v=Ax6xtKmGDyM

53. Stanford Business. "Responsible Supply Chains: building positive impact in a changing world." Stanford Business, Stanford Value Chain Innovation Initiative. 13 December 2018. https://www.gsb.stanford.edu/sites/gsb/files/vcii-event-summary-building-positive-impact-changing-world-dec-2018.pdf

54. Ashoka. "Connecting Refugees with The Global Economy." *Forbes*. 26 October 2017. https://www.forbes.com/sites/ashoka/2017/10/26/connecting-refugees-with-the-global-economy/?sh=893205519732

55. Supply Chain Movement. "AB InBev invests in blockchain start-up BanQu." Supply Chain Movement. 27 June 2019.

56. Murray, Sarah. "Bank You." *Stanford Social Innovation Review.* Summer 2020. https://ssir.org/articles/entry/bank_you

57. Hamse Warfe, interview by author, 27 August 2020.

58. Hamse Warfe, interview by author, 27 August 2020.

59. All things Somali. "Could BanQu, found by Somali Entrepreneur Hamse Warfa, be the future of remittance?" 21 December 2017. https://allthingssomali.com/could-banqu-found-by-somali-entrepreneur-hamse-warfa-be-the-future-of-remittence/

60. UNHCR. "Global Trends, Forced displacements 2018." UNHCR. 20 June 2019. https://www.unhcr.org/5d08d7ee7.pdf

61. Warfa, Hamse. "Creating Economic Identity for Refugees – Hamse Warfa." TEDxFargo. 28 November 2018. https://www.youtube.com/watch?v=AUSMWwhlCvE

62. Maisch, Marija. "Off-grid solar changes lives – but could help many more of the world's energy poor." *PV Magazine*. 24 February 2020. https://www.pv-magazine.com/2020/02/24/off-grid-solar-changes-lives-but-could-help-many-more-of-the-worlds-energy-poor/

63. Maisch, Marija. "Off-grid solar changes lives."

64. Website of Solar Sister: https://solarsister.org/

65. Spielberg, Jonars B. et al. "Reaching the last-mile: women's social and sustainable energy entrepreneurship." *Comprehensive Initiative on Technology Evaluation (MIT)*, February 2018.

66. Impact reported on the website of Solar Sister: https://solarsister.org/what-we-do/our-impact/

67. Spielberg, Jonars B. et al. "Reaching the last-mile."

68. Katherine Lucey, interview by author, 28 July 2020.

69. Mazza , Federico. "Energizing finance, understanding the landscape 2019." *Sustainable Energy for All*. 22 October 2019. https://www.climatepolicyinitiative.org/publication/energizing-finance-understanding-the-landscape-2019/

70. Global Women's network for the energy transition. "Energy Transition Role Models: interview with Katherine Lucey, CEO and Founder, Solar Sister." April 2020. https://youtu.be/tbcjctGTD6w

71. Eason, Amanda and Hokokda, Emma. "Key findings of research case Solar Sister's scaling through partnerships." Miller Centre for Social Entrepreneurship 2019. https://www.millersocent.org/portfolio/solar-sister-5/

72. "Solar Sister CEO and Founder Katherine Lucey." Recorded interview by Clean Technica Talks Last-Mile Solar Revolution. 4 September 2018. https://www.youtube.com/watch?v=6kc5y36VVDk

73. Katherine Lucey, interview by author, 28 July 2020.

74. Katherine Lucey, interview by author, 28 July 2020.

75. Lucey, Katherine. "2018 SDG Live Zone: The role of gender equality and social inclusion in SDG7." Sustainable Energy for All Forum. 11 May 2018. https://www.youtube.com/watch?v=6Bb7tGltMh0

76. Unesco. "Literacy Rates Continue to Rise from One Generation to the Next." Unesco Institute for Statistics, Fact sheet nr 5. September 2017. http://uis.unesco.org/sites/default/files/documents/fs45-literacy-rates-continue-rise-generation-to-next-en-2017_0.pdf

77. Matthews, Brett H. "Hidden constraints to digital financial inclusion: the oral-literate divide." *Development in Practice*, volume 29, issue 8. 16 October 2019, 1014-1028. https://www.tandfonline.com/doi/full/10.1080/09614524.2019.1654979

78. Matthews, Brett. "Hidden constraints to digital financial inclusion."

79. Website of My Oral Village: https://myoralvillage.org/

80. My Oral Village. "FingerMath counting 0-99." My Oral Village. August 2018. https://www.youtube.com/watch?v=5JPsC0Oo0rY

81. Valeccha Richa et al. "Digital Wallet Adoption for the Oral Segment in India." MicroSave Consulting, May 2017. https://www.findevgateway.org/slide-deck/2017/05/digital-wallet-adoption-oral-segment-india

82. Valeccha Richa et al. "Digital Wallet Adoption."

83. Valeccha Richa et al. "Digital Wallet Adoption."

84. Matthews, Brett. Ashoka. https://www.ashoka.org/en-nl/fellow/brett-matthews

85. Gupta, Abhishek and Matthews, Brett. "Oral Users and Digital Payments: Can Existing Interfaces be Adapted?" Centre for Financial Inclusion Accion. 28 February 2019. https://www.centreforfinancialinclusion.org/oral-users-and-digital-payments-can-existing-interfaces-be-adapted

86. Mattews, Brett. "FinEquity member spotlight interview: Brett Matthews, My Oral Village." FinEquity. 02 June 2020. https://www.findevgateway.org/blog/2020/06/brett-matthews-my-oral-village

87. Mattews, Brett. "FinEquity member spotlight interview."

88. Matthews Brett Hudson. "Financial Innumeracy: A Global Problem for Digital Finance?" CGAP. 11 October 2018. https://www.cgap.org/blog/financial-innumeracy-global-problem-digital-finance

89. Dias, Denise and Izaguirre, Juan Carlos. "Risk-Based Supervision Is Key to Financial Inclusion in 2020 & Beyond." CGAP. 20 April 2020. https://www.cgap.org/blog/risk-based-supervision-key-financial-inclusion-2020-beyond

90. Rowntree, Oliver et al. "Connected Women: The Mobile Gender Gap Report 2020." GSMA. March 2020.

91. El-Zogbhi, Mayada. "Measuring Women's Financial Inclusion: The 2017 Findex Story." CGAP. 30 April 2018.

92. Mattews, Brett. "Orality and Usability of Digital Finance." My Oral Village. 26 August 2018. https://www.youtube.com/watch?v=k8dtNdv4q-o

93. Website of Nest: https://www.buildanest.org/

94. Siegle, Lucy. *To Die for: Is Fashion Wearing out the World?* Fourth Estate. 2011.

95. Research and Markets. "Handicrafts Market: Global Industry Trends, Share, Size, Growth, Opportunity and Forecast 2021-2026." Research and Markets. April 2020. https://www.researchandmarkets.com/research/hfp37l/global?w=5

96. Burns Olson, Katherina. "Can a Simple Seal Protect Artisans Working from Home? Nonprofit Nest and West Elm Say Yes." *Architectural Digest.* 1 January 2019. https://www.architecturaldigest.com/story/can-a-simple-seal-protect-artisans-working-from-home-nonprofit-nest-and-west-elm-say-yes

97. Sustainable Brands. "Eileen Fisher, Patagonia, Target Join Committee to Advance Sustainable Artisan Supply Chains." Sustainable Brands. 16 March 2017. https://sustainablebrands.com/read/supply-chain/eileen-fisher-patagonia-target-join-committee-to-advance-sustainable-artisan-supply-chains

98. Nest. "Nest 2019 impact report." Nest. 2019. https://www.buildaNest.org/wp-content/uploads/2020/04/2019-Nest-Impact-Report-for-Download.pdf

99. Nest. "The State of the handworker economy 2018." Nest, 11.

100. Nest. "The State of the handworker economy 2018."

101. Nest. "The State of the handworker economy 2018."

102. H&M Group "Job creation through craftsmanship." H&M Group. 9 August 2019. https://hmgroup.com/our-stories/job-creation-through-craftsmanship/, accessed April 2020

103. Nest standards data from their website: https://www.buildaNest.org/programs/data-technology/

104. Nest. "Artisan Accelerator impact 2018." Nest. https://www.buildaNest.org/wp-content/uploads/2019/09/Artisan-Accelerator-Impacts-for-2018.pdf

105. Rebecca van Bergen, interview with author, 25 June 2020.

106. Rebecca van Bergen, interview with author, 25 June 2020.

107. Rebecca van Bergen, interview with author, 25 June 2020.

108. Nest. "The State of the handworker economy 2018."

109. Website of gojek: https://www.gojek.com/en-id/

110. ILO. "Informal economy in Indonesia and Timor-Leste." ILO. https://www.ilo.org/jakarta/areasofwork/informal-economy/lang--en/index.htm

111. Asian Development Bank. "The Informal Sector and Informal Employment in Indonesia" ADB. 2011 https://www.adb.org/sites/default/files/publication/28438/informal-sector-indonesia.pdf

112. OECD. "SME and entrepreneurship characteristics and performance in Indonesia." OECD. 10 October 2018. https://www.oecd-ilibrary.org/sites/9789264306264-5-en/index.html?itemId=/content/component/9789264306264-5-en

113. Raj Urs, Sumanth. "gojeks impact on Indonesia's gig economy." Gojek. 2 January 2019, https://blog.gojekengineering.com/gojeks-impact-on-indonesia-s-gig-economy-990a60cd23b9

114. Raj Urs, Sumanth. "gojeks impact."

115. Raj Urs, Sumanth. "gojeks impact."

116. Wright, Chris. "Indonesia financial inclusion: GoJek's metal ignition." Euromoney. 5 October 2018. https://www.euromoney.com/article/b1b7bjb93d68tc/indonesia-financial-inclusion-gojeks-metal-ignition

117. Marzuk, Yunni. "Mapan uses traditional financing method to aid rural communities." *Digital News Asia*. 19 October 2017. https://www.digitalnewsasia.com/startups/mapan-uses-traditional-financing-method-aid-rural-communities

118. Wright Chris. "Indonesia financial inclusion." *Euromoney*. 5 October 2018.

119. "Finextra interview Ruma: Fintech will reduce inequality." Finextra Research. 25 July 2018. https://www.youtube.com/watch?v=SJw550GH2R8

120. "Finextra interview Ruma: Fintech will reduce inequality" Finextra Research. 25 July 2018.

121. Das, Kaushik et al. "The digital archipelago: How online commerce is driving Indonesia's economic development." McKinsey&Company. 7 August 2018. https://www.mckinsey.com/featured-insights/asia-pacific/the-digital-archipelago-how-online-commerce-is-driving-indonesias-economic-development

122. Baijal, Aadarsh and Akhtar, Usman. "Promise of digital financial services in Southeast Asia." *The Jakarta Post*. 23 January 2020. https://www.thejakartapost.com/news/2020/01/23/promise-digital-financial-services-southeast-asia.html

123. The Jakarta Post. "The top five e-wallet apps in Indonesia." *The Jakarta Post*. 14 August 2019. https://www.thejakartapost.com/academia/2020/01/23/promise-of-digital-financial-services-in-southeast-asia.html

124. Baijal, Aadarsh and Akhtar , Usman. "Promise of digital financial services in Southeast Asia."

125. Haryopratomo, Aldi. "Building Bridges to Empower People to Help Each Other." gojek. 24 April 2018. https://www.gojek.com/blog/gojek/building-bridges-to-empower-people-to-help-each-other-aldi-haryopratomo/?_escaped_fragment_=

126. "Haryopratomo, Aldi. Spotlight: Going Cashless | Modern Markets Summit." *Bloomberg Markets*. 26 October 2018. https://www.youtube.com/watch?v=YbSiG9t9JbE

127. Wardhani, Dewanti A. "Shaping the future of payment with gojek." 21 May 2019. https://medium.com/life-at-go-jek/shaping-the-future-of-payment-with-gojek-f6552a3c828

128. Ungku, Fathin. "Indonesia's Gojek reorganises management structure to spur growth", *Reuters*. 20 November 2020. https://www.reuters.com/article/gojek-reshuffle-idINKBN2800VA

129. Koh, Dean. "Ride-hailing company Gojek collaborates with Doctor Anywhere to offer medical services for its drivers." *Mobile Health News*. 7 March 2019. https://www.mobihealthnews.com/tag/gojek

130. Haryopratomo, Aldi. "Spotlight: Going Cashless"

131. Suzuki, Jun. "Indonesian informal workers lose work in coronavirus outbreak." Nikkei Asia. 21 March 2020. https://asia.nikkei.com/Spotlight/Society/Indonesian-informal-workers-lose-work-in-coronavirus-outbreak2

132. Samboh, Esther. "Gojek bosses give up 25% of annual salary for drivers, partners as COVID-19 deals blow." *Jakarta Post*. 24 March 2020. https://www. thejakartapost.com/news/2020/03/24/gojek-bosses-give-up-25-of-annual-salary-for-drivers-partners-as-covid-19-deals-blow.html

133. Makarim, Nadiem. "Hiring for a growth mindset." Sequoia India. 12 December 2019. https://www.youtube.com/watch?v=q4drMnvqru0

134. "MAKING THE CUT with Nadiem Makarim." Tech360tv. 2 November 2016. https://www.youtube.com/watch?v=dZSnr6J5JFE

135. Makarim, Nadiem. "Highlights: How to Stay Focused in Managing Your Startup." Tech in Asia. 4 April 2016. https://www.youtube.com/watch?v=R-655np8YK4

136. Nadiem Makarim. "Highlights: How to Stay Focused in Managing Your Startup.

137. Tonby, Oliver et al. "How technology is safeguarding health and livelihoods in Asia." McKinsey. 12 May 2020. https://www.mckinsey.com/featured-insights/asia-pacific/how-technology-is-safeguarding-health-and-livelihoods-in-asia#

138. Wyss, Jim. "How a billion-dollar Colombian delivery app became a lifeline for Venezuelan migrants." *The Seattle Times*. 26 May 2019. https://www. seattletimes.com/business/technology/how-a-billion-dollar-colombian-delivery-app-became-a-lifeline-for-venezuelan-migrants/

139. Tonby, Oliver et al. "How technology is safeguarding health and livelihoods in Asia.".

140. Grab. "Grab's Social impact report 2018-2019." Grab. http://bond.mpc.gov.my/Bond2/download-send/983/113/0.html

141. Website of Healthy Entrepreneurs: https://www.healthyentrepreneurs.nl/nl/homepage/

142. "AHA! webinar 2: Strengthening the last mile." Ashoka. 11 December 2019. https://www.youtube.com/watch?v=N_0_z3EWWkw&list=PL4c_sUqnnlfH3cFJmCw60Aqmgy3eS5mJk&index=2

143. Hoekstra, Borst, et al. "Reaching rural communities through 'Healthy Entrepreneurs': a cross-sectional exploration of community health entrepreneurship's role in sexual and reproductive health." *Health Policy and Planning*. Volume 34, Issue 9. November 2019. 676–683.

144. Website of Healthy Entrepreneurs: https://www.healthyentrepreneurs.nl/nl/homepage/

145. Joost van Engen, interview with author, 2020.

146. "AHA! webinar 2: Strengthening the last mile."

147. Joost van Engen, interview with author, 2020.

148. Joost van Engen, interview with author, quoting a Healthy Entrepreneurs market research in Kenya and Uganda, March 2021.

149. Results of research published at the website of Healthy Entrepreneurs: https://www.healthyentrepreneurs.nl/nl/homepage/

150. "MMH Accelerator Joost van Engen," Boehringer Ingelheim. 29 May 2019. https://www.youtube.com/watch?v=dJMVQ5raw7I

151. Philips Foundation team. "Transforming primary healthcare ecosystems from the inside out." Philips Foundation. 1 November 2020. https://www.philips-foundation.com/a-w/articles/healthy-entrepreneurs.html

152. "AHA! impact report cycle 2." Ashoka. April 2021.

153. Dutch Good Growth Fund. "Healthy Entrepreneurs helpt Oeganda in strijd tegen coronavirus." Dutch Good Growth Fund. 25 May 2020. https://www.dggf.nl/actueel/nieuws/2020/05/25/healthy-entrepreneurs-helpt-oeganda-in-strijd-tegen-coronavirus

154. Ashoka. "Accelerating Healthcare Access (AHA!) Report." Ashoka & Philips Foundation. 2021. 13.

155. Joost van Engen, interview with author, 2020.

156. "AHA! webinar 2: Strengthening the last mile."

157. Joost van Engen, interview with author, April 2021.

158. Website BIMA: https://bimamobile.com/

159. Agartson, Gustaf. "BIMA reaching the unreachable." Leapfrog Investment. 19 October 2015. https://www.youtube.com/watch?v=-nhitTzMPWg

160. Agartson, Gustaf. "Reimagine Financial Inclusion for all and the role insurances play." Digital Insurance Agenda TV. 16 December 2020. https://digitalinsuranceagenda.com/dia-tv/video/financial-inclusion-for-all/

161. "Reimagine Financial Inclusion."

162. "Reimagine Financial Inclusion."

163. Micro insurance Network. "Insights on Mobile Network Operators as a distribution channel for microinsurance in Asia." Micro insurance Network and Munich Re Foundation. 2016. https://microinsurancenetwork.org/resources/resource-13001

164. Stuart, Guy. "The Formula for Mobile Microinsurance Success in Senegal and Pakistan." Centre for Financial Inclusion. 29 August 2014. https://www.centreforfinancialinclusion.org/the-formula-for-mobile-microinsurance-success-in-senegal-and-pakistan

165. BIMA. "BIMA partners with Warid in Pakistan." BIMA. https://bimamobile.com/archives/news/bima-partners-with-warid-in-pakistan

166. Probyn, Justin. "The journey so far: Gustaf Agartson, CEO, BIMA." How we made it in Africa. 22 March 2018. https://www.howwemadeitinafrica.com/journey-far-gustaf-agartson-ceo-bima/61062/

167. Howard, L.S., "Microinsurer BIMA Aims to Close Developing Nations' Protection Gap with Life & Health Cover." Insurance Journal. 19 January 2018. https://www.insurancejournal.com/news/international/2018/01/19/477799.htm

168. Williams-Grut Oscar. "This Swedish startup brings insurance to 24 million people in the developing world through their mobiles." *Insurance Journal.* 22 October 2016. https://www.businessinsider.de/bima-brings-microinsurance-to-africa-asia-and-latin-america-via-phones-2016-10?r=UK&IR=T

169. "Reimagine Financial Inclusion."

170. Cheston, Susy et al. "Inclusive Insurance: Closing the Protection Gap for Emerging Customers." ACCION Centre for Financial Inclusion and Institute of International Finance. January 2018. https://content.centreforfinancialinclusion.org/wp-content/uploads/sites/2/2018/08/Inclusive-Insurance-Final-2018.06.13.pdf

171. Raithatha, Rishi and Naghavi, Nika. "Spotlight on mobile-enabled insurance services." GSM Association. 2018. https://www.gsma.com/mobilefordevelopment/wp-content/uploads/2018/09/2017-SOTIR-Spotlight-on-mobile-enabled-insurance-services.pdf

172. Hook, Lucy. "Insuring remote communities: BIMA's UK product head." *Insurance Business.* 14 September 2017. https://www.insurancebusinessmag.com/uk/news/breaking-news/insuring-remote-communities-bimas-uk-product-head-78938.aspx

173. Probyn Justin. "The journey so far."

174. Hook, Lucy. "Insuring remote communities."

175. BIMA. "A day in the life of a BIMA agent." Bimamobile. 28 June 2017. www.youtube.com/watch?v=sA5s8oa9Zx0

176. Gustaf Agartson, interview with author, 27 October 2020.

177. Website of Tienda Pago: https://www.tiendapago.com/

178. Casanova, Martha. "Credit to Merchants, Tienda Pago's Digital Solution for Fast-Moving Consumer Goods." IFC. 2019. https://www.ifc.org/wps/wcm/connect/industry_ext_content/ifc_external_corporate_site/financial+institutions/resources/digital+credit+to+merchants

179. "Tienda Pago Financial Inclusion Global Grant Prize Winner." MIT Inclusive Innovation Challenge. 2019. https://www.mitinclusiveinnovation.com/winners/tiendapago/

180. Casanova, Martha. "Credit to Merchants, Tienda Pago's Digital Solution for Fast-Moving Consumer Goods." IFC, 2019.

181. Casanova, Martha. "Credit to Merchants."

182. Dan Cohen, interview with author, 15 July 2020.

183. Dan Cohen, interview with author, 15 July 2020.

184. Dan Cohen, interview with author, 15 July 2020.

185. Dan Cohen, interview with author, 15 July 2020.

186. Hardy, Siman. "Unravelling the web of inclusion." Mastercard. 28 March 2019. 24. http://financial-inclusion.com/wp-content/uploads/2019/03/MCC1-FinInc-Report-Screen.pdf

187. Ricciardi, Vincent et al. "How much of the world's food do smallholders produce?" Global Food Security. Volume 17, June 2018. 64–72.

188. ISF advisors. "Protecting growing prosperity, Agricultural insurance in the developing world." ISF and Syngenta Foundation Sustainable Agriculture. 17 September 2018.

189. ISF advisors. "Protecting growing prosperity."

190. Syngenta Foundation Sustainable Agriculture. "Scaling through enterprise, International conference report." Syngenta Foundation Sustainable Agriculture. 5 July 2017. 13. https://www.syngentafoundation.org/sites/g/files/zhg576/f/sfsa_conference_report_717_scaling_up.pdf

191. Website ACRE Africa: https://acreafrica.com/

192. Greatrex, Helen et al. "Scaling up index insurance for smallholder farmers: Recent evidence and insights." CCAFS Report No. 14. https://cgspace.cgiar.org/bitstream/handle/10568/53101/CCAFS_Report14.pdf?sequence=1

193. Index Insurance Forum. "ACRE Africa: Protecting Rural Africa Through Creative Partnerships and Technology." Index Insurance Forum. 28 January 2020, https://www.indexinsuranceforum.org/news/acre-africa-protecting-rural-africa-through-creative-partnerships-and-technology

194. 60_decibels. "ACRE Africa farmers insights Kenya." November 2020. https://acreafrica.com/wp-content/uploads/2021/01/60dB-ACRE.pdf

195. "Reimagining Financial Inclusion."

196. "Reimagining Financial Inclusion."

197. "ACRE Africa: Protecting Rural Africa."

198. "ACRE Africa: Protecting Rural Africa."

199. George Kuria, interview author, 23 September 2020.

200. ACRE Africa. "3-D client value assessment for ACRE Rwanda maize and livestock insurance products." August 2020.

201. 60_decibels. "ACRE Africa farmers insights Kenya."

202. UAP. "Opportunities in Agriculture Kilimo Salama." https://acreafrica.com/wp-content/uploads/2020/04/Opportunities-in-Agriculture-Kilimo-Salama.pdf

203. "Reimagining Financial Inclusion."

204. Business Call to Action. "Inclusive innovative insurance pragmatic solutions for the economically vulnerable." *The Guardian*. November 2020.

205. ACRE Africa, "3-D client value assessment."

206. "Reimagining Financial Inclusion."

207. 60_decibels. "ACRE Africa farmers insights."

208. ACRE Africa. "ZEP-RE is acquire 56% equity stake in ACRE Africa to support the scale up of Agricultural insurance for African smallholder farers." 1 December 2020. https://acreafrica.com/zep-re-to-acquire-56-equity-stake-in-acre-africa-to-support-the-scale-up-of-agriculture-insurance-for-african-smallholder-farmers/

209. Syngenta Foundation of Sustainable Farming. "Surrokkha, a year of experience." 2020.

210. "Simon Winter, Executive Director, Syngenta Foundation | Agriculture Advantage opening event." CGIAR Research Program on Climate Change, Agriculture and Food Security. 8 December 2017. https://www.youtube.com/watch?v=R4W8U1D0E0A

211. Website of Village Saving and Loans Associates: https://www.vsla.net/

212. Website of SOLshare: https://me-solshare.com/

213. Siddarth, Divya and Mishra, Ashish K. "The understated disruption of SOLshare in Bangladesh." *The Morning Context*. 20 May 2020. https://themorningcontext.com/internet/the-understated-disruption-of-solshare-in-bangladesh

214. Ahmad, Reaz. "Bangladesh increases rural access to electricity fivefold in two decades." *Dhaka Tribune*. 21 April 2019. https://www.dhakatribune.com/bangladesh/power-energy/2019/04/21/bangladesh-increases-rural-access-to-electricity-five-fold-in-two-decades

215. Thomas Reuters Foundation. "Solar sharing start-up aims to cut power waste." *Good Day Bangladesh*. 4 July 2020. https://en.prothomalo.com/bangladesh/good-day-bangladesh/solar-sharing-start-up-aims-to-cut-power-waste

216. Fraser, Adam. "Meet the research team transforming lives through renewable energy technologies." Elsevier. 25 April 2019. https://www.elsevier.com/connect/meet-the-research-team-transforming-lives-through-renewable-energy-technologies

217. Groh, Sebastian. "Dr. Sebastian Groh on the Nest." SOLshare. 6 May 2020. https://youtu.be/Pzyelo7vGX0

218. "Dr. Sebastian Groh on the Nest."

219. Siddarth, Divya and Mishra, Ashish K. "The understated disruption."

220. Sebastian Groh, interview with author, 21 July 2020.

221. Groh, Sebastian. "Disrupting the One Billion Energy Market, One Household at a Time." Seedstars. 15 April 2020. https://www.youtube.com/watch?v=LArUSgtRDPU&feature=youtu.be&fbclid=IwAR286nnnzB5MiQvV5Lr_xa9v0d52MVqwLFo-mgsUn3MaEqMYMM1fbCdSRs4

222. Sebastian Groh, interview with author, 21 July 2020.

223. "Disrupting the One Billion Energy Market, One Household at a Time."

224. Singh, Prasanna. "Interview with Sebastian Groh, Managing Director and Founder, SOLshare." SAUR energy. 22 May 2019. https://www.saurenergy.com/solar-energy-conversation/interview-with-sebastian-groh-managing-director-and-founder-solshare

225. Bessaranova, Tatiana. "Solar, Expanded: Building the Future of Utilities in Bangladesh." Next Billion. 2019. https://nextbillion.net/solar-future-of-utilities-in-bangladesh/

226. Bessaranova, Tatiana. "Solar, Expanded."

227. Sebastian Groh, interview with author, 21 July 2020.

228. Bonnet, Florence, Vanek, Joann and Chen, Martha. "Women and Men in the Informal Economy: A Statistical Brief." International Labor Office. January 2019. https://www.ilo.org/wcmsp5/groups/public/---ed_protect/---protrav/---travail/documents/publication/wcms_711798.pdf

229. Statista Research Department. "Number of people with health insurance across India." Statista Research Department. 1 March 2021. https://www.statista.com/statistics/657244/number-of-people-with-health-insurance-india/

230. "Number of people with health insurance across India." Statista Research Department.

231. "When women drive insurance, it's for wellness and not illness | Kumar Shailabh" TEDxtalk Dharavari. 10 September 2019. https://www.youtube.com/watch?v=iDIRNsSXWgA, September 2019

232. Website of Uplift Mutuals: https://www.upliftmutuals.org/

233. "Uplift Biradaree." Uplift Mutuals. 12 June 2017. https://www.youtube.com/watch?v=D2d0E7ugHxU&t=3s

234. "When women drive insurance."

235. "Reimagining Financial Inclusion."

236. "When women drive insurance."

237. Kumar Shailabh, interview with author, 18 September 2020.

238. Kumar Shailabh, interview with author, 18 September 2020.

239. Ashoka. "Pioneering Mutual Aid In India." *Forbes.* 14 October 2019. https://www.forbes.com/sites/ashoka/2019/10/14/pioneering-mutual-aid-in-india/?sh=4bcaf2436e5c

240. Ashoka. "Pioneering Mutual Aid In India." *Forbes.* 14 October 2019. https://www.forbes.com/sites/ashoka/2019/10/14/pioneering-mutual-aid-in-india/?sh=4bcaf2436e5c

241. ICMIF. "ICMIF member Uplift Mutuals launches new mobile app in India as part of ICMIF 5-5-5 Strategy." ICMIF. 22 December 2017. https://www.icmif.org/news_story/icmif-member-uplift-mutuals-launches-new-mobile-app-in-india-as-part-of-icmif-5-5-5-strategy/

242. Kader, Syed Ameen. "India's Muslims develop mutual health insurance scheme as alternative to takaful." Alhaqeeqa. 28 May 2018. https://www.zawya.com/mena/en/business/story/Indias_Muslims_develop_mutual_health_insurance_scheme_as_alternative_to_Takaful-ZAWYA20180527080820/

243. "Reimagining Financial Inclusion."

244. Kumar Shailabh, interview with author, 18 September 2020.

245. Kumar Shailabh, interview with author, 18 September 2020.

246. Prahalad, C.K. (2005). *The fortune at the bottom of the pyramid, eradicating poverty through profit.* Upper Saddle River, New Jersey: Wharton School Publishing.

247. London, Ted, Hart, Stuart L. et. al. (2011). *Next generation business strategies, for the base of the pyramid.* Upper Saddle River, New Jersey: Pearson Education.

248. London, Hart et. al, "Next generation business strategies." 42.

249. Kim, W. Chan and Mauborgne, Renée A. (2019). *Blue Ocean Strategy.* Boston, Massachusetts: Harvard Business Review Press.

250. Tzu, Lao. *Tao Te Ching.* English translation by Ursula K. Le Guin.

ACKNOWLEDGEMENTS

Never underestimate a spark. The spark for this book came from Dr. Ashwin Naik, for which I am grateful. Reading Ashwin's book *The Health Care Gamechangers* got me started, and I modelled mine based on his, adding a few elements of myself on the go. Then came the wind that turned the spark into a little flame. Thank you, Professor Harry Hummels and Wouter Scheepens, without being your co-author writing our book – to be published soon – I would not have realized that I had something else to say myself. Then came COVID and the home schooling of my children as a result, that served as wood fuelling the small flames. It made me realize more than ever that quarantining at home, having a roof over my head and a garden to play in is a privilege. Shouldn't everybody get a chance to build a home that protects you in times of hardship, where your children can play and study? Not just mine, but all of our kids around the word. Life would never return to its old ways, systems do not have to be build back to their old shape. The way my children studied, without their peers, with no teachers around, gave me the strength to do the same. The flames grew into a fire. And Ben, this proves that life is a quest! Who would have thought that I would ever write a book? My heartfelt gratitude for our continued conversations and a safe space to play with fire at our home.

But a fire needs to spark in all directions, for which it had to leave the safety of my home. Roger put in the effort to proofread and provided me with invaluable insights on how to convey my message. Ymke never failed to tell me I could do it. Both of their encouragements blew up the flames. After which this fire became a joint one, more of a campfire with many contributors stirring it up. Ashoka is a fiery place to be; it has been my enabling surrounding, so I could catch a spark and share the fire. Thank you, Alec, for your belief in me and the message of this book. Thank you, Aiyana and Jody, for your patience and teaching me how to write. Thank you, Caroline, for making this book a visually appealing one. Thank you for all your support during the publishing process.

Long before this book came into being, there were these game changers out there lighting fires. A special thanks to them, not just for being supportive and indulgent of my requests. My eternal gratitude goes to you for making this world more just, more inclusive. May the lights of your passion fires reach far and beyond. And to those who read this book, carry it forward, thank you.

ABOUT THE AUTHOR

Photo by Ymke Sie

Erlijn Sie has 15 years of experience working with multi-nationals and an equivalent number of years leading and growing social ventures. She is the co-founder of Micro-credits for Mothers and Credits for Communities, and was managing director of the Banking with the Poor Network and HandsOn Microfinance. Currently, she works at Ashoka – the world's largest international network of social entrepreneurs – with blue chip companies to transform business into a force for good through collaboration with social innovators. Erlijn has devoted her career to contributing to a more just and inclusive economy. Erlijn holds two Masters degrees in Management Sciences and Asian Studies.

BOOK SUMMARY

To live in today's world, you need money; yet the majority of people do not have access to it. The formal financial system is taken for granted, but it also represents the barrier to financial inclusion. This book puts hard-working people at the base of our global supply chains centre stage. *Reimagining Financial Inclusion* features 13 game changers from around the world, who are challenging the status-quo and paving new pathways to financially include low-income families.

Through an in-depth study of their thought-provoking strategies, their intrinsically inclusive innovations and jaw-dropping new ways of organizing, a framework for inclusion is distilled. The framework centres around five levers to tackle the flaws of our financial system. These game changers suggest what the future of finance for all could look like. They show how big brands, banks, insurers, multinationals, telcos, their foundations and CSR arms, fin- and insurtech can contribute. If you are curious about how you can get involved, this book is for you.